The 20 Latin Americas

Americas

VOLUME I

Marcel Niedergang

Translated by Rosemary Sheed

Penguin Books

Penguin Books Ltd, Harmondsworth,
Middlesex, England
Penguin Books Inc., 7110 Ambassador Road,
Baltimore, Maryland 21207, U.S.A.
Penguin Books Australia Ltd, Ringwood,
Victoria, Australia

Les 20 Amériques Latines published in France by Plon 1962
Revised edition published in France by Editions du Seuil 1969
English translation published in Pelican Books 1971
Copyright © Plon, 1962
Copyright © Editions du Seuil, 1969
English translation copyright © Rosemary Sheed, 1971

Made and printed in Great Britain by
Hazell Watson & Viney Ltd, Aylesbury, Bucks
Set in Linotype Juliana

THE PELICAN LATIN AMERICAN LIBRARY
General Editor: Richard Gott

The 20 Latin Americas : 1

Marcel Niedergang is a regular correspondent on
Le Monde, and also spent ten years on *France Soir*.
His particular expertise is the continent of Latin
America, where he has spent the greater part of his
journalistic life; his articles on Latin America in
Le Monde have achieved world-wide fame. The
present two-volume survey has been built out of his
experience on the continent.

Contents

Introduction

Latin America begins at the Rio Grande – a sharp dividing line between an over-industrialized world and a very under-developed one – and ends in Tierra del Fuego, so badly mis-named by Magellan. From 32° latitude in the north to 56° in the south, from the northern frontier of Mexico to the southernmost areas of Chile and Argentina, it covers 8,250,000 square miles – something like fifteen per cent of the world's land surface. Geographically it is easily defined, but its unity is only superficial, though it does have a number of common characteristics, historically, politically, culturally, economically and socially. Towering civilizations as yet large-ly unexplored by us existed in that American sub-continent discovered by Columbus in 1492; Aztecs, Mayas, Chibchas and Incas, the last inheritors of these pre-Columbian civiliza-tions, some of which show remains dating back to ten thou-sand years B.C., have left us some remarkable images stamped in stone or metal. The legend of a 'new' continent did not stand up to the researches of archaeologists. That other America, Latin America, whether Spanish or Portuguese, wanted to achieve political unity at the same time as it became inde-pendent. But a century before the same thing had occurred in Africa : it was the colonial frontiers that ultimately pro-vided the frontiers of its various nations, each jealously guarding its sovereignty. Even today, there are frontier battles between neighbours who are only now beginning to discover one another's existence, after having for so long been oriented either towards the United States or Europe.

The slow development of the various peoples has not taken the same course everywhere. In Argentina, Uruguay, Chile, Brazil, Venezuela, Colombia, the West Indies, Panama and Costa Rica, the great majority of the population come from Europe, or in some cases Africa. In Mexico, on the other hand, and the rest of Central America, in Ecuador, Peru, Bolivia and Paraguay, the vast mass of the people are of Amerindian origin. The Portuguese, the first colonizers of the Brazilian shoreline, felt no repugnance towards miscegenation, whereas the Spanish colonizers, with their greater restraint, did a lot to form the foundations of a feudal, and in places racist, society. But even this is not a universal rule. There was intense miscegenation in the north, chiefly in Mexico, Venezuela and Colombia, though it was relatively slight where it took place at all in the other Andean countries. Because of the busy slave-traffic, the arrival of negroes on the Caribbean coasts of Central America, in the West Indies, along the Atlantic coast of the northern part of South America, and in Brazil, was on a huge scale. A tremendously large number of immigrants from Europe, beginning at the end of the nineteenth century, completely changed the character of the populations of Argentina, Chile, Uruguay and southern Brazil. Colonies of Japanese, extremely homogeneous and fast growing, have arrived in this century, especially in Brazil, and tended to spill over to such neighbouring countries as Bolivia.

The two major languages, Spanish and Portuguese, are Latin and the ruling classes, who rightly lay claim to a western culture, are proud of their 'Latin-ness' – though it is something nebulous and hard to define. Yet in fact nearly thirty million Indians still use languages or dialects which go back to long before the Conquest, and though here and there there have been tremendous campaigns against illiteracy, a large proportion of people still have no access to even the most elementary education.

This statement also applies to religion. In theory, Catholicism is the undisputed faith of two hundred million Latin Americans. In fact, the growing development of churches and missions from North America is only one aspect of the rapid advance of U.S. imperialism throughout the sub-continent. The Catholic Church, having for so long collaborated with the conservative ruling classes, is at last attempting a spectacular renewal, but it is within strict limits, and being fought fiercely by a hierarchy still largely fearful of change. Pope Paul's visit to Bogotá in August 1968 and the second episcopal conference at Medellín in Colombia in fact brought out clearly the tensions created within the Church by the need to apply the resolutions of Vatican II, and the painful alternative presented to all men of good will between ineffective reformism, and revolution which must inevitably lead to violence. As regards actual religious structures, there is a desperate shortage of priests (one per 5,600 people in 1965); and in many cases – particularly in Central America, the West Indies, the Andean areas and Brazil – Catholic beliefs have been superimposed on old Indian ones, or on the fetishism of the former negro slaves. Furthermore, the de-Christianization of the urban masses has been extremely rapid.

Bolívar's dream in the last century only lasted for a few years. The middle years of the twentieth century have been marked by a resurgence of pan-Americanism under the (direct or indirect) influence of a U.S. anxious to secure more firmly its control of an area which it persists in regarding as its particular preserve. The ambitious 'Alliance for Progress' launched by President Kennedy in 1961 failed for a variety of reasons, some of which were only too predictable. But the notion of the need for solidarity has nonetheless taken hold in various ways under the influence of some of the more far-

sighted Latin American leaders. The Latin American Free
Trade Association (ALALC), brought into existence by the
Treaty of Montevideo, has developed with difficulty owing to
the reservations of the most powerful countries, such as
Argentina, whose first ambition is to secure their own
national solidarity, and get their commerce with the outside
world onto a sound footing, before really plunging into any
communal economic enterprises. Furthermore, the creation of
a Latin American Common Market, resolved upon at the conference in Punta del Este in April 1967, and scheduled to be
fully established by 1985, is running into the most tremendous difficulties – psychological, technological, economic and
political. The Central American Common Market, on the
other hand, can boast of some spectacular results, even though
it has not yet been able to make any major change in the
economic structures of the small republics in the isthmus,
nor do much to improve the standard of living of the masses
of poor living there. Spurred on by Chilean and Colombian
leaders, the Andean group for economic cooperation represents yet another new kind of endeavour. Its development has
been hampered by the problem of Bolivia's access to the sea,
and by delaying tactics on the part of Venezuela where the
pressures of American imperialism are especially great. In
short, the basic question posed by the need for economic
integration in Latin America is fairly clear : the problem is to
know whether it is to foster a genuine strengthening of the
economy and sovereignty of the Latin American nations
themselves, or simply to increase the power over them of the
United States. As things are at present, the second would
seem to be the most likely hypothesis. The nature of the
relationships between the two halves of the hemisphere,
which did so much to destroy the Kennedy plan, have not
really altered.

The Alliance for Progress proposed over the course of the
years, to assign twenty thousand million dollars in aid to the

signatory nations, in the form of public loans or private investment. The signatories, for their part, were committed to agrarian reform, to the stamping out of illiteracy by 1970 at the latest, and to raising the average level of incomes. Cuba was of course excluded from this aid programme – whose inadequacy was soon noted by the experts at the United Nations Economic Commission for Latin America (CEPAL) and by various other institutions. Mr Covey Oliver, American joint Secretary of State for Inter-American Affairs, revealed his discovery in 1968 that Washington's financial aid to Latin America was 'relatively modest in relation to the return' the U.S. received from it. According to him, the sum total of investment under the Alliance for Progress in 1968 amounted to 0.16 per cent of the gross national revenue of the U.S., and bilateral financial aid to Latin American countries would not rise beyond 0.6 per cent – an appallingly inadequate figure. All of America's aid through the Alliance for Progress from 1961 to 1968 had grown to no more than 6.7 per cent of all investment in Latin America. At the same time, St Galo Plaza, secretary general of the OAS and a former president of Ecuador, was putting out a dramatic warning to the U.S. that the very existence of the Alliance for Progress was in danger. 'Any further diminution of international aid,' he declared, 'could lead to disaster. Our young people are growing more restless and impatient as they see the increasing gulf between the developed and under-developed nations, not merely in terms of income, but of scientific and technological progress.'

On 22 September 1967, in Rio de Janeiro, Mr David Rockefeller, the President of the Chase Manhattan Bank, one of the three largest privately-owned banks in the U.S., delivered a fervent plea for free enterprise in the underdeveloped countries, defending the notion that 'private foreign aid is necessary for the economic advancement of the poor nations' and that 'private foreign investment has been shown to be an indispensible catalyst in the modernizing of their economy'. To say this is to ignore one essential fact : in the under-developed countries – and this includes the great majority of Latin American nations – the conflict is not between public and private enterprise at all, but between indigenous and foreign interests. Foreign investment can only contribute to the development of Latin America if it is part of a national development plan directed to the economic advancement of the country concerned.

The great majority of Latin American countries have an economy characterized by the interplay of their foreign markets. Their economies remain precariously balanced because of their dependence on the export of one or two raw materials. If you look at the United Nations' statistics of average exports for various Latin American countries from 1959 to 1963, you will see that cereals, meat and leather represent 44 per cent of Argentina's exports, and that in Brazil, though it began to become industrialized as long ago as 1930, 54.2 per cent of all exports is still coffee. Evidently, these percentages become even higher when one considers the poorer countries like Bolivia (tin : 61.4 per cent), Colombia (coffee : 71.7 per cent), Chile (copper : 66.3 per cent), Ecuador (bananas : 61.2 per cent), Guatemala (coffee : 61.8 per cent), Haiti (coffee : 50.4 per cent), Honduras (bananas : 46.6 per cent), the Dominican Republic (sugar : 46.4 per cent), Uruguay (wool : 54.9 per cent), Venezuela (petroleum : 91.9 per cent). Mexico and Peru have a fairly wide range of exports, but these too are still raw materials (lead, zinc, copper, petroleum, cotton, coffee in Mexico; and lead, copper, iron, petroleum, cotton and sugar in Peru). Venezuela is the country with the highest dependence on a single product (petroleum), but this is a special case, since the production and marketing of petroleum are not subject to the same fluctuations as affect most of the other products of Latin America. Apart from the petroleum and banana markets, all other markets involving the basic products of the Latin American nations are unstable in the extreme. It is therefore hardly surprising that most Latin American countries suffer the disabilities of balance-of-payments deficits, diminishing reserves, reduction of imports, and an imbalance in public finance resulting from their enormously heavy dependence on what they can earn from their exports. In ten years the price of raw materials in relation to that of manufactured articles has gone down 26 per cent, mainly because of the increase in the cost of manufactured products. According to Yves Lacoste, 'the economies of Latin America have developed as more or less favourable circumstances have dictated, and their lack of reserves has made it impossible to achieve the level of *per capita* income that would have made it possible to establish any process of self-development. At a period when technology is all-important, where the sources of energy seem to be unlimited, to hope that the Latin American economies will develop simply by the interplay of the market is to condemn them to stagnation.' In effect, the reserve stocks would be satisfactory in a number of countries, but the worth of those reserves is notably reduced by the deterioration in exchange rates which decreases the possibilities of investing in foreign capital goods (equipment). A similar opinion was expressed by CEPAL experts just before the world conference on trade and development (UNCTAD) in New Delhi. 'The rigidity and lack of dynamism in Latin American exports will counteract the efforts that are being made to increase capital reserves and productive capacity. Without financial cooperation from outside to achieve an expansion and a diversification of exports, it will be, in effect, impossible to speed up the formation of capital and increase resources. The process of unification will be paralysed if we cannot solve the problem of our economic and financial relationships with the rest of the world.' And the fact is that Latin America's share in world business continued to decrease from 1958 to 1968; even from 1953 to 1966, it had dropped from 10.3 per cent to 6.4 per cent.

Another serious problem is the withdrawal of profits by the large foreign firms working to exploit the wealth of the area. Even in 1930, the U.S. mainly invested in the sector of raw materials and huge agricultural concerns. They took home, and are still taking home, the larger part of their considerable profits. In 1965, out of a profit of $1,175 million, $306 million were reinvested and $869 million taken home. According to the U.N. Economic Survey for Latin America and the review *Fortune*, North American trust companies made far larger profits in Latin America than in the U.S. The German review *Deutsche Aussenpolitik* tells us that in a given year 'Standard Oil of New Jersey made an 11 per cent profit in the U.S. and 33 per cent in Latin America. In 1948, General Motors made a 25 per cent profit in the U.S., and almost 80 per cent from its Latin American subsidiaries. The Anaconda Copper Company has made 200 times more profit in Chile than in the U.S.' The Chilean economist Alberto Baltra calculates that American monopolies controlling the production of copper in his country have, over the past thirty years, made a net profit of two thousand million dollars. According to the U.S. Department of Commerce's review, *Survey of Current Business*, the profits of the major American firms have in ten years increased by 90 per cent in Chile, 30 per cent in Argentina and nearly 90 per cent in Venezuela. In other words, Latin America goes on getting poorer, while the big foreign monopolies increase their profits and tighten their grip. That it is indeed a grip is illustrated sharply by the following figures: from 1950 to 1965, investments from the U.S. in Latin America rose to 3.8 thousand million dollars. During that same period, the profit from those investments brought back into the U.S. rose to 11.3 thousand million; Latin America thus lost 7.5 thousand million dollars in those years. The statistics of the Department of Commerce in Washington, and those put out by the *Survey of Current Business* also show that the book value of the fixed capital belonging to Latin American subsidiaries of North American trust companies rose to 7.2 thousand million dollars in 1957, to 8.6 thousand million in 1963, and 9.8 thousand million in 1966. In other words, despite the enormous profits they brought back to the U.S., the major American firms in Latin America still managed to make regular increases in the book value of their investments.

It is cruel thus to compare the super-power of a triumphantly technological country with data that show the depth of poverty that exists in Latin America. The true and only real unifying factor in the sub-continent is underdevelopment. It may be useful to make clear exactly what we mean by the term. Some economists, looking at the astounding expansion of Mexico – comparable to that of Japan in the fifties – consider that here we see a country that has achieved its economic 'take-off' and is no longer to be accounted as under-developed in the classic sense. Others, however, notably the Brazilian economist Celso Furtado, assistant professor in the Faculty of Law in Paris, and formerly director of SUDENE (Committee for the Development of the Brazilian North East), link the concept of under-development with that of structural dualism. In this light, Mexico has not yet emerged from a state of under-development, as compared with Argentina and Uruguay, where the labour market is a single structural whole. 'Brazil,' declares Carlos Lacerda, former governor of Guanabara, 'is not an under-developed, but an unequally-developed country.' This is not just playing with words: the general characteristics of the Brazilian federation inevitably class it among what we euphemistically like to call the 'developing' countries, but there are areas of rapid expansion alongside, and in interaction with, areas that are grossly under-developed. What is true of Brazil is also true of Mexico, Venezuela, Peru and, to a lesser extent, of

Colombia. Corresponding to the very varied levels of development all over Latin America, and even within each country, is an equally great disparity of living standards. Neither prosperity nor poverty is uniform. Exaggerations proliferate in both directions, economically and socially, as well as politically. According to the data given for 1967 by the International Bank for Reconstruction and Development, the gross national product per head was 650 dollars in Argentina and 75 in Haiti. Between these two extremes we find Panama (450), Mexico (430), Colombia (270), Uruguay (200) and Ecuador (190). According to these figures, Paraguay, Uruguay and Haiti were apparently moving backwards as regards *per capita* production. Honduras, the Dominican Republic and Costa Rica were 'stationary' and all the rest were (relatively) expanding.

Looked at as a whole, Latin America shows most of the signs of under-development : inadequate or unsuitable diet, wastage or under-use of natural resources, poor returns from agriculture, insufficient or incomplete industrialization, dependence of national economies on foreign powers, archaic social and economic structures, generalized under-utilization of available labour, high levels of both illiteracy and population increase. In 1650 the whole population of Latin America cannot have been more than twelve million. In 1950 it reached 163 million, and by 1967 it was more than 210 million. It is generally estimated that by 1980 there will be 297 million people living there, and by the end of the century there will be 600 million or more. Obviously the average increase of 3 per cent per year in the population of Latin America must temper the optimism manifested by such international bodies as GATT, and certainly estimates of this kind must be seen in their own special context. As Yves Lacoste points out, 'What characterizes Latin America is the extreme contrasts in the distribution of wealth among different groups of the population, which is not a technological but a social problem. The example of Peru is typical : in 1950 there were 8½ million people, of whom one million received something around 55 per cent of the nation's income.' Similar examples could easily be found in Central America, the West Indies, Brazil, and the Andean nations. Infantile mortality takes a terrible toll (108 per thousand in Bolivia, 142 in Brazil, 113 in Colombia, 120 in Chile). In Recife, the major city of north-east Brazil, fifty per cent of all children die before the age of one. There are other black spots in Central America and in the Andes, where sub-human conditions and hunger kill thousands of people every year. Illiteracy rates also vary from country to country, being negligible in Argentina, Uruguay and Costa Rica, yet on the other hand reaching 89.3 per cent in Haiti. On average one can estimate that one in every two Latin Americans is illiterate.

All the experts agree that the way land is apportioned forms one of the major obstacles to any rational development in Latin America. The *latifundio* and the *minifundio* are the two extremes – both equally disastrous. The *latifundio* embodies all the disadvantages of large ownership and small scale exploitation, without having any of the advantages of either,' notes Jacques Lambert. 'A direct descendant of the system of slavery, or more generally of the kind of servitude represented by the Indian *encomienda*, the latifundist regime with its relationship of personal dependence on the part of the workers towards the landowner, and its traditional obligation of the master to protect his subjects is a total system of social organization that can only be compared with feudalism. ... The economic function of the *latifundio* is only incidentally that of producing for the market. Its prime purpose is to satisfy the social and economic needs of its people which, up to now, owing to the isolation and ignorance in which they live, are rudimentary in the extreme.' It must be pointed out that this is true of the pre-capitalist agricultural areas of which there remain very few examples now (north-east Brazil in particular), and that the modern large-scale landowner is well geared to exporting his produce. Even so, and despite the exodus from the countryside, something like half of the active population of Latin America still consists of non-landowning peasants. It is the exceptional landowner who does anything to improve the level of production on his property. They do not buy manure or tractors (there are ten tons of manure and one tractor for every thousand hectares in Brazil as against 50 tons of manure and 45 tractors in France, for instance). Except in Mexico, Cuba and Bolivia, only a tiny minority of landowners and large businesses own the majority of cultivable land. Thus, according to CEPAL, 1·47 per cent of estates covering 74 per cent of all cultivable land belongs to landlords each of whom owns more than a thousand hectares, while 72·64 per cent of holdings of less than twenty hectares cover 2·75 per cent of the cultivable land. But all plans for agrarian reform, except in the countries I mentioned (Mexico, Cuba and Bolivia), have, up to now, met with implacable hostility from the landowners. It is noteworthy, however, that projects for agrarian reform have been worked out and applied in some places ever since 1960, especially in Venezuela, Colombia, Peru, Ecuador and Chile. But, apart from Chile, where the Christian Democrat government had planned to have 100,000 families farming their own land by 1970, they are essentially projects of colonization which do nothing to alter the present iniquitous system of land tenure. Even where agrarian reform has been enforced, as in Mexico, where it has been carried out with ups and downs since 1917, there is always the risk to be reckoned with of the large estates being reconstituted by devious means. This is especially the case in the northern Mexican states of Sinaloa and Sonora. Even once the reform has been applied, as in Bolivia, it remains unsteady, due to the lack of agricultural credits and of competent technologists, coupled with the sheer ignorance of a large proportion of the peasants involved.

Spengler showed very well how economic growth is related to the dynamism and mobility of social groups. This is as much the case with industrial development as with the necessary radical reform of agricultural production in Latin America. As Raúl Prebisch, one of the most influential economists in CEPAL noted, 'well-equipped firms are operating alongside others run at vast expense, in a kind of tacit mutual benevolent society, whereby the latter preserve a precarious existence, while the former amass vast profits from the difference between them'. The absence of civic consciousness, the lack of any confidence on the part of the landowning oligarchy (with very few exceptions) and the new industrial middle class in the capacities or futures of their own countries, the appalling lack of education at all levels, the incompetence of politicians, and the still all-too-common corruption of governments, all help to explain the undue importance given in so many Latin American countries to the armed forces, and the increase in direct or indirect interventions which, though intended to assist renewal and democratization, mostly do no more than connive with the ruling classes they are by way of overthrowing.

Developments of this kind obviously facilitate an increase in control by American imperialism – which began to replace the imperialism of Britain around the turn of the century. This handing over of power is particularly in evidence in Argentina which for so long had a special relationship with Great Britain. The plan to reform higher education in Brazil, the various grandiose projects for 'colonizing' the virgin lands of Latin America proposed by U.S. research institutes, the close connections between the Pentagon and the commanders of the South American armed forces, the intensive training given to thousands of Latin American officers in the military

academies of Panama or Fort Benning, the establishment of autonomous institutes or universities whose purpose is to create
leaders who believe in 'the American way of life', the researches into birth control carried out by religious and lay
bodies, the acquisition of vast areas for farming and investments in mining concerns, an ever increasing monopoly in the
key points of the economy (steel, heavy industry, metallurgy, cars), sociological investigations of the public-opinion
poll type, direct or indirect control of the organs of press,
radio and television, the proliferation of firms running on a
mixture of indigenous and American capital : all these are the
manifestations (and there are many others) of a powerful and
increasing will to conquer. If this can be achieved, then the
kind of direct intervention which took place in Santo
Domingo in 1965 and shook the comfortable assumptions of
the OAS very badly for some time, will not be necessary.

The anxiety to exploit the factors of mobility in Latin
America to gain better control, not merely of the sources of
wealth, but also of the human element, is a fundamental
aspect of the workings of American imperialism south of the
Rio Grande. To quote Henri Edmé, it is true that 'imperialism
does not only gain ground by way of the violence it metes out
to revolutionaries. It fights with them over the very masses
from whom they claim support.' Ever since 1960, U.S. policy
in Latin America has tended to fit in with new conditions
wherever necessary, while continuing to carry out the recipe
as before wherever that may still be possible. In suddenly
agreeing to support the establishment of a South American
Common Market, which it had formerly opposed, Washington was following the advice of American businessmen : it
was a question of rationalizing the system of exploitation
complicated by the economic balkanization of the continent.
There is certainly a risk that a genuine and powerful Latin
American economic entity may come into existence. But it is a
slight and distant one. On the other hand, the short- and

slightly longer-term advantages are considerable. Trusts like IBM which have already set up assembly-plants for calculating machines in Brazil, Argentina and Chile, cannot but have a certain objective interest in the unification of the entire sub-continent.

The fact is that the few tangible crumbs from the banquet which the American technocrats have promised can never be adequate to feed the local populations which are continuing to increase. What one can glimpse of the possibilities for 1980 are far from encouraging. If present trends continue, agriculture, which in 1968 represented 23 per cent of total production, will by then represent less than 20 per cent. On the other hand, the population working in the industrial sector will have grown from 18 per cent in 1968 to 25 or even 30 per cent. It seems most unlikely that the conditions governing Latin America's international commerce will change significantly in the foreseeable future. Therefore, given the probable continuance of the present rate of population growth, there seems little ground to hope for any notable improvement in the standard of living of the poorest of the masses.

'It is undeniable that there exists a revolutionary situation in many parts of the Latin American continent, a situation which calls for urgent, thorough-going and basically revolutionary changes.' This conclusion – in the document presented to the second episcopal conference in Medellín in August 1968 – is an excellent illustration of the ever-growing awareness of the situation to be found in the most varied circles, religious and secular, all over the continent. 'We Christians cannot stand aside or declare our neutrality as we see our people going forward to their historic destiny. The average *per capita* income is barely 300 dollars. This is a state of affairs which results from our continent's subjection to foreign capital, whose power never ceases to increase.' The document also recalls 'the existence of privileged groups made up of barely 2 or 3 per cent of the population, who between them receive an enormous proportion of the national income. The Latin American who has so long borne his poverty in silence has suddenly woken up to the situation, and his needs now far outstrip the pace of development. What was unconscious poverty is now conscious destitution ...'

Thus Christians, quoting the Gospel, and revolutionaries who draw their inspiration from Marx and Lenin, are saying more or less the same thing. Though such Christians are still very few in number, their declarations are all the more forceful in that they cut right through the fog of traditional Christian positions. They may only be a tiny indication, but they are an important one: the extreme example of Fr Camilo Torres, who chose to live as a guerrilla 'because there could be no other solution', and died, does not necessarily receive the approval of all the most revolutionary of the younger clergy who are demanding changes, but it has certainly made them think.

In university circles a long tradition born out of the Córdoba Manifesto of 1918 still inspires new generations of intellectuals, having previously contributed to the establishment of such reformist movements as the APRA in Peru. In Latin America, universities have always been centres of intellectual and political concern. It is obvious today that the various departments of those universities are training-grounds for the revolutionary leaders of tomorrow. During the decade ending in 1970, the reformism so warmly encouraged by American liberals failed. Reformism, whether of the Christian Democrat kind reigning in Chile since 1964, or the democratic kind favoured in Venezuela since 1960, with its apparently equal condemnation of communism and capitalism, does not seem to have managed to find any of the solutions for which the circumstances are clamouring. It has made certain reasonable and limited progress possible. It has also made it possible for a new generation of political men to come to the fore, men who are in general efficient and disinterested, who present a distinct improvement on the rule of the earlier demagogic patricians, or mindless tyrants – though their breed has not yet totally disappeared. It must be admitted that the kind of negative politics and armed insurrection of the diehard revolutionaries has not really achieved much more during that same decade. Certainly the leaders of the various revolutionary movements have lacked imagination and not really thought out fully what they are trying to do. The wish to apply the Cuban pattern to countries of a very different sort has paralysed their efforts and obscured their objectives. Evidently the Cuban revolution, despite the most enormous economic problems, did achieve radical agrarian reform, and there has not been anything, anywhere, to compare with its successes in the vital area of education. But the conditions which enabled the Cuban revolutionaries to succeed in 1959 cannot be assumed to have existed anywhere else in the same combination in any other part of Latin America between 1959 and 1968. The failure, or stagnation, of so many of the armed risings thus resulted in bringing to light a sharp division between the old Latin American Communists, like the Brazilian Luis Carlos Prestes, and such young Marxist revolutionaries as Douglas Bravo in Venezuela or Fabio Vásquez in Colombia. It is clear that the older communists have been left behind by the speed with which the Cuban revolution has precipitated history, and their faith in a 'democratic phase achieved through an alliance between the working class and the bourgeoisie of the country' does not correspond to what is actually happening in most of Latin America. Equally, those who favour direct and immediate action have often tended to overlook certain vital elements in their approach to the problems. Both sides have clung to their errors with tenacious Latin passion, with the result that there has been a weakening, temporary only, perhaps, but very real, of the revolutionary left. The fragmentation of the different leftist tendencies was particularly evident in the Dominican Republic three years after the April rising, and from every point of view the death of Guevara in eastern Bolivia in October 1967 was deeply symbolic.

The prospect looks gloomy, and could well justify the predictions of certain leading Americans of the 'danger of anarchy among the proletariat'. For in fact, apart from a few noteworthy exceptions, no real re-examination has been made of the structures handed down from colonial times though all over the continent the magical word 'revolution' can be heard on all sides. It is possible however that the ever-more-numerous voices clamouring for a 'destructive revision' – so reminiscent of those of their forerunners in eighteenth-century Europe – are the heralds of some sort of violent but salutary upheavals . . .

THE AUTHOR

CHAPTER 1

Brazil

STATISTICS

Area: 3,286,487 square miles
Estimated population in 1967: 87,305,000 inhabitants
Population density: Almost 27 people per square mile
Annual rate of population increase: 3 per cent
Annual increase in average per capita income: 0·6 per cent.

PRINCIPAL PRODUCTS

Coffee (Brazil is the world's leading producer), mandioca (or cassava), black beans, cane sugar, cotton, cocoa.
Iron, manganese, bauxite, amianthus (fine asbestos), copper, precious stones.

Brazil, a federal republic made up of 22 states and four territories directly administered by the central government, is really a continent within a continent. Its 3,286,487 square miles occupy pretty well half of South America, and it is the largest of all tropical countries. Its population was more than 87 million in 1967, and if it continues its present rate of a 3 per cent growth *per annum*, it will be approaching 100 million by the end of the century. In the last census of 1960 there were two cities – Rio de Janeiro and São Paulo – with over 3 million inhabitants. Four others had over half a million; Recife, Belo Horizonte, Salvador and Porto Alegre. Twenty-five more had over 100,000, and Brasilia, the new federal capital, was approaching that figure. Four of every ten Brazilians live in the triangle between Rio, São Paulo and Belo Horizonte, and more than two thirds of the national income comes from the labours of this industrialized area which virtually supports the rest of the federation. Finally, with 35 thousand million dollars gross national product (the sum total of the country's production of goods and services), Brazil must henceforth be seen as the major market in the Third World after India. From 1939 to 1965, industrial production went up by an average of 8½ per cent per year, and it now represents 30 per cent of the national product. Yet the *per capita* income remains low. In 1966 it was no more than 400 dollars. This quite inadequate sum, the unequal development of the different areas of the country, and the fact that a large part of the population live outside the orbit of political and economic life, mean that, despite all this, Brazil must still be described as an under-developed country.

It would seem however that Brazil, two thirds of which is still virtually uninhabited, has been invested with all the superlatives which the geography textbooks used to apply to North America at the end of the nineteenth century.

It is thought but not yet known for sure that something approaching a sea of oil extends under the great forest of the Amazon, from Belém to the borders of Peru and Venezuela. Drilling is now going on, and derricks are rising at Nova Olinda. And it is quite certain that huge reserves of iron ore are buried in the state of Minas Gerais, which has already given the Old World more gold than Mexico and Peru together; 60 per cent of those reserves consist of hematite, known to metallurgists as the *filet mignon* of iron.

More than 1,800 different kinds of fish have been found in the rivers of Brazil, including the fearful man-eating *pirhana*, and a dazzling variety of butterflies, insects, parrots, ants, giant termites and reptiles. There is nothing in the world to compare with Butantan, which stands in the middle of a forest of rosewood trees, near the Pinheiros river. There, since it was set up by the São Paulo state government in 1902, inoculation serums are being produced and there are special laboratories for studying the poisons and viruses of scorpions and spiders. Coral snakes, ringed with red, black and bright yellow, lie dozing in the sun. In a near-by pit, snakes that look like coral snakes but are harmless are almost as splendid. Every year about 20,000 snakes are delivered to Butantan by planters or farmers, who receive ampoules of serum in payment.

But the Brazilians are not doing this just for home consumption. They point out that they only have 43 different types of snakes, whereas in Mexico, for instance, there are 72; and while Brazil only has one species of rattlesnake, the United States has 37.

It can give offence to talk too much in terms of malaria or the tropical heat. Certainly the construction of the Madeira railway to the edge of Bolivia cost the lives of thousands of workers from epidemics. But what may be true in the northern Amazon basin is far from being so in Rio, São Paulo or Santa Catarina state. It is a fact that the average temperature in Rio at the height of summer is barely higher than that of the Riviera in July. The offence is caused not only by the fact that modern Brazil, having succeeded in creating the first tropical civilization, rejects anything that might be reminiscent of the colony – or the prejudices – of the eighteenth century; but also because to a man living in Rio or São Paulo, the Amazonian jungle seems as far away as Greenland does to a Parisian.

The Brazilians are quite justified, therefore, in claiming that we do not really know them. The vital difference between Brazil and the other Latin American republics is one we often forget: Brazil was discovered and colonized by the Portuguese.

*

The history of Brazil began at the end of the fifteenth century, when Pope Alexander VI arbitrated between Spain and Portugal over the matter of the control and conquest of their sea routes. By the treaty of Tordesillas in 1494 the Portuguese won from Spain the right to exercise sovereignty over all land discovered up to 370 leagues west of Cap Verde and the Azores. This imaginary line ran more or less from Belém to Santa Catarina – with the result that the approximate frontiers of Brazil were marked out even before it was discovered – which was only in 1500.

This fact gave rise to controversies which are still going on. What is quite certain is that the first Portuguese settlers, four hundred brave men under the leadership of Afonso de Souza, landed in Pernambuco thirty years later. The colonization was slow, gradual and relatively pacific – at least as compared with what was going on elsewhere in America.

The first product to be exploited was wood : it was red wood used for dyeing, *pau brasil* – a colour like glowing embers, the colour of that unknown shore with its border of wind-bent palm trees discovered by Pedro Alvares Cabral and his sailors on 22 April 1500. So this far land from which this brazier-flame wood came was called Brazil, and the people who sold the wood were *Brasileiros*. Cabral himself did not give it the name though, for he thought he had just discovered a small island, and called it the True Cross and later, Holy Cross. In the end the whole country was called after this wood and its colour. Then, after the wood, came sugar. Then gold and diamonds. Then coffee. Then rubber, then more coffee, which of course continued to have its ups and downs. There are few examples of any colonization or civilization so closely linked with the intensive and successive cultivation of a single crop.

From its birth in 1500 up to the middle of our own century, the history of Brazil has been a long series of fantastic booms followed by appalling and unexpected slumps. And each time Brazil has risen again with that passion, that sense of panting, almost of mania, which is its peculiar characteristic. And then there will have followed another disaster, another calamitous crash. Yet each time a new miracle starts the machine up again. The Brazilians have one certainty they never waver in : God is Brazilian.

The exploitation and exporting of wood from Brazil did not last for long. For thirty years the Portuguese, preoccupied by the countries they had recently conquered in Asia, did not trouble much about this land of Vera Cruz, supposedly on their route to India. Then competition, the greed of foreigners, the distance of Asia and the longing for Eldorado, and, to some extent, chance, gradually transformed this land discovered almost with indifference into a colony to be populated. The wood, the *pau brasil*, was seen mainly as a product that needed only to be cut down and taken back to the metropolitan country. It was sugar that symbolized people's actually settling there to live. By 1534 there were colonies in Recife, Bahia, Vitorio and Rio de Janeiro. The first capital to be chosen was São Salvador da Bahia, and the first bishop appointed by the Pope arrived in 1551. This slow conquest was disturbed first by the French, and then the Dutch.

In 1503 Pommier de Gondeville, a gentleman from Normandy, got together an expedition to the shores of Brazil. He was copied by other Normans who longed for adventures in far-off lands, for spices and dark-skinned girls, men like de Varengeville. François I had never recognized the treaty of Tordesillas. Villegagnon, a knight of Malta and an enthusiastic theologian, tried, in about 1555, with the blessing and financial support of the King, to lay the first stone of a southern French empire by establishing himself with armaments and belongings on a rocky island in Guanabara bay, opposite Rio. This burlesque interlude, undertaken in the name of religious freedom and endangered by arguments about the sex of angels between Villegagnon and his Huguenot companions, came to an end in 1567 when the Portuguese attacked and won the rock with their Indian troops. (Today the naval academy stands there.) The Dutch epic was a slightly longer one. Dutchmen occupied Bahia and Pernambuco in 1624, but by 1654 their dominion over the northern coast of Brazil – which had not been without its advantages – had come to an end.

*

The sugar period lasted for a hundred years – from 1600 to 1700. For the whole of the seventeenth century it was Brazil that provided Europe with most of the sugar it used. It was introduced in the middle of the sixteenth century, and though it failed in the south it grew magnificently in the rich and fruitful soil, the *massapé*, of the north-eastern shoreline; and it was sugar that gave Brazil its first image: a colonial land, languid, sensual, paternalistic but slave-owning, cruel and mystical, greedy at once for gain, for easy pleasure, and also for the consolations of religion. Daguerrotypes of a Portuguese family in Bahia in the last century show faces extraordinarily like those of the kind of people who lived in the southern states of America on the eve of the civil war.

The cane-fields called for a labour force, and it was not long before the Indians ceased to be numerous enough. Having made use of the Red men, they moved on to the Blacks. Traffic in negroes from the Sudan, Guinea, the whole western coast of Africa and even from Angola began in 1538, and though legally forbidden in 1850, it continued in practice right up to the end of the nineteenth century. In less than three centuries it is estimated that more than three million Africans were landed in Brazil as slaves. In the fifty years which preceded abolition, almost half a million 'objects for sale' from India or Guinea crossed the Atlantic cooped up in the holds of slave ships where they were whipped till they bled or rubbed with gunpowder and pimento-juice if they showed any signs of revolt, and decimated by scurvy and the loss of all will to live.

The Brazilian sociologist, Gilberto Freyre, gives a minute description of the colonial society of the 'sugar civilization' in *The Masters and the Slaves*. The home of the landlord, the *casa grande*, was the manor house of this fuedal microcosm. The white patriarch, owning plantations often covering thousands of hectares, was equally master of the male and female negro slaves herded together in the *senzalas*, huts put up near the sugar mill. His children and grandchildren were their masters too, as they grew up in the arms of negro nurses, and lived in a comfortable proximity to the attractive little negro and mulatto girls. *The Masters and the Slaves* is an anlaysis of how the first modern tropical society came to be created by the Portuguese. Whether from temperament, from atavistic character or from taste, the Portuguese avoided the psychological mistakes so frequently made by the English, French and Dutch colonizers. In particular, they overcame the taboo on sexual relations with native women. *The Masters and the Slaves* is a damning assessment of racism, of the slavery that so debased the negroes, and a brutally honest explanation of the sexual liberalism of this particular form of colonization.

Freyre sees the blackest shadow in the picture as having been syphilis. 'That,' he says, 'was the chief illness in the master's houses and the *senzalas*. The son of the mill-owner would contract it, almost playfully, with the negro and mulatto girls, as he lost his virginity at the early age of twelve or thirteen. For at that age, he was physically a man, and could be teased if he had not yet had any women. Indeed he might even be teased for not yet having caught syphilis.'

The advantage of this easy mixing of the races was, to Freyre, counterbalanced by the terrible disadvantages of syphilis. A lot of Brazilian sociologists and anthropologists would not assent to Freyre's analysis or his conclusions.

They claim that he overstresses this sexual aspect of the relationship between the Portuguese masters and their Indian or negro slaves. They also criticize him for describing only one area of Brazil, the north east, thus denying his comments any relevance to the rest of the country. But one essential fact can at least be maintained: the sugar civilization was supported by a one-crop agriculture, on large estates, and by slavery, which gave it two results of capital importance in Brazil's development:

1. The mixing and mingling of black, white, and red races marked the beginning of the unique human success that modern Brazilian society represents.

2. The colony of economic dependants grouped round the sugar mill of the white master became the colony of political and electoral dependants of the landed proprietor.

The first result was a good one. It has enabled twentieth-century Brazil to know almost nothing of racial conflicts. A man is not judged by his race, but rather by the colour of his skin. As there are infinite shades, the kind of sharp distinctions between two clearly-defined racial groups such as one sees in the U.S. or in South Africa, are impossible. Segregation is not totally non-existent, as official propaganda would like us to believe, but it is negligible. There are of course problems in everyday life, and too dark a skin can be a real handicap to quick advancement in any sphere, but it is never an impenetrable barrier.

There is no law formally forbidding negroes from getting any jobs in the public service, but it must be admitted that, for instance, of the 4,000 students admitted to medical school each year, only thirty are black. There are no black Brazilian diplomats, and naval officers are 100 per cent white. Is this just chance? Is it purely due to economic factors? That seems unlikely. In effect, Brazil has for the past fifty years been gradually 'whitening' – though less than the Brazilians

themselves may think. But the most recent and most important statistics do suggest that the development is tending in
the direction they wish. Finally, the barrier is in fact more
an economic than purely a racial one. The richest people are
generally white, and the poorest black. The real solution to
the racial problem lies in the economic rather than the psychological sphere. It is less a matter of counteracting prejudice which barely exists, than of improving the standard of
living of the mass of the people.

The consequence of the second result I mentioned is a bad
one : it was among the sugar mills that the *coronelismo* from
which modern Brazil is only just beginning to be freed first
began.

There is obviously no point in wondering what Brazil
would have been like had there not been this forced mass
immigration of African negroes right up to the middle of the
nineteenth century. It is simply a fact that there are more
Africans in Brazil than in any other Latin American country.
Africa itself is there – in the simple demonstrations of the
ordinary people of Brazil, in the candles the negro servants
put up at night on the balconies of the ultra-modern homes
of Copacabana to drive away evil spirits, in the roll of the
candomblé's drums, in the violent and sweet-smelling exuberance of the markets in the old town of Bahia, in the stirring
Carnival in Rio with its beating rhythms of negro music. It
is there in the catlike movements of Brazil's best footballers.
It hangs over the whole north-east coast in that sweet smell
of *cachaça*, the sugar-cane firewater with which the workers
on the huge plantations would drink themselves into insensi-
bility; and one can still, on summer nights, on the beaches
of Leblon and Ipanema near Rio, hear nostalgic memories of
the dirges which the slaves on the old plantations used to
sing.

For more than half a century the north east sacrificed
everything it had to the god Sugar – its forest, all other crops

except tobacco, and its money to buy slaves, and especially men. 'Sugar cane', wrote Josué de Castro, 'devours everything around it. It demands fertile lands and eats them up. It destroys the humus. It annihilates small helpless crops, as well as human potential which it slowly bleeds white. It is this kind of autophagous régime that most characterizes the various sugar-growing areas, and marks out their successive stages – rapid rise, passing glory, and then irreversible decay.'

Competition from the West Indies in the eighteenth century put an end to the era of sugar in Brazil. Further competition from sugar beet and the abolition of slavery precipitated the collapse of a highly lucrative monopoly. The crisis in the sugar industry in the north east has got worse and worse since 1940. A great many factories (forty in the Pernambuco area alone) were closed down because their owners could not see their way to modernizing or carrying out the necessary reorganization. Some landowners managed to save their undertakings, but such islands of relative prosperity made the standard of living of the masses of country people worse than ever. During the time of the great droughts the north east was known as the country of land-eaters. In 1957 they were selling ants in some of the coastal markets in Pernambuco. The plan for industrializing the north east under the guidance of SUDENE certainly resulted in the appearance of some ultra-modern factories in the suburbs of Recife, but such industrialization is not fitted to the needs of the area, and has not up to now succeeded in solving the serious social crisis whose deepest roots must be seen in the colonial sugar society, whose incredible wealth is still visible in the gold, the marble, and the wooden sculptures of the 228 churches of São Salvador da Bahia, which yielded to Rio its place as capital city of Brazil in 1763.

Salvador survives, despite having lost the glories of its past, though the sea wind regularly fades the pinks and greens and mauves of its pastel walls with great blasts of humid air. But there has recently come a new hope : the bay of Bahia is the centre of production for Brazilian oil. Furthermore, SUDENE has assisted the establishment of about sixty new industries, and Aratu, twenty kilometres from the town, has become a centre which will control the electricity for the Paulo Afonso grid, and also a new ultra-modern port. In twenty years' time Aratu should have a population of half a million.

The traffic in negroes did not completely put a stop to the search for Indians. The slave raids organized in the seventeenth century from Recife, Bahia, Rio and São Paulo began as expeditions of discovery. Preceded by a standard-bearer, and blessed by the Church before they went, the *bandeirantes* went up the Amazon, driving out or capturing the Parana Indians. The first such trip was in 1637. Pedro Teixeira crossed the whole interior of Brazil, still unknown land and, having crossed the first barrier of the Andes at Quito, capital of Ecuador, found that he had collected a troop of 2,000 people – soldiers, Indians, slaves, women. Behind their *bandeira* (often a somewhat ragged flag), the *bandeirantes* set about covering every area in search of gold, diamonds and Indian slaves. During their expeditions, they founded towns, some of which are still standing, others long since abandoned and empty. Those who started out from São Paulo went up to the highlands of Minas where the discovery of gold in 1696 opened the second phase of Brazilian economy and history : the Eldorado period. That lasted until 1800. A new boom, a new adventure, had begun.

*

Brazil, the first provider of sugar to the world, became in the eighteenth century its chief provider of gold. The high plateaux of Minas attracted a wave of tough adventurers, bringing with them women and slaves, fighting their way up rivers to take possession of the new lands, quarrelling over the trails and stopping-places used by their various convoys of slaves and mules. This new discovery, begun by the people of São Paulo, benefited first of all the people of Rio. In fact the town's wealth began as the first convoy arrived bearing gold and diamonds, and it became journey's end for the riches drawn from the interior. During one year, 1762, Brazil despatched to Lisbon a ton and a half of gold, and the Portuguese capital, which had been destroyed by an earthquake in 1755, was largely rebuilt as a result of this manna from Brazil.

A new metropolis grew up: Ouro Prêto, studded like Bahia with Gothic churches, and spilling down the mountain slopes as Bahia had rolled down to the sea with flights of steps looking rather like the benches of an abandoned amphitheatre. At its height this mining capital had a population of 100,000; its decline began with the ending of the nineteenth century. Belo Horizonte, so well named, spread out on a sunlit plateau, replaced it as the political capital of the state of Minas Gerais in 1897. The enthusiasm that had fired the blood of Ouro Prêto's people gradually waned, leaving a weary town, whose geographical position forcibly prevented any further growth. That fact also preserved it, and Ouro Prêto became a museum piece, named in 1933 'a national monument' because of the variety and magnificence of its baroque churches, its multi-coloured tiled roofs, its bridges, and the old houses jumbled together along its steeply sloping, narrow streets.

The close of the sugar civilization had been hastened by competition from abroad. The end of the Eldorado period was caused, on the contrary, by the obstinacy of the miners. The mining processes were rudimentary in the extreme, and consequently demanded an ever-growing number of workers. When the river beds had been exhausted as a source of gold, the tools and muscles of the negro workers were strained to breaking point against the mountainside itself. The work yielded less and less reward. By the end of the eighteenth century the mines, rivers and galleries in the Minas mountains had been abandoned. Bustling towns like Vila Rica, Sabara and São João del Rei declined within a few years into the idleness of forgotten cities at the foot of disused quarries. But for the first time the goldrush in Brazil had actually made men go into the interior.

As the wave of avarice receded, the solid traces of a living population stayed behind. A new kind of riches, a new future, was opening up for Minas. Gold was finished – or nearly so. But there were iron, phosphates, lead, platinum, emeralds, bauxite, antimony, nickel, zinc, tin, chrome, cobalt, and the entire range of radio-active minerals.

The government in Lisbon gave the appearance of grandly ignoring the *bandeirantes* – though they were carving out for it a veritable empire, extending its frontiers gradually as far as the Guaporé and Javari rivers. But the Jesuits, setting off from São Paulo where they had been established since 1554, moved south, north west and north. The gulf that still exists today between the two Brazils – north and south – is a heritage from the two styles of life and two differing mentalities of the first centuries of colonization. As against the dynamism and energy of the men, whether religious or pioneers, who set off to the interior from Rio and São Paulo, one sees the monotonous, static and pleasure-loving rhythm of life of the planters of Bahia and Recife.

To conquer the land in the south and in the centre the former had had to cope with distances, untamed nature and totally unknown Indian tribes. All these had to be faced and overcome. Whereas on the north-eastern shoreline returns came easily, and the vast and docile body of black labour induced laziness, languidness and leisure in their masters.

*

One of the first Brazilians to rattle the chains – light though they were – of the metropolitan power, was a remover of teeth, that hairy, bearded and bold 'Tiradentes' who was finally hung, drawn and quartered in a public square in Rio in 1792. Tiradentes – his real name was Da Silva Xavier – now a national hero and the subject of many a municipal statue, was only a few years before his time.

At the time of Bolívar, when the revolt of the Spanish colonies against Madrid broke out, Brazil proved its patience and wisdom. At the very same time as the Spanish governors were being driven out by the *Libertadores*, the court came from Lisbon to seek refuge in Rio de Janeiro from the Napoleonic troops under Junot's command who were advancing to the banks of the Tagus.

Suddenly the establishment of the Portuguese monarchy in the violent context of Rio made Brazil a new and special kind of country. Internecine arguments were dropped, and the Brazilian ports gradually became more and more open to international trade. This wholly unexpected transfer of a rather musty old Court into the most colourful and least conformist country in the world incidentally favoured the birth of an independence for which the countries beyond the Andes had had to fight hard. King Juan VI having somewhat unwillingly rallied Lisbon to try to save the tottering remains of his throne, his son Pedro uttered the famous cry of Ipiranga : 'Independence or death !' That was on 7 September 1822 : Pedro I became the emperor of a Brazil which won its liberty with an ease that other countries might well envy.

A unique case in the history of both Americas, Brazil won its independence through the action of a Portuguese sovereign born in Portugal. Dom Pedro I went on to show himself a wise and politically astute head of state. But his son, Dom Pedro II, was an absolutely extraordinary man, so that while their neighbours in Argentina and Paraguay were living as best they could under the cruelty or dishonesty of their

caudillos, the Brazilians were lucky enough to become subjects of a king more enlightened than any Europe had ever
before seen.

Dom Pedro II, who ruled from 1850 to 1889, is remembered
as a man of peace, a liberal, a lover of the arts and literature,
translator of Hamlet. The petty tyrants then ruling the republics liberated from Spain considered Napoleon their ideal :
Pedro II considered Pasteur and Victor Hugo the greatest
men of the day. In 1850 he stopped the legal importation of
slaves into Brazil. Having conquered the Paraguayans in 1870
with the help of the Argentinians and Uruguayans, he
demanded not a single inch of their land, nor a penny of
their money. His liberalism contributed to the loss of that
empire. The complete abolition of slavery in 1888, and the
rise of the great republican movement led to the fall of Pedro
II. Abandoned by the land-owning oligarchy who were enraged by the loss of their cheap black labour, the scholar-
Emperor had to go back to Europe.

The republic very soon entered on a period of violence,
disturbance and revolution. Brazil had never yet had a
caudillo. It had *coronels* – not necessarily soldiers, indeed
most often landed proprietors – who could dictate the law
because they were rich, powerful, daring and unscrupulous.
From 1906 to 1930 Brazil had eight presidents, whose political fortunes depended wholly on the goodwill of the *coronels*
who could pull strings behind the scenes in the Tiradentes
palace. Yet despite all the troubles, immigrants continued to
arrive – Portuguese, Italians, Germans, Slavs, Japanese,
Lebanese, Syrians and Turks. This mixture of nationalities
gradually created a new race – Brazilian man – who is today in
a position to estimate both his strengths and weaknesses.

Sugar throve in the dark, rich soil of the north east. Coffee
spread over the red earth of São Paulo, from Paraná de Santa
Catarina almost to the borders of Paraguay. Sugar saw the

birth of a tropical, static society, dependent on the mill. The gold and diamond rush helped bring into existence a multitude of small centres of population which remained alive even after the *ciclo de mineraçao* had ended, and became the nuclei of modern industrial development. Coffee completely overthrew all the structures of the past. It was a crop demanding a huge labour force, and resulting in the migration of negro slaves from the north east, and the arrival of many of the European immigrants who were flooding into the south. 'Coffee,' said Roger Bastide, 'is a *bandeirante* plant, a plant that keeps moving on, invading new areas, leaving behind it used up earth and deserted towns.'

Starting from Rio, the coffee wave rolled over the state of São Paulo through the Paraíba valley in about 1830. The history of its progress, which fills the end of the nineteenth and beginning of the twentieth century, is also the history of the fantastic development of São Paulo. In 1900, São Paulo had a population of only 80,000. By 1920, it was 580,000; by 1925, 720,000; by 1940, 1,500,000; and by 1952, 2,250,000. In 1961 it had become larger than Rio with its 3½ million inhabitants. The state of São Paulo, covering no more than 9 per cent of the country's land area, contains almost 20 per cent of its population. It provides 44 per cent of its industrial and 32 per cent of its agricultural revenue. It would be a mistake to explain this fantastic growth only in terms of the development of this one magical crop. Other factors contributed to making it *the* mushroom city of Brazil, the first industrial centre in the whole of South America : the proximity of the port of Santos, to which it is linked by a magnificent motorway, the rapid development of considerable hydro-electric power, and, above all, its being so near the mineral wealth of Minas State and the iron-ore centre of Volta Redonda. But certainly it was first and foremost the development of coffee-growing that marked the beginning of its prosperity.

Up until at least 1930 the periodic crises arising out of the low price or over-production of coffee played a considerable part in Brazilian political life. It is no less clear that the development graph of São Paulo is a fairly close reflection of that of coffee production. In 1900 there were reckoned to be at least 600,000,000 coffee trees, and from the turn of the century coffee might well be described as the new master of the Brazilian economy. The crop, which was no more than 147,000 60-kg sacks in 1836, filled over 15 million such sacks by 1906. The social and personal revolutions resulting from this new population area were in the same proportions. Coffee, like sugar or mining, called for a large labour force. Like the owners of the sugar mills in the north east, the *fazendeiros** of São Paulo began to demand negro slaves.

Historians are not agreed as to the precise numbers of negro slaves forcibly brought into São Paulo. It seems probable, however, that several hundred thousand moved from the north east to the south in the space of a few years, from the sugar-cane to the coffee plantations. It is, furthermore, fairly certain that the slave traffic was carried on in secret for the richer of the plantations well after all trade in negro slaves had been forbidden by law. But illegal slave-dealing became more fiercely repressed during the final years of the nineteenth century, and instead the free immigration of workers from Europe and the whole Mediterranean basin supplied the labour that was needed. From 1887 to 1900 the area of São Paulo alone received 863,000 immigrants. This white labour force, these *colonos* as they were then called, worked alongside the negroes, who slowly and gradually became free. Big estates, slavery, paternalism: the society brought into being by the coffee period has many major features in common with the tropical society created by the sugar civilization; but there is a different note in it which is one of the bones of contention between Gilberto Freyre and

* Estate owners.

other sociologists. Freyre sees coffee, two centuries after Bahia and Recife, as having produced the same kind of patriarchal society in São Paulo. Those who disagree with him see the Brazil which has been built up, first around São Paulo, and then the southern state, as being an entirely new country, completely different from the archaic and rural civilization of the north east. In effect, as Jacques Lambert has pointed out, the two countries, the colonial and the modern, are indissolubly interlinked, even though the areas in which each was established are quite clearly defined. It was not only the north-eastern and northern states which stood out against the economic revolution of São Paulo and its dynamism; the same thing happened in country areas relatively close to the heart of São Paulo where the *caboclos* – Brazil's *mujiks* – live.

The forward march of coffee went on during the first thirty years of the twentieth century. From São Paulo it spread over into Paraná, where the land was better. The erosion of the early coffee-lands, successive crises of over-production (coffee was burnt in Brazilian locomotives for the first time in 1905), and the depression of 1930 which was all the more of a disaster for Brazil in that it coincided with a further period of over-production : all these helped to explain the decline and transformation of the coffee boom. The large estates were broken up. Such secondary crops as cotton, tobacco, vines began to appear. And, more important still, the *fazendeiros* began to invest their declining but still considerable profit in mining, industry and trade. So, though it had tragic consequences in many American countries, the 1930 crash gave the economy of São Paulo a completely new impetus. God was now no longer just Brazilian : he was from São Paulo. Buildings, banks, skyscrapers and industries rose up almost overnight in the city.

From 1930 onwards the process of industrialization marked the beginning of a new phase in the development not only of São Paulo itself, but, as a consequence, of all Brazil. The world depression forced the country to develop its own internal markets, and the government's policy of supporting coffee, which at that time represented three quarters of the country's exports, made the period of transition easier than it might have been. Price guarantees for all coffee produced went hand in hand with the destruction of stocks. According to Celso Furtado, the total amount of coffee destroyed in ten years was as much as 80 million 60-kg sacks. But the necessary reduction in imports contributed to the development of Brazilian consumer industries (textiles, foodstuffs, and so on). Then the contribution from the interior to total industrial production which had been 19 per cent in 1940 fell to 5·1 per cent in 1965. This phenomenon was visible in every sector of industrial activity. Celso Furtado distinguishes two phases in the development of Brazil since 1945. The first, until 1955, was a time when the annual growth rate was about 6 per cent. The second, from 1960 onwards, has seen that rate go down to less than 5 per cent. Thus, in the building industry, for example, the growth rate went down from 6·4 per cent in 1950 to 2·8 per cent in 1965. In agriculture, in the same period, the rate rose painfully from 5 per cent to 6·9 per cent. Furthermore, industrial development has not yet had any notable repercussions on exports: in 1967 coffee still represented 40 per cent of the income from exports, while other raw materials (cotton, sugar, iron ore) provided a further 50 per cent. To make matters worse the continual lowering of the prices of raw materials from 1955 to 1968 (cocoa, for instance, fell from 748 dollars a ton to 505) virtually cancelled out the profits that a 40 per cent rise in the volume of exports should have brought. It is evident that the industrial sector in Brazil is finding it hard to get into the international trading world, despite the modernizing of its traditional industries, and the establishment of new and more technologically advanced ones.

So, over the past forty years, Brazil has seen both the benefits and the problems of planned industrialization. Clearly the structure it has built up must now be strengthened by the support of an infra-structure which is still badly deficient in too many areas. Here again, thanks to its being so very much wealthier than any of the other states, São Paulo has set the lead. On the river Paraná, 700 kilometres from São Paulo city, two vast dams are planned to produce 4,600,000 kilowatts. The second section of the Urubupangá complex, which is intended by itself to produce 3,200,000 kilowatts by 1978, will be the third largest power station in the world. But even by 1971 Brazil should have twice the available power it had in 1962.

*

A Brazilian sergeant major, Francisco Palheta, actually smuggled the first coffee plant in in the eighteenth century from French Guiana, and took it to the state of Parà on the north-east coast of Brazil. By a curious coincidence, the end of the Brazilian rubber boom was reminiscent of the beginning of the coffee era. Henry Wickham, an English settler in Santarém by the Amazon, received a letter one day from a botanist in London, begging to be sent seeds of the *hevea*, or rubber tree. That was in 1876. For about twenty years wild rubber from the Amazon had been the chief source of supply for the world market, which demanded it in ever greater quantities. Wickham organized a secret expedition up the Tapajós, a tributary of the Amazon, and gathered thousands of seeds of the *hevea brasiliensis* – a tree whose smooth trunk can rise to a height of over ninety feet. From England where he sent them the seeds were sent out to Singapore and Java, and those which survived this astounding secret journey were the start of the rubber plantations in the islands of the Sunda Strait; these at once began yielding four times more than these same trees in their wild state in the Amazonian forest; furthermore, they were close to the sea, so that transport was cheaper, and there was plenty of local labour. All these advantages made them well able to compete with Brazilian rubber, though it was not for a few years that the triumph of south-east Asian rubber became obvious.

In 1890 south-east Asia still only produced a mere 500 tons of latex, while from the Amazon 16,000 tons were reaching the market. By 1913, on the eve of World War I, these proportions had been reversed, with Brazil exporting 37,000 tons, and Asia 47,500. At a blow the price of rubber fell by nearly two thirds.

Once again disappointment in Brazil was in proportion to the previous excitement. During the forty years of Brazil's monopoly in the world rubber market, there had been a new rush of *bandeirantes* and adventurers to the Amazon area. Tens of thousands of men penetrated deep into the jungle to find *hevea* trees. 'They came from the dry lands of the north east,' writes Josué de Castro, 'sturdy, hopeful and reassured to find such ample water supplies. They were going into virgin forest. They tended the rubber trees, and drew off the precious liquid. They smoked rubber. They sold it for fabulous prices. And just as they were beginning to feel that they owned the world, the ground fell away beneath their feet. Their legs were suddenly feeble and soft, and the weakness rose from their feet to their stomachs. Their chests felt as if they were held in a vice: it was beriberi, and it took possession of their bodies, destroyed their nerves, killed their vitality ...'

The brief and thrilling rubber boom brought fantastic excitement to a town that had been barely more than a village: Manaus. The townspeople, drunk on the sale of rubber, longed to have their streets paved, like those of Rio, with mosaic; they wanted bridges, electric trams, palaces, churches and even an opera house where Pavlova herself might come one day to dance. The rubber boom began in

1860, and ended more or less on the eve of the First World War, but the *seringueiros* refused to accept that Amazonas was no longer supreme. On two occasions all Manaus believed that the miracle was to be repeated. In 1927 Henry Ford, irritated by having to put up with the disadvantages of the new British monopoly in rubber, invested 20 million dollars in trying to revive two plantations alongside the river Tapajós. But working conditions in this difficult area remained so appalling, and tropical diseases wrought such ravages among his workmen, that the enterprise lasted only a short time. During the Second World War the Japanese got control of the *hevea* plantations in south-east Asia. But it was too late for Amazonas. The last flickerings of a fire that had been burning Brazil's blood for twenty years had died out. And Manaus was once more a provincial equatorial town 3,000 kilometres from the Atlantic and completely surrounded by forest. Yet there still remains something of that last wild yearning for quick money. The rubber boom made it possible for Brazilians to explore areas they had hardly known before. Offices were set up, towns established, and a network of waterways for transport put into operation. The first steps had been made for the next economic – and human – adventure: oil.

The imperative need to keep the Amazon area safe from foreign covetousness has, since 1960, inspired a daring plan for developing all the riches of that vast forestland. It still remains to be carried out. But to inhabit the area is the best way to prevent infiltration by the Americans: both military and intellectual circles in Brazil are convinced that the Pentagon has its own plan for 'neutralizing' Amazonia, in order to gain control of its vast potential resources, and dominate an area whose strategic importance is obvious. Manaus became a free port in 1968, and this contributed to a new start for trade in the former rubber capital. It is now linked by regular air routes with Miami and Rio. Iron has been found beneath the banks of the river Madeira, and a steelworks is being built on the banks of the river Negro which flows into the Amazon. In 1970 it will produce 120,000 tons of steel. Other projects are under consideration (especially hydro-electric schemes) in addition to the extraction of oil and manganese now taking place in the Amapá territory, the Brazilian section of the 'green hell'.

*

If one analyses it, old Brazil is concentrated in the north-east, where nearly 50 per cent of the population still lives. It is an area where negroes, mulattoes, *mamelucos*, people of mixed blood with skins of every shade, abound. The other new Brazil is in the south, in São Paulo, in Minas, and in the states of Paraná, Santa Catarina and Rio Grande do Sul, where the massive immigration of Europeans, north Africans, Lebanese and Japanese has entirely changed the population. Obviously it is not just as simple as that. Poverty and wealth are not divided by a straight line. There are *favelas** below the residential areas of Rio, slums in the suburbs of São Paulo, and forgotten *fazendas* living on in their old way in Minas Gerais. There are, too, islands of prosperity and modernity in Bahia, Recife and even in the heart of the Amazon states. But, in the main, after four centuries of conquest, of the pioneering – and at times bloody, heroic or disastrous – adventures of the *bandeirantes*, after the successive or coinciding booms in sugar, gold, diamonds, coffee and rubber, we are beginning to see the whole picture a bit more clearly.

The state of São Paulo is still the moving force of the federation. Like a locomotive, it draws the other states behind it, reluctantly at times. In the United States the progressive conquest of the land created a country in which the industrialized north confronted the agrarian and slave-owning south. In Brazil it was the other way round. In 1932

* Slums or shanty-towns.

São Paulo for the first time gave evidence of its power by having a revolution in the name of the Constitution.

The locomotive refused to fulfil the function of leader which nature, men, and luck had combined to give it, thus giving Brazil its small-scale and brief war of secession – only in reverse. In any case, São Paulo was brought to heel by the federal capital and the other states which combined against it. But the defeat was only temporary; for the only way in which the latent antagonism between south and north can be removed, the only way to raise living standards for all in Brazil – even those living on the old sugar estates, in the *favelas*, the townships, and the poor farmland of the interior – is to industrialize and diversify the economy of the country. The 1930 slump and the gradual decline of the single-crop economy – a source of easy money, but also of unexpected disaster – combined to direct Brazil along this wise path.

*

Brazil's future depends on a continual improvement of agricultural technology and a well-planned industrial expansion. There are plenty of indications that this process is in fact taking place, and that it will go on despite the most difficult obstacles and grave handicaps. The Kubitschek government developed agricultural credit through the Bank of Brazil. The Quadros government planned to create a central bank for agricultural credit. Definite results have already been achieved in the sphere of mechanization. From 1951 to 1959 more than 60,000 tractors were imported. This mechanization is indispensable, for in 1950 three quarters of all farming was still being done by hand. But these are only palliatives in relation to the agrarian reform which absolutely must be brought about. A few figures will be enough to indicate how badly reform is needed : the area cultivated annually is not even 2 per cent of the total area, and 45 per cent of the cultivated ground consists of estates of over 1,000 hectares;

more than 15 per cent of that is occupied by estates of over 10,000 hectares. And these vast estates are still being worked by archaic methods which make it impossible to increase productivity, and in fact can only tend to make more and more farm workers migrate to the cities. The large landowners are naturally hostile to any sort of reform, while holdings of less than 20 hectares occupy only 5 per cent of the agricultural land. The vast estates are on a particularly horrifying scale in the north east, where their ridiculous under-production is the sheerest waste of what could be tremendous agricultural wealth. Yet 40 million Brazilians still live off the land, and in utter destitution. The vast majority of these *caboclos* live almost like serfs, working, when they can get work, in conditions one can hardly bear to describe, especially in the north east – conditions of exploitation similar to those imposed on the peasants by the large landowners of Peru, Colombia or Ecuador, to name but a few.

The problem of agrarian reform has often been mooted in Brazil, but there has never been even the tentative beginning of a solution. The attempt of the Goulart government, though modest enough and quite inadequate, met with insurmountable obstacles in March 1964, and was in fact one of the reasons for that government's fall. Goulart's plan was that all lands lying alongside the main roads and railways should be expropriated to a depth of ten kilometres. Only estates not being cultivated and more than a hundred hectares in size were to be affected. In other words it was planned to take over 9 per cent of the agricultural land and give it to, at the most, 150,000 peasants. The 'land statute' passed in November 1964 by the Castello Branco government gave the federal authorities power to expropriate land where it was in the interest of society and pay for it with national bonds. In 1968 the work of census-taking and surveying which were to make the application of this plan possible was not yet completed. Brazil is thus one of the few countries in Latin America not yet to have made any serious attempt to deal with the problem, despite its urgency.

The inadequacy of means of transport, and the paucity of the capital at the nation's disposal are the chief things that are strangling the Brazilian economy, together with the extreme weakness of the internal consumer market. Thus it is not surprising to discover that even the most basic industry did not seriously begin until during the Second World War. Needless to say São Paulo has the most impressive figures to show, and its people are proud of the fact. A million and a half workers are operating 40,000 factories in this richest state. A single trust, the Matarazze, controls 300 enterprises and employs 30,000 workers. There has been no diminution in the gulf between north and south. Yet from the most northern area to the deepest south, one can see certain significant developments. The steelworks of Volta Redonda, in the Paraíba valley, 145 kilometres from Rio, was established in 1942. Today it is the leading producer of steel in the whole of Latin America. In 1955 Brazil did not make a single motor vehicle; in 1961 it produced 180,000 cars, and sold 110,000 washing machines, 150,000 television sets, half a million radios, 350,000 sewing machines, 300,000 refrigerators, and 120,000 air-conditioners. From 1963 onwards there was a certain stagnation : 196,000 vehicles in 1964 and 195,000 in 1965. But the production of steel is increasing, and was due to be between 6 and 7 million tons in 1970. And the plans for future expansion include the setting up of several large steelworks to function in cooperation. All this is mainly the work of Usiminas, which has been in operation since 1964, and whose annual production capacity could reach a million tons, and COSIPA, founded in 1965, which should produce 800,000 tons. The Volta Redonda steelworks itself should have raised its output from 1·3 million to 3 million tons of steel within ten years. The definite diminution of the general dynamism of the Brazilian economy to be seen since 1960 has not stopped the Brazilians from making plans which some economists consider both daring and illogical, their view being that the accent should be put on reinforcing the infra-structure and redistributing the national income more fairly.

It is true that cement-works, chemical industries and mechanical industries now proliferate in the valleys where not so long ago gold-hungry prospectors were hard at work. The chemical industry in particular has developed remarkably: following the example of Mexico and Venezuela, Brazil has concentrated especially on petro-chemical installations which yield tremendous savings in dollars.

The former negro slaves and immigrants attracted by rumours of an Eldorado in Brazil have become workers, organized into unions, whose ever stronger and more coherent demands make it clear that Brazil is ready to put the *coronel* and the *patriarche* into the antique shop once and for all. Smoke from the factories rises at the feet of mountains still bearing scars where gold was clumsily and too hastily hacked out. Food is being produced in areas where not so long ago the only visitors were the *garimpeiros*.* Gold is being mined by modern methods at Nova Lima, the deepest gold mines in the world. The sub-soil of Minas, which has produced 14 thousand million tons of iron ore, still has vast untapped resources. Metallurgical factories have been set up in Sabara and near Belo Horizonte. Buildings of glass and steel, those symbols of industrial development, have altered the whole peaceful skyline of Belo Horizonte, the mushroom town of the past decade, and are also going up in Macapá. The Paulo Afonso falls into São Francisco river have been channelled to complete the hydro-electric centre for the states of Rio, São Paulo and Minas. This is perhaps the most profitable of all the recent changes in Brazil.

Macapá, the capital of Amapá territory, is only a stone's throw from the Amazon jungle, in the shadow of the legend-

* Prospectors.

ary Tumucumaque mountains which inspired a whole generation of explorers. Today Amapá territory has a network of
roads, a hydro-electric power station on the river Araguari,
paved streets where once there were only muddy clay paths,
and a port with all the equipment needed to export the millions of tons of ore from the magic mountain, the Serra do
Navo; indeed the fact that such a mountain could be tamed
is proof that there is no portion of the vast land of Brazil that
cannot make a contribution to the enrichment of the country
as a whole.

Kubitschek in 1956 said this : 'I shall do for Brazil what I
have done in my own State.' Every president of Brazil has
since made the same promise. Juscelino Kubitschek was
elected in 1955 by the Vargas party's electoral machine, but
the wave of support which bore him to the presidency would
not have been so powerful had he not achieved a radical
modernization of the State of Minas Gerais where he had been
governor. He launched an ambitious five-year plan for public
works which was based on four main elements : energy,
transport, food and basic industries. Even Jânio Quadros, who
hated plans, statistics and definite promises, also fixed a final
date for what was in effect a further five-year plan : this involved tripling the mileage of asphalt roads, producing 9 million kilowatts an hour by 1965 and 15 million by 1970,
reducing the proportion of the illiterate among the population from 62 per cent to 30 per cent, and doubling the output
of steel to 6 million tons by 1965. Quadros, the empiricist,
also started out with planning. The records he was setting
himself to beat may have even seemed a bit too ambitious to
the more realistic technologists in Brasilia. But this 'new
broom's' challenge was not to be put to the test, since he
decided to give up his office after only six months.

*

Brazil certainly has everything; all the most essential cereals, the most exotic fruits, lead, and all the other minerals needed to produce atomic energy. Clearly it possesses almost all the conditions which could make it one of the great powers in the future. But what is not so clear is whether the average standard of living of tomorrow's 200 million Brazilians will be any nearer to that of the average north American – whether it will not still be more like that of the poorest of the poor in Egypt, or over-populated India. In Rio and São Paulo rich connoisseurs have created outstanding museums of modern art. But one in every three Brazilians is still illiterate. 'Poor little Niagara,' cried Mrs Eleanor Roosevelt as she looked at the incredible Iguaçu falls by the border where Argentina, Paraguay and Brazil meet. Yet in 1966 Brazil was still producing no more than 5 million kilowatts an hour in any dependable form. Families like the Matarazzos or the Lunardellis have built up vast fortunes, yet less than two hours by plane from São Paulo there are Indians still living in the stone age who shoot arrows at the planes that fly overhead. Quite close to the magnificent air-conditioned buildings in Copacabana men live in *favelas* and eat the same food as primitives in the equatorial forests of Africa. Half the population of Brazil in fact suffers from chronic malnutrition. And it is not just a chance that the man who has been fighting world hunger so passionately and effectively is a Brazilian : Josué de Castro. In his book, *The Geopolitics of Hunger*, Castro has some overwhelming descriptions of the destitution and physical disintegration of the peasants in Brazil, brothers in misery of the peasants of India, the West Indies, Black Africa, and southeast Asia. Half the people have no shoes. One Brazilian child in three will be lucky enough to get to any school. Only one in six will have the chance of secondary education.

In the Mato Grosso, in Campo Grande, in the southern states and in the red lands where the coffee grows, rich *fazendeiros* have their private planes and airstrips. Yet it is questionable whether the aeroplane can really solve the fundamental problem of communications, despite the immense development of air transport (three quarters of all the air travel in the world takes place in the sky over Brazil). The rivers too are insufficient: there are 54,000 kilometres of navigable waterways, but the available craft are unsuitable or completely out of date. Yet, paradoxically, it is more profitable and more practical to send commodities from Belém to Santos by water than by road. Boat traffic is developing proportionately far faster than any other kind. Railways, especially, have made only the most modest inroads into the industrialized areas of the south (37,000 kilometres of railway line). Consequently the construction of good roads is an absolute priority. Pierre Monbeig says, quite rightly, that 'the lorry driver is the *bandeirante* of today'. Nowhere in the world are roads harder to build or more expensive to maintain. Nowhere in the world does road transport have so many or such varied obstacles to contend with. Yet only roads can give an adequate solution to this key problem of linking the various regions. It is not just a matter of the long distances to be covered; first and foremost it is a problem of neighbourly relationships – the real basic political unit in Brazil is the small town, and for a long time first Salvador and then Rio were capitals only in theory of a land in which the different states either knew nothing of one another, or were positively antagonistic. Brasilia, the new federal capital, is certainly a challenge to nature and a risk for the future; but it is also historically, politically and economically a necessity. Most of the 90 million Brazilians live in poverty along a narrow shoreline. The only way in which Brazil can improve the standard of living for the 200 million people it may well have in the year 2000 is to start *now* to make use of the virgin lands of the interior. The Brazilians believed they had everything. They are now in the process of discovering the *marcha para o oeste* – the 'Go west, young man' – which could be the opening of a new epic for the *bandeirantes* of the twentieth century.

*

More legends, more witchcraft, more prophets, more mystery and violence have come out of the *sertão* than any other area in Brazil. More people too. The *sertão* does not actually have any clearly defined boundaries. It could be said to begin 50 or 100 or even more kilometres from the coast. It is, first and foremost, a magnificent piece of scenery – the style of the *caatinga*, an Indian word which can be roughly translated as the white forest. In the *sertão* the trees are like dried bones, as though they had just been through a terrible fire. Bushes, cacti and thorny plants spread over dry and hard soil with scattered stones, and long stretches of sand. A fiery sky flames above this grand and mysterious country, a place where everything is sharp and bony, painful to the touch, hard on the eyes. Men as wild and harsh as the land, dressed in skins or ragged old clothes, trail round on bony horses seeking any possible source of water for their cattle. Geographers have given a fearful name to this area, which extends along the river São Francisco, and all the land east of a line from Bahia to Fortaleza : they call it the polygon of drought. It may have less than 400 millimetres of rainfall in a year; indeed there may be several years running with no rain at all. So the *sertão* fully justifies all the curses and cries of despair it has inspired for centuries. The *vaqueiros*, the cowmen of the area, tell their children and grandchildren terrible tales of the agonies they have undergone as a warning. The drought of 1877–9 killed 58,000 people and drove another 125,000 away from the place. The drought of 1915 killed 30,000, drove away 32,000 and saw the total disappearance of 700,000 cattle, 200,000 horses and more than 2 million goats and sheep. The last major drought was in 1952–3, and then again the dusty trails of the *sertão* were filled with pitiful streams of people dying of hunger and thirst, trying to get to the promised land of the south, to flowing water, and green grass. Men, women and children looking like skeletons pushed forward along the endless thirsty road, littered with the whitening bones of dead animals, as vultures flew overhead. And though it is only as dramatic as that from time to time, there is in fact a permanent stream of people moving out.

Every year thousands of people leave the *sertão* to look for work and food in the rich states of São Paulo and the south. But they hate leaving, for their love of their cruel stony homeland is in proportion to the suffering it has inflicted upon them. A man from the *sertão* loves his desert as a sailor the sea, or a mountain-dweller his glaciers. Around 1900, nearly 50,000 cowmen set off for the Amazon during the rubber boom, in the hope of exchanging a life of certain misery for the illusory security of the rubber worker. From 1940 to 1960 the chief states through which the *sertão* extends – Ceará, Rio Grande do Norte, Alagôas, Pernambuco and Paraíba in particular – continued to lose people by the thousand to São Paulo, Rio and the states of the south. The civilization of the *sertão*, characterized by the mournfulness and taciturnity of the Indian, is harsh, pitiless and a continual battle to survive. It is also a civilization depending on cattle rather than horses, whose true home is the pampas land of Rio Grande do Sul. There are no herds. Barbed wire enclosures have barely begun to appear; animals wander about under the empty sky looking for thorny plants that are edible, and water holes dug by the cowmen in the beds of rivers long since dried up. As droughts approach, people and animals disperse still more, and only the strongest remain. So the folklore of the *sertão* pays honour to the independence of the bull as to that of the *vaqueiro* who looks after him : blind singers, their sight destroyed by the burning sun, go from farm to farm singing the exploits of famous bulls – so proud that they prefer death to becoming domesticated. The death and resurrection of the bull is the central theme of the *Bumba-meu-boi*, a kind of farcical mixture of dancing and acting which is put on in *sertão* villages on festival days. There is nothing in the *sertão* that is not a symbol, a sign or a warning; people watch the sky, the stars, the moon, the birds, the movements of ants, and even the way their goats kick, in order to try to divine whether or no it will rain. For life and death are closely linked with the clouds and wind which can from one moment to the next bring greenery and life back to their dry land. Primitive singers repeat over and over the despairing laments of those who walk forever to meet death in their burnt-out country.

The *sertão* is also the land of the *cangaceiros* – highwaymen of a kind whose glamour is dear to the hearts of the people. The first *cangaceiro* appeared quite suddenly after one of those periods of exceptional aridity which turn the *sertão* into a real hell. At first, groups of *cangaceiros*, half mad with hunger, poverty and despair were no more than gangs of thieves. They killed and robbed, spreading panic and confusion in the villages throughout the interior. Continually picking up new members as they went on their desperate way, they would attack isolated *fazendas* and commit horrifying atrocities. But the modern – and mythical – image of the *cangaceiro* bears little relationship to this tale of blind and bloody violence; the modern *cangaceiro* is blood-brother to the Mexican bandit who defends widows and orphans, assists exploited peasants, and redistributes ill-gotten wealth; he is violent, generous and poor. Like the Mexican he wears a great hat with a rolled-up brim, pistols in his belt, and wide trousers over his boots. The last of the *cangaceiros*, who is still much talked of, was called Lampião. The death of Lampião, struck down after one last strong Brazilian drink, coincided with the coming of written laws, and the arrival of motor vehicles to the *sertão*. A great many people there still believe that Lampião is not really dead, and that one day he will return, as perhaps also will *Conselheiro*, the Counsellor, one of the most famous of the innumerable prophets created by the strange ecstasy of the *sertão* and its droughts.

*

Around 1896 Antonio Conselheiro was preaching the end of the world to thousands of disciples who were caught up in his mania and fervour. He even built a capital, Canudos, and three military expeditions which the government of the new republic of Brazil sent against him were decimated by his cowmen supporters, and by the hazards of the desert with which they were wholly unfamiliar. Finally Canudos, Conselheiro, and his flock were exterminated as the result of the kind of apocalyptic massacre the prophet himself might have dreamt up. But the laments and cries of those who bit the dust in the *sertão* finally reached the ears of all Brazil. No longer can any central government let itself ignore the north east in any of its planning. In one sense the situation is completely absurd : for the *sertão* is no exception to that cruel but immutable law of human societies whereby hunger only serves to increase procreation. Despite famines, vendettas and emigrations, the *sertão* still produces more human lives each year than it destroys. To save those lives, the government is building dams, and promises agrarian reform. Indeed the money spent on the north east in the past twenty years would have made it possible to re-settle the whole population of the *sertão* in the virgin land of the western part of central Brazil. Celso Furtado was commissioned before 1964 by the Goulart government to run SUDENE, a state organization specially concerned with the development of the north east by means of heavy public and private investment – with private capital to be attracted by the promise of vast returns. SUDENE was proposing to investigate ways and means of developing this area, so long neglected, whose population has an annual average income of only a quarter that of the people in the south east. To industrialize, to irrigate, to develop mining and farming – all these objectives determined by experts in the Goulart government were adopted by the directors of SUDENE appointed by the Castello Branco and Costa e Silva governments since April 1964, when Celso Furtado lost all political power and escaped to France. (It is significant that Furtado was invited by the Brazilian congress in June 1968 to present his views on the problems of development.) Dissatisfaction, despair and fanaticism have turned that over-populated triangle of land into one of the areas most ripe for revolutionary ideas. There is no longer complete isolation, since motor vehicles now travel along the old earth roads and new highways. The lorry driver, the man driving through the *sertão*, would describe in the villages there what was happening in the rest of the world. Of all Latin America, the north east of Brazil was one of the areas in which the agrarian reforms in Cuba were discussed with most excitement. In the various Indo-American capitals, in Quito, Bogotá, Lima, La Paz, as well as in Venezuela and Uruguay, students demonstrated in the streets with shouts of 'Cuba, sí; Yankee no.' But in general the masses of the country people have been undisturbed – except in the Brazilian north-east where farm workers had been getting organized into unions from 1948 up to 1964.

Francisco Julião was a lawyer. His fame had not yet extended beyond the bounds of the north east, but his name was often heard in the corridors of the presidential palace of Brasilia. In the hope of discrediting him his enemies accused him of Castroist and communist sympathies; but Julião was no disciple of Castro – he was if anything his unknown forerunner. The 'peasant leagues' of the north-east had begun to come into being spontaneously in 1948. When the first dispute between farm workers and landowners was brought to arbitration before Francisco Julião the legal expert, Castro was still only a young and impatient revolutionary in the making, preparing to attack the Moncada barracks.

On the great estates where sugar cane was grown (three quarters of the land that was cultivated at all), the workers had almost no means of redress; everything was decided, given or refused by the boss. They got no money, but only tokens they could spend in shops belonging to the landowner. This vast area given over to sugar could have been used for growing food. Instead the food products, which had to be imported, were relatively expensive; furthermore, the fact that there was plenty of labour to be had made it easy to preserve the most appalling conditions of employment. The further into the interior you went, the worse conditions in the *fazendas* were. Farm workers got no money; they would work three or four days for the boss, who allowed them a scrap of land which they barely had time to cultivate. They lived in mud huts, put up and grouped into 'villages' by the *fazendeiro*. Sometimes, however, the sugar harvest near the coast would only last three months; for the rest of the time the mass of casual labourers became an addition to the sub-proletariat whose general conditions were quite certainly a lot worse than those of any of the old negro slaves. Anonymity and contempt now took the place of the protective paternalism of the seventeenth-century feudal landlords. With speech after speech, Francisco Julião gradually won the confidence of the farm workers, and became their leader. He was forty, of mixed blood, impassioned, brave and dynamic; and he finally determined on direct action.

The first trial of strength took place in 1956 on the Engenho Galilea plantation: the day-labourers took possession of the estate and the factory. Armed with guns, knives and sticks, they repulsed an attack (not a very wholehearted one) by soldiers sent by the authorities. The rebels held firm, and the government of Pernambuco state gave way. The state indemnified the owners of the plantation, and distributed the land among the workers. It was a decision with certain political overtones about it, since it was the eve of the presidential election campaign, and the state governor supported Jânio Quadros, and wanted to have a solid vote for him from the north east.

Only later did Francisco Julião have occasion to go to Cuba, together with Quadros. This encounter with the Cuban revolution on the part of the peasant leader and the political demagogue did not end very happily, for Julião became more convinced that Cuban agrarian reform could be applied in Brazil, and on that account he fell out with Quadros.

Following the Engenho Galilea affair there were further rebellions, though none so important. Such anarchist movements could only succeed to the extent that they were of advantage in the political game of the moment. Julião realized this, and therefore determined to work on a long-term operation of organization and propaganda.

The 'peasant leagues' managed to bring together a great many farm workers in the north east, and in 1963 their leader claimed to be assured of the support of 500,000. The centre of the spider's web was Recife, and there was a permanent staff in every 'town in Pernambuco state and along the coast. Julião's programme was a beautifully simple one : 'To transform the *latifundios* into collective farms.' Needless to say the 'peasant leagues' were little more than a joke in the wider political arena, and Julião himself at one time almost gave up in despair.

In the meetings he organized, the portraits most commonly put up for the admiration of the multitude were those of Fidel Castro and Luis Carlos Prestes, head of the Brazilian Communist Party. The unrest inspired by the 'peasant leagues' grew, and the federal government decided on large-scale military activity as being the only way to deal with possible trouble. In the spring of 1961, following student demonstrations, the town of Recife was occupied by the army.

The Goulart government, on the other hand, was quick to realize the value of this movement for self-defence on the part of the north-eastern workers whose leader, or more precisely whose adviser, was certainly now more definitely Castroist than he had been. Colleagues of Julião went to Cuba to study the methods and results of the agrarian reforms brought about by the revolution there. Within Goulart's government were people closely and sympathetically following what was happening in the 'leagues' which were, for the first time, putting the big landowners and ruling classes of the north east on the defensive. The contagion spread to the neighbouring states of Pernambuco, Alagoas, Ceará, Maranhão and even Paraíba. The period when Miguel Arraes, a liberal from Crato, involved in Catholic circles, was governor of Recife was a particularly favourable one for the 'leagues'. Their spokesmen at last found in the governor's palace a man with power who genuinely and passionately wanted to hear the voices of the oppressed. The coup of April 1964, largely caused by the need to put a stop to agrarian reform that was judged to be 'subversive' by the landowners, could not fail to destroy the 'leagues'. Repression was particularly harsh in the weeks following Goulart's fall. Julião fled, and, though he was taken in by a deputy friend of his, was in the end arrested. In prison he joined Miguel Arraes who had refused to yield to the will of the military rulers. The two men's paths were later to diverge: after he got out of prison, Julião went to Mexico and worked for a time with the Cubans. Arraes, after a year in prison, got out of Brazil with some difficulty, and settled in Algiers to think out new forms of revolutionary action.

*

A common tourist trip of Brazil will begin in Copacabana and end in Salvador (Bahia). Copacabana is something of a disappointment. Behind its six kilometres of beach with the great Atlantic rollers foaming in, its mosaic footpaths and white buildings, there is – nothing. Bahia, on the other hand, has so much that can be gradually explored, one flight of steps after another, one church after another. It is a dead, a has-been town, and yet it is more lively than any of the others. Though in the north, its people are as talkative and truculent as any in the south, and it has the most gifted writers and subtle politicians. Bahia is more African than American. In 1968 it had nearly a million inhabitants, almost 60 per cent of them negro or mulatto. Broken into two by the vast cliff that runs almost to the bay, its upper and lower towns are linked by lifts as in Sorrento – yet the two differ little, both filled with the same smells of cooking and palm oil.

The country most closely linked with Bahia is Guinea, from which the first slaves came, and wood from there is still used to make the little hands that act as charms against bad luck. The *condomblés* of African worship, Guinean or Dahomeyan, can be heard through the heavy Bahian nights more loudly than anywhere else. Not just at Carnival time, but all the year round, Bahia dances, sings, hums, and is constantly astir for one or another of those colourful festivals, some touching, some totally surrealist, which have grown out of the combined influences of Christianity, paganism, animism, of the white man, the Indian and the negro. For a long time Bahia was the capital of Brazil. Thomé de Souza, the first governor, established himself there in 1549, with a few men-at-arms, some lawyers and a handful of Jesuits. The splendour and the political power of Bahia were contemporary with the sugar monopoly; as the sugar mills fell into disuse, it too began to decline. In 1763, Rio replaced Bahia as the capital. But baroque art still reigns triumphant in Salvador (as the town is now called). At the top of steps littered with baskets, with greasy cakes and fish stews, turbanned mulatto women sit outside the blazing and agonizing façades of Nosso Senhor do Bonfim or São Francisco. According to Arthur Ramos, a Brazilian authority on negro affairs, the majority of the coloured people in Bahia are Sudanese in origin, which may well serve to explain their peculiarly dynamic quality. Whether this is so or not, the negroes in the Salvador area have in fact contributed with immense energy to the economic transformation of what were the sugar-growing lands. Small-holders on their own cultivate one of the finest Brazilian tobaccos, as well as cotton, cassava and maize.

The north-eastern coast provides a striking contrast with the *sertão* of the interior. Tremendous droughts are followed by abundant rains. From the bay of Todos os Santos to Cabo São Roque in the state of Rio Grande do Norte, the rainfall is never less than 900 millimetres a year, and is sometimes even over 2,000. It is a coastline of cocoa palms shaken by the wind, of *restingas*, narrow strips of sand separating lagoons from the open sea, and of *recifes*, reefs, one of which gave its name to the capital city of Pernambuco. With its million inhabitants, Recife has preserved in its stonework and its canals something of its Dutch history. This long, low-lying and humid coastline of the states of Paraíba, Rio Grande do Norte and Ceará, where a good year means no more than 113 days of rain, and the shores of Maranhão, where the memory of the early French sailors still lingers, form a single long beach where, in the evenings, the *jangadeiros* haul up their triangular-sailed rafts, to leave again each morning on those fragile-looking *jangadas*. Their equipment is of the most rudimentary kind : they take a large reed basket to hold the fish, a *cabaça de agua* of fresh water, a pot for food, a net, a stick, the *araçanga*, which can prove useful in beating down over-curious dolphins, and a kind of wooden spoon for wetting the sail, with which to enable it to take more wind. The *jangadeiros* sometimes have to tie themselves to their rafts when the sea is rough, or they may get thrown overboard. Thousands of negroes seeking freedom used this method of travel to get down the coast from one state to another at the end of the slave period, shaking with fear, and hanging on for dear life to those fragile craft as the waves washed over them.

Despite the economic and political decline of the north east as the south developed, the population density there is still the highest in Brazil. In places it reaches over 100 people per square kilometre. Despite – or perhaps because of – famines, mortality and incredible poverty, the north east undoubtedly remains the main fund of human resources in the country.

*

A quarter of all the trees in the world grow in the vast forest of the Amazon which extends – frightening, flourishing and partially in swamp-lands – over 300 million hectares, filling the two states and four federal territories of the north. Nowhere on earth is there a landscape which gives one a more agonizing sense of the extravagant omnipotence of primitive nature, and the merciless battles of the great reptiles of the mesozoic age. Everything is in proportion to the Amazon itself – 6,500 kilometres long. The Indians who paddled their canoes up and down it naturally gave it the same name as the ancient Egyptians gave the Nile: the sea. The river has 1,100 tributaries. It rises in the Andes at a height of 5,000 metres, and descends so steeply to the warm plains of the interior that by the time it makes its majestic entry into Brazil it is only 65 metres above sea level. At that point it still has 3,000 kilometres of forest and grassland to cross before reaching the Atlantic. Thus, despite the enormous volume of water – 100,000 cubic metres a second at Obidos, and 200,000 at its mouth when it is at its highest – it is relatively slow-moving. At Obidos, before the bend of Santaré, it is only 130 metres wide, but by Belém it is 30 kilometres from side to side; and even 100 kilometres out to sea its muddy waters have not been completely absorbed into the ocean. Its mouth proper is 350 kilometres wide, and contains an island, Marajó, as big as Belgium.

One may sum up the character of the Amazon area in two figures: it covers 45 per cent of the total land surface of the Brazilian federation, and only contains 4 per cent of its population. Dreadful things have been said about it: it was the fearful enemy without a single weak spot, there were malarial swamps, fierce Indians, deadly morasses, man-eating plants, fishes that would eat cattle, and monstrous anacondas. The names of its tributaries – the Tapajós, the rio Negro, the rio Maderia, the Itacuai, the rio Branco and the Xingu – did not have the friendly gentleness of the streams that came down to the Plata, but the same mysterious and vaguely disturbing harshness as the naked brown men who sought a patch of daylight to live in among the few sun-pierced areas of the vast forest. It is perfectly true that Amazonia contains one of the most fantastic reserves of flora and fauna in the world. We have not yet put a name to every species of tree and animal to be found there; for instance, the jaguarondis is an apparently ordinary feline, yet so little known that zoologists are not sure precisely what category to put it in. The jaguar, king of the jungle, rules over animals as curious as the sloth or the *tayra*, as ancient as the *jacaré* or the iguana, as persistent as the great ant-eater, to say nothing of the multitude of marmosets, squirrel monkeys, and chattering parrots. Brazilian literature actually contrasts the green hell, the *selva*, with the rio Mar, the great river Sea which makes it possible to travel into this primitive world in which trees and water form one as they did in prehistoric times. Such few men as have ventured into the area have done a lot to help to invest the great equatorial forest of Brazil with a halo of

incredible legends. The first Portuguese *bandeirantes* to pene-
trate it had only one objective : to capture Indian slaves from
their plantations in Belém do Pará and Maranhão. Those who
went after them in search of the natural products of the forest
– vanilla, cinnamon, and still later that latex that was rolled
into huge balls in the rudimentary encampments of the
seringueiros – discovered a world of fear and phantasmagoria
in which the demarcation between land and water, between
fish that walked and flowers that swallowed seemed sometimes only imaginary. The Indian mythology of the ancient
Tupis or Arawaks told of the endless fight and the terror of
man, naked and primitive, struggling through the vastnesses
of that green and watery cave.

The stories of this pre-human world were taken up first by
the mestizos, then by the whites, and everyone did something
to improve on them, filling the Amazon jungle with caval-
cades of Indian Valkyrie – the famous Amazons – who would
rise up in the patches of light that came from the glimmering
of the moon goddess. Travellers swore on the Bible to having
seen terrifying battles among these Amazons, women who
would give themselves to their menfolk only once a year in a
special place. The Indians, gradually pushed further and
further back by the invaders and slave seekers, discovered that
the most pitiless of all the enemies in the great forest was in
truth the cruel hunter of human quarry. In the revised and
corrected edition of their Great Book, the Indians' promised
land soon became a land with no white men in it. The fate of
the Amazonian Indians, and those of the distant lands of
the north west would undoubtedly have been the same as that
of their brothers who were massacred in the West Indies had
it not been for one man who embarked on courageous and
effective action. His name was Rondon and he was a Brazilian
general, a student of Comte's positivism and also an adherent
of the non-violent methods put forward by Gandhi. The

Service for the Protection of Indians, whose exploits and successes have never been matched anywhere in the Americas, grew out of a crisis of conscience which Rondon underwent when sent on a mission to the Brazilian interior.

He suddenly saw the realities of Indian life for the first time and determined to dedicate himself to defending these people whom no one else was helping – indeed for whom many people felt nothing but contempt. From 1890 to 1930 Rondon went on foot, on mule-back or by canoe through over 50,000 kilometres of bush. He laid down 5,000 kilometres of roads, and along them he set up the telegraph wires which today link Rio with Bolivia, Ecuador and Peru. Before his death in 1958 at the age of 93 he was the prime agent in achieving peace on the Brazilian border. Strictly speaking it was he who first conceived the idea of giving technical aid to under-developed peoples. In 1910, when his Protection Service was given official recognition, the fine groups of scouts whom he sent to meet the last Indian tribes still left unscathed by the inroads of explorers and adventurers were given only one order: 'Die yourselves if you have to, but never kill anyone.' It was too late however. Illnesses imported from Europe were killing the Indians as surely as guns or machetes.

And not all the people working on Rondon's Protection Service were equal to the mission as conceived and planned by him. Men sent into the Mato Grosso to protect the last of the Brazilian primitives took advantage of their position to despoil communal lands, and what can only be called massacres were tolerated, or at least ignored by them. This 'genocide' was publicly denounced in 1968 and the government undertook an enquiry which revealed that for many years there had been terrible extortions, and that whole peoples had been simply wiped out. But these were exceptions, and Rondon's own name emerged unstained from the torrent of mud-slinging.

*

There are chalets like those you find in Triberg or Donaue-schingen in the Black Forest; there are restaurants bearing signs of bears or stags serving sauerkraut and German beer; there are shoemakers called Müller or Schmidt. One town in the state of Santa Catarina is even called Blumenau, in memory of a doctor who had established the first German community in southern Brazil by 1850. A massive influx of Germans into this southern land produced a country radically different from other areas. The long-established European settlements and the fragmentation of large estates have made southern Brazil an area of small industry and small-scale farming in sharp contrast with the vast *fazendas* in the states of São Paulo, Minas Gerais, or the north east. The arrival of German immigrants in Brazil continued unbroken from the mid-nineteenth century. The crises and upheavals in German political life, the setbacks to liberalism, Bismarck's *Kultur-kampf* and the Nazi persecutions combined to send waves of fair, blue-eyed men to Paraná and Santa Catarina. After the First World War the German colony had grown to more than half a million. Since 1920 another 100,000 or more immi-grants have arrived, bringing with them their courage, their dynamism, their bitterness and dreams, their individual characteristics and local disputes, as well as a vast appetite for work and regular advancement. They found the same grey skies, cold winters and long periods of rain as they had known at home, and they began to colonize the land that was still free in the directions of Paraguay and São Paulo.

These close-knit and individual communities of Germans caused a certain concern to the central governments when Nazism was at its height; in fact, the Germans who had come to Brazil were Nazi-minded only in their triumphalist wish to see Germany a great nation again, and they were ready to shut their eyes to its crimes and cruelties. There was a genuine risk of a fifth column between 1938 and 1943; the German con-suls in the south suddenly became propagandists for separatism. Though their campaign met with some degree of response in the towns, it failed totally in the countryside. Then, too, the fall of Nazism came soon enough for that separatist enthusiasm to die a natural death. But a prudent Brazilian government decided after the war to offer Brazilian nationality to all immigrants after only a very short time, and almost unconditionally.

In 1872 the three southernmost states, Paraná, Santa Catarina and Rio Grande do Sul, contained 133,446 inhabitants, representing only 7·25 per cent of the population of Brazil. In 1950 this figure was 7,940,000, or 15 per cent. By 1960, with almost 10 million inhabitants, this proportion was maintained. The German immigrants have since been joined by Poles (especially in Paraná, where there are a great many of them and they tend not to mix with other people), Russians, and also Japanese who have mainly specialized in market-gardening and have been spectacularly successful.

You find Japanese colonies of a very homogeneous kind not only in the south of São Paulo state, but also of recent years in Minas, the north east (where they have proved that tomatoes can flourish in what was thought of as exclusively sugar-land) and even in the Amazon area. Thus, alongside the Portuguese, who mainly come from the Azores, and the *gauchos* who are related to the Uruguayans, there has been a recent tremendous increase in the European population which has contributed enormously to the longed-for 'whitening' of the country as a whole. However, even in the south, so individually minded and individualist, the atmosphere remains fundamentally Brazilian. The skyscrapers in Curitiba and Porto Alegre are very like those in São Paulo and Belo Horizonte. The immigrants' descendants no doubt keep a fragment of their old homes somewhere in their hearts from the tales their grandparents tell. But they are at the same time passionate nationalists, and it is clear that they want to be considered as wholeheartedly Brazilian. This became quite obvious after the fall of the Goulart government. Vargas and Goulart were both southerners. Porto Alegre, the capital of Rio Grande do Sul, played an important part in bringing Getúlio Vargas to power, and in supporting Goulart as president after the unexpected resignation of Quadros in 1961. Leonel Brizola, Goulart's brother-in-law, and the governor of Rio Grande do Sul during the presidency of the man who saw himself as the heir of 'Getulism', even tried in April 1964 to rally the final efforts of the south to try to prevent the military coups in Minas, Rio and São Paulo. It would be an exaggeration to say that the south was punished after 1964 for the leading part it had played beforehand. But the state of Rio Grande do Sul was watched with some care from 1964 to 1967. The states of the south, looked upon in the forties as having prior claim on the profits from Brazilian expansion, suffered to no small extent from projects set on foot by the federal government to give special help to development in the north east. Southern businessmen complained bitterly as they saw the financial benefits granted by SUDENE drawing to the north capital which they needed, yet the spectacular development of towns like Porto Alegre, Florianopolis and above all Londrina (the new boom-town of the south) between 1964 and 1968 seem to indicate little reason for thinking southern dynamism was losing its impetus.

*

The characteristic noise in São Paulo is the noise of work. From a balcony on the twenty-fifth floor of the Hotel Jaraguá, the view to the north comes up against a proud and jagged line of skyscrapers. Closer in one sees green patches like the Praça da Republica. Further to the north, beyond the line of the Tietê river, the smoke from perhaps thirty factory chimneys floats into a single mist lying over the vast suburbs where the poorer people live. In the other direction, facing the narrow rua da Consolação one sees more skyscrapers, more factories, and bare earth where foundations are to be laid for yet more buildings.

Rio has a stupefying kind of beauty. The *cidade maravilhosa* is too lovely, leaning up against the bay, flanked by the sentinel of its bare Sugar Loaf mountain, dominated by other peaks covered in dense greenery, and protected by the open arms of the statue of Christ at the top of the Corcovado. It is a city of fascination. In the centre, the ancient and comfortable houses of the old Brazilian families appear to be stifled by the proliferation of skyscrapers. From time to time one of the gentry will sell a bit of ground surrounding his stately old home. A new building then rises alongside it. But though they fight against it, the citizens, old and young, share an American view of life if nothing else: 'A chance for everyone.' The simple and heartwarming picture of the workman driving his Cadillac, or owning a high-rent block of flats after only a few years of gruelling hard work, still obsesses most businessmen in São Paulo. The example of colossal fortunes built in record time by the sons of immigrants, often Italian – the Matarazzos, the Lunardellis, the Borghis, the Morgantis – stimulates their belief that there has as yet been no hardening of social barriers, no firmly-grounded class structure.

Much has been written about the competition between São Paulo and Rio de Janeiro. The former has power, energy, vast size, and a magnetism which has in it something both of Chicago and of Genoa; the latter is famous for its beauty – a beauty perhaps exaggerated, but never in dispute. In size São Paulo definitely has the lead. The third competitor, recently established in the middle of the Goiás plain – Brasilia – will take some time to achieve any comparison with these two. The 'coffee town' which in the last century had barely 26,000 inhabitants has grown with a speed hardly imaginable elsewhere in Europe or America. Hurrying crowds of working people go their way past banks built of marble and steel. And in the heart of this steaming, bubbling metropolis are the last old squares, oases already due to be destroyed. The failure of the services (communications, drainage, telephones, etc.) to keep pace with the demands on them have made it abundantly clear how disadvantageous it can be to have had such spectacular but unplanned expansion in the economic capital of the Federation. In 1968 the 'problems of São Paulo' reached their high point, and there were vast projects on foot to provide – at long last – a proper infra-structure for this overgrown city.

Rio on the other hand, despite its turbulence, and its many abortive attempts to build tunnels to Copacabana, is still more in touch with nature. Rio would not be itself without its frame of lush green hills and the rolling of the breakers along its beaches. It is not, however, a place to be described; nor is it possible to take in its jumble of hills, beaches, quays and *morros** just by looking at a map – you have to see it for yourself. The most spectacular way to discover the city is to see it from the air at night. The sparkling lights of Ipanema, Leblon, Copacabana, Flamengo and Botafogo shine out between the bay and the ocean, dominated by two flickering beacons from the Sugar Loaf and the Corcovado statue. One of Rio's biggest attractions is its beaches which extend for 32 kilometres, from La Urca to the *barra da Tijuca*. Those at the foot of the Sugar Loaf and in front of Flamengo are used by the mass of the people; those in Copacabana are full of athletic footballers; in the south, they become smarter, and are exclusive indeed by the time one gets to Ipanema. But Copacabana soon disappoints those who really love Brazil and Rio. Its amazing façade of white buildings, all of equal height, facing the waves beating in from the Atlantic all the year round has nothing behind it. Once you leave the boulevard with its famous mosaics, Copacabana is just one more ordinary, modern and somewhat lifeless district. Yet it is there that

* Hillocks.

T.L.A. I—4

officials will go to find an apartment, which often costs more than they can afford, because it is fashionable.

Few bays in the world are equal to the bay of Rio. To build the city involved a continual struggle against the inroads of mango-trees, palm-trees and *bagaceiras** – an army of greenery. The forest lost the battle, but it is not far away. You find it at the first bends of the road up to Petropolis, which used to be the summer residence of the Brazilian government. The battle now to be fought is against the sea and the bay. To gain breathing-space, the city is growing wider, and a huge esplanade across the water near Santos Dumont airport has altered the appearance of the graceful Praça Paris. Apparently Gobineau, who was the French minister to Brazil in the days of the Emperor Dom Pedro, did not like Rio. In his reminiscences, he talks only of the cockroaches and scorpions which seem to have been continually finding their way into his house. But parasites and snakes alike have beaten a retreat before the onslaughts of concrete, steel and glass which now spread along the whole of the two wide avenues, Rio Branco and Vargas. People have sometimes thought of Rio as only existing at Carnival time; and certainly with the approach of February excitement mounts to the *favelas* and bit by bit the whole town puts on fancy dress. But the Carnival, with its smell of alcohol and sugar cane, its powdering of confetti, lasts little more than a week; and it is in the huge 250,000-seat stadium of Maracana that you will find permanent expression of the exuberance and excitement of the *cariocas*.†

One newspaper – which either had no sense of humour, or perhaps too much ! – made a great fuss in June 1962 over the expulsion of a French correspondent who had written that the world of football made it possible for the Brazilian leaders to get their people to forget the sharp rise in the cost of living.

*Undergrowth.   † The people of Rio.

In a sense it is quite true that Brazil no longer has a monopoly of this deification of national sporting teams : during that same World Cup match, played in Chile and won by the Brazilians, other supposedly far calmer nations like Germany, Czechoslovakia and even the U.S.S.R. gave more space to the success or failure of their teams in Santiago de Chile than to any political news. But the Brazilians do have a specially impassioned approach to football. In 1958, when Brazil won its first World Cup, the Kubitschek government adjourned their political work to welcome the victors to Rio as though they were a delegation who had won ten years of peace for their country in some great international conference. In June 1962 the team returning from Santiago were escorted through Rio by a crowd as wild and joyful as any one might see in the Carnival. The great Brazilian football players are far better and more important than any idols : the Maracana is not so much a stadium as a temple. After all, the Carnival is over in four days and nights – from midday Saturday until Ash Wednesday; certainly the *cariocas* think about it months ahead of time, and it has really become a kind of way for the black man to come down from his *favelas* and briefly pay the white man back by imposing his music, his own special mixture of gaiety and sadness on the whole city. But from 1 January to 31 December football is something that makes it possible for the *cariocas* and their Brazil to lead the world.

*

At dawn on 24 August 1954, after a night spent in deep thought in his rooms in the Catete, the presidential palace in Rio, Getúlio Vargas shot himself in the heart. The previous day he had replied to the heads of the armed forces who demanded his resignation : 'I shall only stop being president when I am dead.' But no one thought of it as any kind of promise. The military leaders who wanted to get rid of Vargas had found a formula which seemed to them satisfactory for everyone. They proposed that Getúlio take three months' holiday, intending this to be in fact a final departure. For him it would have been nothing of the kind, and when he heard from his brother Benjamin, whom he wanted to appoint chief of police, that they really wanted him out, Getúlio asked to be left alone. He was a man of single passion – the passion for power. A sentimental man who had never let his affections dominate him, he discovered loneliness and betrayal at the end of the road. What was going through his mind as day broke? What was the real reason for his action? Was it that he did not want to end up forgotten like his predecessors, that he wanted to depart proudly? Whatever the reasons, his suicide had a tremendous and long-lived effect on politics in Brazil. His shadow still lies along the corridors of power. The whole thing was such a complete surprise; it produced an emotion not felt in Brazil in the previous twenty-five years. Sobbing crowds came down from the *favelas* and poor districts of Rio to kiss Getúlio's face for the last time. Thousands of people provided a tragic escort for his coffin on its way to Rio airport. The smiling old *gaucho** went to his last resting place in São Borja in the Rio Grande do Sul, which he had left a quarter of a century earlier to become the master of Brazil. He left a letter that was both a political testament, a last declaration of love for the people of his country, and an accusation against north American capitalism:

After so many years of domination and exploitation by international economic and financial cartels, I led a revolution and I won. I began the work of liberation, and established the rule of freedom in society. I had to abandon it. Then I was returned to power by the people. The clandestine campaign of the international cartels then became allied with that of the national groups

* His popular nickname.

fighting a regime which gave guarantees to the workers. The profits of foreign businesses rose to 500 per cent per year. I fought month after month, day by day, hour after hour; but they did not want the workers to be free. They did not want ordinary people to be independent. I have nothing left to give now but my blood. I was a slave to my people; I fought against the exploitation of Brazil; I fought for the people; now I give my life.

*

What he gave was in fact his death. For a time it looked as though Brazil would for the first time give the lie to its long tradition of peaceful politics and have its first real bloody revolution. But, apart from Porto Alegre, nowhere were there disturbances of any real seriousness. Vargas's death certainly looked like a settling of accounts: it was the epilogue to a long and complex crisis, beginning as rivalry of a classic political kind, but degenerating into corruption, nepotism and political assassination. The first move was an armed attack on Carlos Lacerda, editor of a small-circulation opposition daily, the *Tribuna de Imprensa*. Lacerda, dynamic, excitable, as fanatical in his friendships as he was virulent and unjust in his enmities, made up for the smallness of his readership by a violence of language which infuriated the placid Vargas. Lacerda escaped the guns of his attackers, but a young airforce officer with him was killed – which gave the whole affair a new twist. The inquest was held by the air force, and it was discovered that the murderers were members of Vargas's entourage. The opposition, whose spokesman (though at times only barely tolerated) Lacerda was, went mad. It was discovered that the attack had been planned by a certain Gregorio Fortunato, chief of the president's guard and much in favour with him; he was a huge negro, and went everywhere with his boss – almost like a kind of black Rasputin, who had amassed a vast amount of money through dealing in prostitution, gambling, and blackmail. Brazilians can cope with scandals in the ordinary way, but this was something exceptional. No one in Rio believed that Vargas himself had ordered the attack, but nevertheless it contributed to the fall of this man who had been in power for far too long.

A week after Vargas's death the opposition leaders could breathe again. There was not, after all, going to be a revolution. 'Getúlio died for nothing,' they said. 'What kind of victory is that?' They were only partly deceiving themselves; in effect nothing was really changed in Brazil by Vargas's death – yet 'Getulism', like 'Peronism' in Argentina, left traces not soon to be effaced, though the large landowners remained as powerful as ever. There remained a vast gulf between the wealth of the happy few in São Paulo or Rio and the incredible poverty of the *caboclos* and farmers of the north east. The prevailing social and economic structures remained unchanged.

*

Getulism is not really an original political doctrine: like Peronism, it is a doctrine of intentions. However, its one essential characteristic was a certain effort to improve the standard of living of the masses. Fixed working hours, social security, paid holidays, a minimum guaranteed wage, and insurance against risk of sickness or accident – all these social measures were brought in for the first time in Brazil during the Vargas administration. Of course he did not manage to get nearly as much done as he had promised; no doubt, too, this social legislation was only really put into practice in the cities and not in the country, though the lot of the agricultural workers was far worse and should have been given priority. Nevertheless, though incomplete, though not making it possible to build a new society, it was a revolution that did really do something to shake the foundations of the old society, known in Brazil as the 'old republic'. For the first time the justice of such social claims was actually admitted. Needless to say this was not possible without some degree of equivocation, support from the army, considerable police harassment, and the supposedly temporary suppression of a great many freedoms. And, though little given to action, the most violent opponents of Getulism in the later years of Vargas's dictatorship came from among the old families of Brazil and those liberals most strongly attached to European democratic ideas and culture.

Vargas's whole political career was really a succession of calculated hesitations followed by spectacular reforms. He was born in 1883 at São Borja, near the Argentine border. His father and grandfather had been farmers, but he studied law, and when he was elected to Congress it was said of him that he could 'listen to the grass growing in the pampas'. In other words, he knew when *not* to speak. He was a robust man, beardless, with a short nose, metal-rimmed glasses and a keen gaze; he spoke little and smiled a lot. Almost apologetically he took power in 1930. He was not the official candidate of those in power at the time. There was a firm tradition in Brazil of having the president's successor chosen in advance, and the departing president, Washington Luis, had designated Julio Prestes to succeed him. That particular election year in Brazil was also the year of the great crisis which shook all of Latin America like an earthquake, and resulted in coups d'état in Bolivia, Peru and Argentina. Brazil did not escape the disturbances; it too had its *golpe*,* its *pronunciamiento*, but without bloodshed. It was a revolution in which no bullets were fired, and was received enthusiastically by the mass of the people. Washington Luis's choice of a successor was a challenge : logically, he should have been succeeded by someone from Minas Gerais, since it was that state's turn to take

*Coup d'état.

over the leadership of the federation; and Prestes was from São Paulo. In answer to this insult, the mountain-dwellers of Belo Horizonte asked that the Rio Grande do Sul support their leader, Getúlio Vargas. It looked as though an alliance of that kind could not fail to win the election; yet Washington Luis's party machine was stronger still, and Vargas was beaten. In Porto Alegre, the crowds rushed into the streets shouting, 'We want Getúlio!' So Getúlio bought a railway ticket to Rio. Wherever the train stopped, crowds appeared with the same cry, and when he arrived in Rio, President Luis had resigned at the polite but firm suggestion of the army leaders. The way was clear.

In theory, Vargas was supported by a party known as the Free Alliance. This was a curious mixture of officers, liberals, democrats, academics and even some communists, whose sole common denominator was the rather uninspiring slogan: 'Things must change'. Ever smiling, the skilful Getúlio made wonderful use of this 'cocktail' of the political spectrum. He did not support, but never actually denied, the communists of Luis Prestes, or the fascist greenshirts of Plinio Salgade. His first big test came in 1932. It was obvious that the business of getting him into power, carried out by the *mineiros* of Minas and the *gauchos* of Rio Grande, was really paid for by the people of São Paulo; therefore, the state of São Paulo demanded a return to the constitutional order that had been set aside by the first acts of the Vargas government. Bertholdo Klinger, the former chief of police, rallied the 30,000 troops of the state; and Vargas gave an indication of his brilliant ability to compromise: while on the one hand he prepared the federal troops for the fighting they might have to do, on the other he offered a comfortable retirement to the leaders of the uprising. Once the rising was over, he carefully avoided taking any reprisals against São Paulo, and promised that he would provide the kind of constitution its people demanded. These, though inspired with extraordinary patriotic fervour, were forced to yield – but their defeat was due not so much to the new and temporary alliance between Minas and Rio Grande do Sul, as to the sheer military superiority of the central government troops.

The second test came in November 1935. The third infantry regiment, stationed in the capital, suddenly hoisted the red flag, and their example was followed soon after by a number of officers of the Air Force Academy, who had the previous night murdered those officers who remained loyalists. They were probably hoping that all the garrisons in Rio Grande do Sul would follow suit, but precisely the opposite happened. The revolt of the São Paulo liberals in 1932 had failed because the States were divided among themselves. The communist coup in Rio in November 1935 also proved to be abortive, lasting only a single night, but its consequences were more serious. A month after the red revolutionaries had been put down, Vargas proscribed the communist party in Brazil. Its leader, Luis Carlos Prestes, was arrested and sentenced to 46 years and 8 months in prison – and we still do not know today just how the jury worked out such a complicated bit of arithmetic !

When he actually gave the order to revolt that November, Prestes had just returned from a visit to Moscow where he had been made a member of the Comintern Executive committee. Most of his aides were against the rising. 'It's too soon. It's just playing into the hands of the fascists.' But Prestes paid no attention.

Brazilian communism is a curiosity. Up to now it has drawn its most fervent and determined supporters from among the army, the intellectuals and even the bourgeoisie, whereas it has made almost no progress among the workers and peasants who should, in theory, be its richest seed-bed. As in other Latin American countries, the powers that be have always been liable to lump together the Communist Party proper and all revolutionary movements of the left. By doing so the dictatorships have been able to continue to dismiss the demands and threats of the *peones*, and get support from Washington in putting down genuinely liberal movements. This policy explains how such evidently senseless and in fact bloodthirsty dictatorships as those of Jiménez in Venezuela, Trujillo in the Dominican Republic, the Somozas in Nicaragua and Batista in Cuba could be kept in power for so long.

Clearly Brazil provides one of the most favourable possible areas for the spread of revolutionary ideas. The conditions in which vast numbers of Brazilians live are absolutely appalling, and the desperate gulf between poor and rich is such as to shock all intellectuals and liberals. Then, too, Brazilian communism has had the luck of having an impressive and competent leader, unlike some of the other Latin American countries; indeed Prestes's name has become something of a legend. Among the people he is nicknamed the 'cavalier of Hope'. This might appear odd but for the fact that the Brazilian army has a long tradition of liberalism, and enthusiastically took up the positivist doctrines of Auguste Comte – and, also, Prestes's father was once an officer cadet. Luis Carlos himself belonged to that generation of the thirties so passionately concerned with liberty and justice; they were the men who helped to diminish the power of the *coronelismo* of the past, as also of the system of landlord-dictated voting inherited from colonial society. Even in 1924, Captain Luis Carlos Prestes was leading his batallion to revolt; that was the start of an adventure that has been recounted most lyrically and vividly by Jorge Amado, one of the major Brazilian writers of our time. To 'keep the revolution alive all over the country' Prestes, now the leader of a group, took his army on an apparently pointless march from south to north. For some years, the exploits of the Prestes band caught the imagination of the country, and inspired songs in every village. At one point Prestes used a hideout on the Bolivian border, where he discovered the intense poverty of the *caboclos*, and made use of every quiet moment to read the classics of Marxism. When his long march came to an end, somewhere in the Mato Grosso, Prestes discovered what he felt to be his true calling: he set off for Moscow.

*

Vargas's ban on the communist party had the corollary effect of giving credence to the propaganda of the extreme right-wing political movements which dreamt of aping Hitler and Mussolini in Brazil. The fact of there being a large colony of German immigrants in the south was a great advantage, and indeed one of the essential elements in a plan for conquest that was never actually put into effect. It was in 1933 that Plinio Salgado founded the 'integralist' party, South America's version of European fascism. Its supporters wore special green shirts, scarves, belts, boots – a whole cumbersome and ridiculous para-military outfit. They also underwent a para-military training. Fortunately this tropical fascism had a Brazilian flavour to it, and was thus never as dangerous or violent or brutally efficient as its leaders would have liked. However it soon collected plenty of money, and enough equipment to alarm the government. Vargas decided at that point that he himself would present Brazil with new laws, and on 10 November 1937 everyone was utterly astonished to hear the president's voice on their radios, announcing the proclamation of the *Estado Novo*.* The preamble to this new constitution was simple enough: 'The President of the republic of the United States of Brazil, wishing to fulfil the legitimate aspirations of the Brazilian people, is determined to ensure national unity.' He was proposing a strong democratic government. The world believed Brazil to have become fascist, but in four days Vargas used all the power at his disposal to dissolve and proscribe the integralist

* 'New State'.

party. Article 1 of the new constitution enabled him to ban any flag other than the national flag with its Comtiste device : 'Order and Progress'. He himself loved order.

Really it is impossible to put any kind of label on Vargas. 'My friends,' he used to say 'are more dangerous than my enemies; for an enemy may always turn into a friend.' It was with simple maxims of this kind, with limited ideas and a lot of empiricism that he ruled his immense country from 1930 to 1945.

He had carefully prepared for one indispensable change by getting his most faithful colleague, Oswaldo Tranha, to go to Washington in 1941 to meet Roosevelt. It was Rio that was host in 1942 to the third meeting of American Foreign Affairs Ministers, convoked mainly to discuss the fight against Nazism. In July 1944 Brazilian troops were among the Allied contingents that landed in the bay of Salerno; they were the only South American soldiers to take part in the liberation of Europe, and their officers made such good use of their experiences that they came home with very clearly defined ideas about the kind of government which would suit their country best. One of those ideas was that Vargas had been around long enough; they told him so, and he accepted it. But before he left the Catete*, he made several decisions which he thought would assist his ultimate return to power. He allowed all political exiles to come back. He freed Luis Carlos Prestes from prison as the recognized secretary general of the Brazilian Communist Party.

The 1945 general election was won by General Gaspar Dutra, the candidate Vargas supported. The Communist Party got 568,000 votes – so all of a sudden it found itself the fourth largest party in the country. Of course a lot of those who voted communist did so for reasons quite unconnected with the revolution; Prestes's personal prestige had a lot to do with it, and he himself was elected a Senator. His eloquence,

* The presidential palace in Rio.

though enormously improved by his nine years of reading and thinking, was not given scope for long. The Dutra government decreed the Communist Party dissolved in 1947; the election of the fourteen Communist deputies was annulled, and once again Prestes was obliged to flee. The period was not suited to the same kind of long march he had organized in 1924, and he lived in hiding, going from one safe spot to another – glimpsed here, sought somewhere else, but in fact being allowed enough freedom to make sure that he was never actually found.

*

Vargas's campaign for the presidential election of 1950 was a model of its kind. He travelled systematically all over Brazil, spending a few minutes in every village, a few days in the more important states. In comparison with this the movements of his two opponents, Brigadeiro Gomes, unwearying, the permanent runner-up, and the official candidate Cristiano Machado, looked very disconnected, clumsy and inadequate. Vargas won by an impressive margin; people voted him back in to 'get things changed'. But what had changed during the five years of his relative absence was really the world itself. Ever faithful to his fundamental principles, Vargas declared that thenceforward Brazil would draw its inspiration from Scandinavian socialism and the British Labour Party. There was a chronic economic crisis : the combination of an endless outflow of capital, the deficit in the balance of payments, frost in the São Paulo coffee plantations, speculation, a desperate drought which laid waste the north east, and the increasing cost of living in a short time presented those who had come to power in the 1950 elections with an intensely difficult situation. Vargas should have adopted rigorous and well-tried methods. What he did was to double the wages of the lowest paid workers; he decided to refuse to allow foreign capital to be invested in the exploitation of Brazilian petroleum, in 1953, the *Petrobras*, Brazil's own national petroleum company, made it difficult if not impossible for foreign money to come in, even indirectly. Vargas also tried to get a law passed which would have greatly limited the enormous profits being made by foreign companies. Thus the target so mercilessly attacked by the increasing opposition (whose moving spirit was Lacerda) was a man trying to cope with ten enemies and ten problems at once. Yet again the army was to play the determining role. In January 1954 the military leaders had been urging the dismissal of João Goulart, the Minister of Labour, and successor designate of Vargas. Goulart was young and dynamic, and had begun to transform the trades unions into a really powerful workers' movement. Shortly afterwards the colonels sent Vargas a memorandum to warn him against the 'dangers of his dema-gogic form of politics'. Thus the conflict between the president and the 'silent power' in Brazil became sharper.

Nothing major had been done for twenty years without the army's taking part. In 1937 the army had helped Vargas to dissolve Congress and effectively become master of the country. In 1945 the army forced him to resign. Then, in 1950, his triumphal return followed a reconciliation with General Gois – the very man who had led the attack on him five years earlier. It is revealing to note the moment chosen by the military in 1954 to begin showing signs of nervous-ness. The campaign for elections to the Senate and the Chamber of Deputies had just begun. The memorandum from eighty-two colonels and lieutenant-colonels (all of them officers in command of troops in the federal district) was a clear warning. Nor was it the only one. Another memoran-dum had been prepared by a group of lower-ranking officers. General Juarez Tavora, the commandant of the military academy, in his turn cast doubt on the effectiveness 'of the economic and social measures' being taken by the Vargas government. In thus gradually becoming shriller, the army was certainly not just protesting against the social policies of what they considered a demagogic government; they also had claims of a 'professional' nature to make.

The increased cost of living had a particular impact on this military caste which had for so long been the defence of the country. Goulart's policy of trying to make the workers' party a genuinely popular and well-organized movement disturbed and angered them. The sudden disappearance of Vargas on 24 August thus looked at first sight as at least a short-term victory for that group in the army which was allied to the most conservative factions in the country. But the pistol shot in the Catete only ended the life of one man. Ever since 1954 the mass of the people in Brazil have been continuing to look for someone who would take up the work begun by Getúlio.

*

Since Vargas's death there have really been two men who have made a mark on the Brazilian political scene: Kubitschek and Quadros. The former, president from 1956–60, was an administrator for whom popularity was a major preoccupation. The latter, a puzzling and complex personality, provoked innumerable attacks in his brief six months of power. Juscelino Kubitschek was undoubtedly the political heir of Vargas when he came to power. The party machine was powerful enough to get him in despite the obvious hesitation of the army and the conservatives who wanted to make the most of their victory over Vargas. Quadros, whose political career had begun in very different conditions from Vargas's, tried to seize hold of the advantages of the emotional capital amassed by Getúlio. It is difficult to assess Quadros's short period of power: Kubitschek's name will always be associated with Brasilia.

It is harder again to pronounce judgement on Goulart who was, from 1961 to 1964, faced with an exceptionally difficult situation. As for the two officers who were in power from 1964 to 1968, even the Brazilians considered them inept as heads of state. Castello Branco was dismissed as a 'little Caesar' by some of those who had worked to get rid of Goulart, and Costa e Silva, whose charm seemed so magnetic in 1967, was soon overwhelmed by events in 1968.

The Brasilia project really dates back to 1853, for it was as long ago as that that the idea of transferring the federal capital from the Atlantic coast to the high plateau of Goiás state was first put forward. In 1891 the possibility of such a change was embodied in an amendment to the Constitution. The first Constitution of the first Brazilian republic actually stated the place where the future federal district was to be: on a plain of 14,000 square kilometres, at least 200 kilometres from the present state capital, Goiana. But it was to be forty-three years before this even began to be put into effect. In 1934 a special government commission visited the area in order to settle on a precise site for the administrative buildings and the Chamber of Deputies. Curiously the archives say that the commission was to take all necessary steps to get the work begun as soon as possible. None the less Brasilia disappeared under further layers of administrative dust. Vargas's *Estado Novo* did nothing about it at all. Commissions, projects and counter-projects, one of which envisaged extending the federal district as far as the borders of Minas Gerais and Bahia, followed one another with varying success from 1946 onward.

In 1953, exactly a hundred years after the idea had first been projected, Congress passed a law stating that the site chosen for Brasilia must have a good climate, be easily reached both by land and water, and have soil suitable both for building on, and for the cultivation of vegetables. It was further stipulated that the future capital should spread over 5,000 square kilometres, and have about 500,000 inhabitants. Gradually the dream was becoming a reality. But of course all these abstract details and theoretical decisions did not make any impact on the *caboclos*; it looked as though the good old *amanhã*,* something that must be done tomorrow, or sometime or perhaps never, would apply to this crazy obsession of the government, as to everything else. Rio is used to the sight of work forever 'in progress' : more than ten years after it had been begun, the vast Maracana stadium still looked as if it were waiting for the workmen to put the finishing touches. Several beginnings of buildings still stand shapeless in the middle of the city as tactless reminders of the general nonchalance. Someone was needed to harness people's energies, and move from the stage of interminable memoranda to that of bulldozers; that someone was Juscelino Kubitschek.

His winning of the presidential election of October 1955 was something of a surprise; even a week beforehand no one would have given much for his chances, despite his energetic electoral campaign which took him to the most remote villages of the Amazonian jungle and the north east. Against him there was a coalition which, though oddly assorted, mustered the force of all those who hated Getúlism. As the candidate of the social democrats, the workers and the communists – in other words the effective leaders of the left-wing part of the electorate – Juscelino had all the moderates against him. A large part of the army – the same men who had engineered the fall of Vargas – was doubtful if not definitely hostile. In the end Juscelino won, but only by a margin of 400,000 votes over the conservative candidate, the austere and clever Juarez Tavora. A careful study of the results makes it clear that the shadow of Vargas was ultimately the determining factor. João Goulart, leader of the workers' party, former Minister of Labour in the Vargas administration, got more votes for the vice-presidency than Kubitschek got for the presidency. And the Brazilians were shocked and horrified

* Literally 'tomorrow': the Portuguese equivalent of the Spanish *mañana*.

to find that Plinio Salgado, former leader of the fascist green-shirts, had got 700,000 votes. Salgado, who was brilliant both as a writer and a speaker, certainly had considerable prestige in the states of Paraná and Santa Catarina, where the German immigrant groups dictated policy; but it had to be accepted that at least half of his votes must have come from elsewhere, from people who hankered after fascism but had not the courage to admit the fact.

Juscelino's election enraged some of the leaders of the services so much that they attempted a coup – the first in a series, all planned along identical lines, and put down for similar reasons. The coup failed because Henrique Teixeira Lott, the Minister of War, trained in the military academy in Paris, refused to be a party to it. It was the naval and air force leaders who were involved, and he simply brought the army and its tanks into Rio; so, this first '*pronunciamiento* in favour of legality' made it possible for Kubitschek to take effective possession of his presidential office in the Catete in January 1956. But he remained indebted to his War Minister.

During his campaign for the presidency, Kubitschek had covered a record distance; as president he continued to travel all over the country. He was soon nicknamed 'Travellers-chek' – a typical bit of Rio humour. As the grandson of Czech immigrants who had settled in Minas Gerais, he certainly had travellers' blood in his veins. His mother was a stocky woman with light eyes and fair hair, and the extraordinary energy typical of her Moravian ancestors. The people of Minas were still to some extent nomads; in the villages they sang late into the night under tropical skies, perhaps about a friend, or a harvest, or a festival – one song, for instance, was the song of the *peixe vivo*, the living fish, and it was the rallying song for Kubitschek's supporters. 'How can the living fish live out of water? How can I live without you?'

Forty years ago, Diamantina was a sleepy hilltop town oblivious of the fever of the gold rush. A narrow gauge railway, powered by burning wood, linked it with Belo Horizonte. In 1919 Kubitschek took the train to the big city to study for his doctor's diploma, which he received in 1927, having supported himself and paid for his studies by night work as a watchman or telegraph operator. He went on to do more specialist courses in Paris at the Hôpital Cochin, in Berlin and in Vienna. He also made a brief trip to Czechoslovakia, but only in the tourist's sense of seeing the most important sights. Back in Brazil, he was elected a deputy for his state, then *prefeito** of Belo Horizonte; then, as Governor of Minas from 1950 to 1955, he doubled the state's output of electricity, and built an asphalt road from Belo Horizonte to Rio. Even as president of the federation, Kubitschek's prime concern remained the building of roads, dams and power stations; but his greatest achievement – or disaster – was Brasilia.

This was not of course the first instance in history of a capital or great metropolis rising up from nothing: Alexandria, Byzantium, Peking and even Washington are, or were, what one might call purpose-built capitals. Kemal Ataturk, the father of modern Turkey, decided one day to establish Ankara in the centre of the high arid plateau of Anatolia, to get away from the fogs and also the political overtones of Istanbul with all its ancient splendours. But Kemal had all the power of an intelligent and ruthless tyrant. Kubitschek had to cope with the sarcasm, the apathy and the utter indifference of the majority of Brazilians. As he took office he announced that he intended to cram fifty years into the five he would have, starting with Brasilia. His first step was to set up a state body to study and develop the *Novacap* project. By October 1956 the first building workers were starting their labours on that tropical plateau with the soft and unvarying climate that goes with being a 1,000 metres above sea level.

*

* This is an office equivalent to that of our Mayor.

Lucio Costa and Oscar Niemeyer, pupils of Le Corbusier, and already well known among rising young Brazilian architects, had designed the amazing Ministry of Education building in the centre of Rio with its revolutionary sun-visor and beehive construction. There was an open competition to submit plans for Brasilia, and they won it in March 1957. The future city was soon given a patron, Dom Bosco, founder of the Salesians. Among his prophecies was one of a promised land in the new world somewhere between the 15th and 20th parallels, precisely the situation of Brasilia which lies on the watershed of the Amazon basin, the Plata and the São Francisco rivers (the latter the only major river whose entire length lies in Brazil itself).

Lucio Costa began by tracing a cross on a blank sheet of paper – a symbol of land conquered. The horizontal axis, designed for residential areas, eventually became a curving line. And from the sky what Brasilia most looked like, by the time of its official opening in April 1960, was a great bird. The vertical axis was given over to official and public buildings, ending in the symbolically named Square of the Three Powers, where the executive palace stands between two semi-circular areas designed one for the Chamber and Senate, the other for the Courts of Justice.

940 kilometres north east of the former capital of Rio, Brasilia, with its red earth and sparse vegetation, remains a continual source of fascination. It was built at a fantastically quick pace: it took only three years for 50,000 workmen to finish the major work on the new capital. The monotonous concrete cubes of the *superquadras* and the residential areas rose up on their piles. The palace in the Square of the Three Powers, the cathedral fashioned in the shape of an exotic flower, the palace of the Alvorada – all architectural masterpieces, poems in glass, steel and concrete – were in place close by the artificial lake formed by drawing together the waters of half a dozen streams. Everything was planned for: the

railway station (leading as yet nowhere), the cultural centre, the gigantic tower of the television station, the area for the university, the race-course, the golf-course, the botanical garden, the observatory, the cemetery, and one avenue, twenty kilometres long, set apart for embassies to be built by each government to its own specification.

The official opening of Brasilia took place in an incredible atmosphere of thoughtfulness, surprise and admiration, despite whirlwinds of red dust brought in by the winds from the savannah, and the incredible masses of official visitors. Israel Pinheiro, the main organizer, appointed *prefeito* of Brasilia, marched at the head of an impressive file of *candangos* – all those who had taken part in building the city. People had come from the distant north east along the now 2,000-kilometre road from Belém do Pará to Brasilia, crossing the Tocantins river, and part of the Amazonian jungle. Two other ultra-modern highways connected the new capital with Rio, São Paulo and Belo Horizonte. Later there will be a motorway from Brasilia to the far-off and up to now inaccessible territory of Acre, running along the foothills of the Andes, and crossing the great Mato Grosso.

If the new capital can succeed in bringing large new populations into the interior, and assisting the creation of new arterial roads, new towns and new centres of life there, then there is some point in its existence. That is how the U.S.A. went about the same job in the nineteenth century; railways penetrated farther and farther west, and towns, people, and cultivation followed in their wake. Kubitschek was trying to use roads to achieve the same purpose north America had achieved with railways. To use his own words, 'Six million square kilometres of our land must have a share in the general progress of Brazil.'

Certainly Brasilia presents one of the finest subjects for contemplation you could want as a twentieth-century philosopher considering the eternal theme of the city. But ordinary people in Brazil see it more prosaically as the direct cause for the catastrophic fall in the value of their currency. The opposition has not yet been wholly silenced: they say, and it is quite true, that there are two Brasilias, one an administrative and official city in which officials twiddle their fingers in tiny apartments whose only view is the wall opposite, and another, wholly unforeseen by those who planned and built Brasilia. That other is the already 'old town', where families are huddled together in rough huts made of planks, known to all Brazilians as 'the Far West': these are the slums of Brasilia, but they are alive, moving, full of human warmth, noisy with shouting and cries for help, and stand out in their disorderly rhythm against the cold silence of official Brasilia.

Even before Quadros's surprising resignation in August 1961 it was obvious that no one could put the clock back. Even had Quadros really wanted to, he could not have brought the capital back to Rio de Janeiro. And if there is one thing upon which both the supporters and the opponents of Brasilia are agreed, it is that Rio, with its overcrowding, its long narrow lines of land between the Atlantic and the forest, and its endless traffic jams is no longer a place where anyone can work efficiently. In Brasilia, on the other hand, there is peace; you can hear yourself think. But the people who actually have to live there, officials and diplomats, are not happy. Kubitschek, in the last five months of his administration, shut himself up in the Alvorada palace, and concentrated on getting the transfer of all the legal and other machinery through with the utmost speed. All the archives of the Senate, the Chamber of Deputies, and the Supreme Court, as well as all the staff and equipment of the presidency, were taken by air from Rio to Brasilia. Quadros followed him into the now established presidential offices there in 1961; he did so with an ill grace, but he could do no other. In his first, sadly pessimistic presidential speech he deplored the wild spending of his predecessor – meaning of course Brasilia. He was to have many future occasions to complain about its obvious inconveniences. The pace at which the big administrative bodies were being transferred slowed down; a number of deputies and senators took to spending only two or three days a week in the capital, and going back to Rio for a very long weekend. And the diplomats, for their part, were not much delighted with the avenue reserved for their embassies, and complained endlessly of the housing problem, and the lack of entertainment.

It certainly looks as though it will be some years before Rio is really replaced as the capital city. On the day of Brasilia's official opening, Rio's *cariocas* wore their Carnival masks and held a funeral procession for the burial of their town – yet a certain malign and ironic glee could be noted under their apparent demeanour of mourning and lamentation.

*

Quadros's induction in 1961 as state governor surprised some of his supporters, for his rapid and apparently irresistible rise to the highest political offices always gave a sense of being adjourned from one day to the next.

Quadros won his first victory in the election for the key post of governor of the state of São Paulo. He got over 600,000 votes, thus winning by a margin of some 20,000. Adhemar de Barros, the former governor, was a truculent and dynamic politician with an electoral machine that had proved its power and had many faithful friends, but he was beaten, and in 1954 this came as a surprise. So three months after Vargas's death, Jânio Quadros was one step nearer the presidency.

He fulfilled his new obligations with a discretion that rather belied the chaos which had characterized the earlier years of his career. Adhemar de Barros had left memories of a governor who promised great things, achieved far less, and openly indulged in dubious dealings. By contrast the austerity and efficiency of Quadros seemed good omens to the people of

São Paulo, and it was without any real opposition that he won the election to the presidency in October 1960. He took possession of the presidential palace in Brasilia in January 1961 but, alas, the charm lasted no more than eight months. On the following 25 August, the Brazilians were stupefied to learn that President Quadros had decided to resign: this curious, inconsistent, restless and yet ambitious man left the country, swearing never again to enter the field of politics. But those who thought his resignation merely a tactical move proved right; early in 1962 Jânio Quadros came back to Brazil to fight again for the presidency.

One American journalist made this caustic comment: 'He is like Marx – and I don't mean Karl; I mean Harpo.' Certainly Quadros made no effort to win sympathy. His face was thin and bony, continually twitching; his hair was long and un-kempt, and he had a bedraggled moustache; it was a long time since he had taken any trouble over his appearance. As he began his political ascent he looked more like a worn-out hermit than an assured candidate haranguing a crowd who would treasure his every word. He always wore the same threadbare suit, a shirt with frayed collar, and an untidily tied tie. His enemies declared in those days that he was making use of his lean and hungry look to win sympathy from the people. 'When he leaves a dinner party, he takes out a hunk of bread in his waistcoat pocket. He then goes to a political meeting in one of the working-class districts of São Paulo, apologizing for being late, pretending that he hasn't had even the time to eat, and ostentatiously munching his dry bread during the meeting.' Other equally uncomplimentary rumours accused him of actually spreading hairs round his jacket collar to look even more careless of his appearance. But in the event all these calumnies, whatever their basis in truth, rebounded against those who were repeating them. The victory of this determined ascetic cast an even deeper shadow upon the figure of Adhemar de Barros, whose method of attracting crowds was precisely the opposite – one of cynical honesty. Adhemar would stand on a public platform, roll up his sleeves, and jovially call his public to witness: 'I am accused of being a thief? Well, so I am. After all, who isn't. Do *you* know anyone ...?' And as the audience rocked with laughter, Adhemar, fiercely jeering, would name names and quote details. Then, with a sudden change of tone: 'I am the only one who steals from the rich to give to the poor. I'm a thief, okay. But I'm building roads and motorways, dispensaries and stadiums ...'

Vargas used to flatter his enemies. Café Filho, vice-president at the time of his death, and therefore provisional president until the 1955 elections, was a conscientious and unambitious civil servant. Kubitschek was the efficient administrator and planner who came forward with a complete reform of the state structures of Minas Gerais to his credit.

But Quadros remains an enigma. He has been called left-wing, right-wing, and middle-of-the-road; people have said he was a political chameleon. He has also been accused of a tendency to be dictatorial, and even of paranoia. Carlos Lacerda, the man whose pamphlets did so much to precipitate the fall of Vargas, and who having at first supported Quadros later went on to attack him, wrote this: 'He is the most changeable, unstable and perfidious man ever involved in Brazilian political life.' On the day of his inauguration in Brasilia the independent daily *O Globo* of Rio expressed a rather more cautiously worded judgement: 'Jânio may not be a great president. He will certainly not be an easy one.' The author spoke more truth than he knew.

Quadros was not even a native of São Paulo, but the son of Catalan immigrants who had settled in Campo Grande on the Mato Grosso, that flat, infertile country, rich only in promises. He was born there on 17 January 1917. His father was a pharmacist, always on the run from his creditors, who finally ended up in São Paulo having tried one place after another. When the family got there, Jânio was only sixteen. He studied, and then became a teacher, and finally got a good job in a private college, the Dante Alighieri Foundation. One Carnival day, he almost completely lost his left eye in an accident in which he got a bottle of burning ether full in the face. Half blinded, he vanished from the scene in despair and spent some months alone, during which he wrote poems which were really a kind of testament: 'You can tell me nothing of suffering ... for I am a young man old before my time ...' However, he returned to his studies, and, following the example of Abraham Lincoln, he became a vague activist in the obscure Christian Democrat party in São Paulo – a movement which certainly did not represent more than 2 per cent of the total Brazilian electorate. In 1947, he was in forty-seventh place on a list of candidates for the town council of São Paulo, on which there were forty-five seats. But it was then that the Dutra government decided to ban the Brazilian Communist Party, and all communist names had to be removed.

*

Suddenly Quadros was fourteen places higher on the list, and this chance made him a councillor in São Paulo. At council meetings he revealed a totally new and violent manner which surprised his colleagues. He had suddenly found a purpose in a life which had up to then seemed to him merely pointless, and arrogantly declared his intention of fighting for the poorest of the poor in that great industrial city. He set out to visit each area, organizing meetings and promising even more than Adhemar had. His fame grew, and the slogan he chose proved enormously successful: he was 'the councillor with the broom'. This 'madman from the Mato Grosso', as his opponents irreverently nicknamed him, declared that he would 'clean out the stables of the governor Adhemar de Barros'. In March 1953 he managed to get himself elected *prefeito*, mayor of São Paulo. He lifted his broom higher still:

'I shall sweep out all the thieves. . . .' The communists did not want to stake their chances on this one man, so they in turn attacked him – denouncing the contracts he had made with Standard Oil, and describing him as 'the valet of Wall Street' in the left-wing journals. But neither communist attacks nor the disquiet of the moderates could diminish his prestige.

As governor he used the same methods which he had found so successful as mayor of São Paulo. He had been thought of as vaguely socialist; but, on the contrary, he at once set about attracting foreign capital and signed agreements with various North American trusts to launch development plans for the state. In Brazil the office of state governor is quite rightly seen as a step towards the federal presidency. The *mineiro* Kubitschek, governor of the state of Minas Gerais, had made Belo Horizonte Brazil's boom city in 1955 before becoming president. Quadros followed a similar course, and in this case it was all the easier in that the convention of alternating different states in political control of the federation made São Paulo the natural successor to Minas in 1960.

The dishevelled, noisy, aggressive, ill-shaven Quadros of 1953 vanished during the presidential campaign. As medieval artisans would make their journey round France, so he made his journey round the world. For weeks he was in the headlines, visiting Hirohito, Nehru, Ben Gurion, Pope John XXIII and Khrushchev. He made a controversial but popular visit to Fidel Castro. He tried to win support from progressives as well as moderates. The UDN, that citadel of the opposition to Vargas, was prepared to support him on condition that he accepted a moderate as his vice-presidential candidate; this being a reasonable condition, he accepted; later he refused. But by then the moderates still had to support him despite his determination to go it alone. The communists were almost the only ones not to fall victim to his campaign of charm. They rallied to the banner of Marshal Teixeira Lott, the candidate of the workers and the outgoing president Kubitschek.

The election results were as expected, with a triumph for the 'candidate with the broom'. Quadros got five and a half million votes, which was 1,700,000 more than Lott. Adhemar de Barros was far behind. Quadros alone received 48 per cent of the votes.

*

He was thought to have Castro sympathies; on his return from Cuba, only a few weeks before the election, he had declared that it was ridiculous to accuse Castro of communist tendencies. But he also told those close to him that he would be the first to support the U.S. in Latin America if Cuba really were to become a 'People's Democracy'. It was thought too that he gave encouragement and support to the Portuguese refugees from the Salazar regime who had been in São Paulo for some years. Chance events made it possible to put up fairly speedily part of the smokescreen that concealed the true intentions of the new president. On 31 January 1961, the very day of his inauguration, the Portuguese ship *Santa Maria*, captured in Venezuelan waters a week earlier by Captain Galvão, appeared in the sea off Recife. It was evident that Galvão was depending on promises Quadros had made him. Thus faced on his very first day with a situation of enormous delicacy, Quadros determined to act as a head of state should. He offered political asylum to the Portuguese and Spanish desperadoes of the Iberian revolutionary government, but returned the *Santa Maria* to her rightful owners in Portugal. However, worried officials in Brazil realized that the new president had no intention of abandoning his extremely individualist way of going about things; in the vast reception rooms of the Alvorada palace, where the paint was barely dry, Jânio was evidently still hanging on to his broom and had every intention of using it.

'It is my definite intention to clean everything up here', he said coolly to Kubitschek, as he symbolically received from him the keys of the palace. And he was as good as his word. From April 1960 to January 1961 Kubitschek had had time to impose a certain style on the place – it was marked by a general open-handedness, a permissiveness, a table ever ready to accommodate anyone and everyone who might wish to come. Jânio decided to begin by bearing out all that was said of him, and got rid of the famous chef engaged by Kubitschek on the grounds that he preferred plain beef, rice and beans to complicated gourmet food.

He sent the grand piano from the reception room back to its maker, and countermanded the gala dinner which was to be brought from Rio to Brasilia by special plane for the inauguration ceremonies. 'Economy,' as he said, 'must begin at home.'

By the end of March, two months after his official inauguration, he had already dismissed some 20,000 government employees, and decreed an obligatory seven-hour day for all officials. A banal enough measure, it might seem, but in fact it was a minor revolution. In Brazil officials had always worked barely half-time, and would have a second and generally more lucrative job to supplement their inadequate salaries. There are innumerable stories about wicked officials and the 'champion of the lead-swingers', Maria Candelaria – indeed there is a well-known carnival song about her. It had always been easier, quicker and more effective to approach a *despachante* than try to make direct contact with any government official. The *despachantes* are extremely important figures in Brazilian life, who exist alongside the adminstration proper; as busy and subtle intermediaries, they know how to pull strings and get things done. Their key-word is *jeite*, or knack, trick, dodge. Whether the Quadros government succeeded in completely getting rid of them is uncertain, but the fact of his daring to attack such deep-rooted customs and habits was significant indeed. Quadros ordered all government expenditure to be reduced by 30 per cent, and he also cut down the subsidies on such essential imports as wheat and petroleum. Brazil's diplomatic and technical missions abroad also fell under the knife: ambassadors were ordered to reduce their standard of living and cut the costs of the receptions they gave. Quadros declared to a group of industrialists in April 1961: 'We must take firm steps if we are to save the country. I don't care what people think of me for it. My only wish is to work for Brazil, and to do my job well.'

The gates of the presidential palace in Brasilia were firmly locked and guarded. A complicated system of green and red lights was installed to let ministers know whether or not they could go in to the president. Back in the mayor's office in São Paulo, Jânio had had a notice put up on his office door: 'I am not here to get work for you. Please do not waste my time.' In Brasilia, as in São Paulo, his first demand of his colleagues was that they work hard. He had his office fitted up with direct telex communications to all the regional governments of the country. He would summon his assistants at any time from 7 a.m. onwards, and one day gave a severe dressing down to a minister who was a quarter of an hour late. Perhaps nothing could give a better cameo of the kind of regime Quadros wanted to establish in Brasilia than this story: a political old-stager who had campaigned for Quadros and was waiting with increasing impatience to be given a new job now that his man was in, asked the president: 'Well, what place am I to have in your team?' And Quadros replied with a sweet smile: 'Your place is in my heart.'

The communists' attitude after his victory was interesting. They continued their attacks unabated; even Prestes himself emerged from his retirement to present the official point of view of the party: 'It should be clear to the people of Brazil that with Jânio Quadros's victory in the election, the most reactionary political forces have come into power – people who want to hand Brazilian petroleum over to Standard Oil, or, under pretext of fighting inflation, will devalue our currency in whatever way suits the International Monetary Fund.' To Prestes, Quadros was still the candidate of the big banks in São Paulo, who were in turn simply instruments of north American capitalism. Furthermore, it soon appeared highly doubtful whether Quadros, in spite of his declared sympathy for Castro and the Cuban revolution, had any intention of doing much to counter the domination of the U.S. economy in Latin America. He accepted the Kennedy Plan enthusiastically almost at once.

Yet, on the other hand, he indignantly refused an American loan of a hundred million dollars offered by Kennedy's government on the grounds that it had all the marks of a present from Washington to celebrate the inauguration of a president upon whom Yankee big business pinned its hopes. The loan would have made it possible for Quadros's government to 'deal with the expenses of its first three months in power'. It would, also, as the American leaders intended, give Quadros a chance to begin to repay the debt left by the outgoing administration which was in the region of 176 million dollars.

'Brazil,' Quadros replied drily to Kennedy's special envoy, 'will only accept economic aid when it is offered as genuine aid. We are not beggars cap in hand.'

Since 1930 Washington had with some justification considered Brazil as one of its firmest and most loyal allies. Now Quadros was saying all over Brazil that in future they must reckon with a less obedient neighbour. In fact he actually said so in so many words to Adolf Berle, Kennedy's special envoy. Berle's behaviour was very ill-judged: he wanted to find out what attitude Quadros's government would take if there were a direct or indirect attack on Cuba. He was counting on a private interview, but Quadros gave his answer that same evening and it flew round the diplomatic community like wildfire: 'Brazil is opposed to any form of intervention, whatever its nature, in the internal affairs of other countries.'

From January to August 1961 the American press played up the rather too simplistic theme of the rivalry between Quadros and Castro for the leadership in Latin America. At a time when Quadros was seen as being a pleasant but ineffective dreamer, Castro aroused enthusiasm and sympathy from American commentators. Washington decided seven years later to pit the 'madman from the Mato Grosso' against the 'Ivanhoe of Cuba', but the duel never actually took place. And when Quadros decided to resign, the reasons he gave were reminiscent of the things said by Vargas on the eve of his dramatic suicide.

Quadros sent missions to iron-curtain countries to make economic agreements with them. He entered into diplomatic relations with Rumania, Bulgaria, Albania and Hungary. He ordered the Brazilian delegation to the United Nations to vote in favour of the admission of communist China to its great glass palace in Manhattan.

*

'If we don't make revolutionary reforms,' said Quadros to his ministers, 'then one fine day another Castro will appear on the scene from a mountain hideout.' Unlike Kubitschek, Quadros liked to tackle obstacles one by one; he wanted to have built by 1965 nearly 12,000 kilometres of asphalt roads; he wanted also to build more primary schools and fewer universities. In April 1961 he gave Western Union a contract for installing a whole new telecommunications system in Brazil. He also gave Ford the go-ahead for building a tractor factory. But the authoritarian and revolutionary democracy which he also wanted eventually to build must undoubtedly have been forced sooner or later to intervene in the financial affairs of foreign businessmen.

From 1955 to 1961 Kubitschek had launched a plan for

public works, given a completely new stimulus to the car industry, and built the skeleton of the new federal capital. But he did all these things at the cost of the country's currency; consequently one of Quadros's major objectives was to stop the fall of the *cruzeiro*. Kubitschek had given the world a picture of Brazil as generous, prodigal, rich enough to do anything. In the few months of Quadros's administration it became a country that counted its every penny, was determined wherever possible to 'make do and mend', and put every farthing produced by such economies into its Savings Account. It might well have proved the best thing that ever happened to Brazil to have as president so punctilious an accountant, thus enabling its balance sheet to be put into good order before returning to the forward leap.

The unexpected departure of Quadros, however, turned all such possibilities into speculations as to what might have been. On 25 August his resignation was announced in a short message that he himself read on the radio. His voice shook as he said, 'I feel myself destroyed. Hidden forces are even now mustering against me. Were I to remain at the head of the government, I should not be able to preserve the peace and tranquillity I need to do the job. As I turn this page in my personal and my public life, my thoughts go out to the students, the workers, and the whole vast family of people who make up Brazil . . .'

Eight months after his resignation the country was still divided as to how this statement was to be interpreted. A tiny number still thought that, under strong pressure from the army and the conservatives, he had withdrawn to save his country from being plunged into chaos and civil war. The vast majority remained convinced that he had not really resigned for good, but was doing 'another Vargas' only in order to come back stronger than before. Events proved them right. When he embarked for London on the *Uruguay Star* with his family, Quadros stated categorically: 'What has happened is final. I shall never enter politics again …' Yet as soon as he got back to Brazil in the spring of 1962 he immediately got in touch with the leaders of the 'peasant leagues' of the north east, in readiness for the next elections. In April 1964, together with Goulart and Kubitschek, he was deprived of all his rights as a citizen, but by then his time had passed. He behaved with amazing discretion during the Castello Branco administration, and only decided to criticize the military regime in 1967 – whereas many of those involved in the 'revolution' of March 1964 had been denouncing it for some time. He spoke a bit more loudly in 1968, and was then kept under house surveillance in Corumbá by the Costa e Silva government for four months. In the fifties Corumbá was, wrongly perhaps, thought to be an isolated and not very healthy little town serving mainly as a border post from which to keep an eye on Bolivia. By 1968 it was only two hours' flying time from São Paulo, and where there had been dirt roads there were asphalt highways. Certainly as a punishment, Quadros's 'imprisonment' there was not as harsh as it might have appeared.

*

The man who played the determining part in Quadros's resignation was the same man who had attacked Vargas so violently : Carlos Lacerda. He was rabidly right-wing, and made no secret of the fact. His whole career was directed to an unrelenting attack on communism : Vargas's tragic death justifiably earned him some bitter dislike, and indeed he was more or less sent to Coventry for months which, for so active a man, was painful in the extreme. But to expect him to give up the fight would have been to misunderstand the man. He was soon on the attack again, and managed to win the election for the governorship of the state of Guanabara (incorporating what had been the federal district and state of Rio after Brasilia had taken Rio's place as capital).

He began by seeing Quadros as the champion of order and austerity, the friend of the important bourgeois families of São Paulo and the protagonist of private enterprise; therefore he passionately supported the party of the 'candidate with the broom'. But Quadros's attempts to make friends with the communist bloc countries surprised and disturbed him, and eventually he turned against the new president with the same violence he had previously brought to his support. Having rallied enthusiastically to the man, he now furiously set about denouncing him. Which, in fact, was not hard to do. To be the governor of São Paulo is far easier than to rule a country as vast and complex as Brazil. In eight months of power, Quadros showed that he was unable to produce plans for a rational financial policy; he did not even envisage the fiscal reform that was indispensable. Though he deplored the inflation that had assumed such alarming proportions during the last months of the Kubitschek government, he actually printed as many banknotes in seven months as Kubitschek had in five years. He toured all the states to consolidate his popularity, asking every governor what he needed in the way of dams, schools, industries and so on. However, what Lacerda attacked most skilfully was the doubtful direction of Quadros's foreign policies – not his failures as an administrator. The best occasion of all for Lacerda arose when Che Guevara was on his way back from the Pan American conference in Punta del Este: Quadros invited him to Brasilia, and decorated this lieutenant of Castro's with the highest honour the country had to bestow – the medal of the Southern Cross.

Vargas had been carried away by a 'torrent of mud'. It would not have been difficult for Quadros to have refuted Lacerda's accusations, but his failure to do so must be understood in terms of the psychological state he was in. In fact, on 25 August 1961 the three military ministers, Marshal Odilio Denys, Admiral Silvio Heck, and Brigadeiro Grum Moss had assured Quadros of the loyalty of the armed forces. But the president was exhausted, in a state of nervous and mental confusion, and stuck to his determination to resign.

The real crisis only began afterwards. The man who would normally succeed him was the vice president, João Goulart, and he was at the time touring communist China. Goulart had not been elected on the Quadros ticket, but had run as second to Marshal Teixeira Lott, the candidate of the workers' party and the communists. The fact that he was seen as Vargas's spiritual heir won him more votes than Quadros's number two. Having been vice-president in the Kubitschek administration, Goulart felt quite at home in the job under Quadros; as an aide to Vargas, and a native of the same district in the Rio Grande do Sul, Goulart founded his political fortunes on a close connection with the trades unions and the machinery of social security. At the moment of Quadros's resignation, Goulart was giving a courtesy speech in favour of the communist regime in China; the unfortunate expressions he used in his toasts to Chou-En-Lai gave the army just the excuse they needed to veto his accession to the presidency – clearly he was nothing more nor less than a communist agent. Goulart came back to Brazil post haste and landed in Porto Alegre where his supporters were in a huge majority, and anger against the military leadership was mounting dangerously. Troops were sent by the federal government against the third army of General Machado Lopes which was in support of Goulart. But the three military leaders and Goulart himself were all wise enough to recoil at the thought of civil war, and the crisis ended in a typically Brazilian compromise. Goulart would be made president, but would not have the kind of presidential power enjoyed by Quadros or Kubitschek: both houses of the legislature were summoned immediately in Brasilia, and agreed to the plan. The only man to speak against this 'non-solution' was Leonel Brizola, governor of Rio Grande do Sul; he rightly pointed out that the European parliamentary system could never be perfectly adapted to a country like Brazil, and demanded that the Constitution be strictly adhered to, and full presidential power given to Goulart. But his voice was ignored amid the louder and more forceful pressure of Marshal Denys and Admiral Heck. The 'hidden forces' mentioned by Quadros, though they would not have deterred a man of stronger character than his, now made themselves visible. The military could never have overthrown a man who had more self-confidence and cunning than Quadros; but they were sufficiently determined to impress the senators and deputies. The Chamber voted this new amendment to the Constitution by 233 to 55, and the Senate followed them by 47 to 5. The military ministers put a good face on it, accepted their semi-victory, and finally allowed Goulart's plane to land in Brasilia.

The crisis left a country unsure of its own political future. By having thus openly intervened, the army had done itself a grave disservice; it had proved that military pressure, the traditional scourge of public life in Latin America, still existed in Brazil. And once again, it was Kubitschek who passed the most severe judgement on Quadros, whose resignation had been the signal for an inevitable and dangerous crisis : 'The crisis he induced by resigning has cost us three times the price of building Brasilia. There has been no greater criminal in the whole history of Brazil . . .'

The compromise which brought the crisis to an end, and by the same token destroyed the classical and traditional role of the presidency, soon became quite obviously inadequate to the real needs of the country, just as Kubitschek had predicted. Goulart, though officially president, had to work in harmony with the president of the Council, and was not long in discovering his ambiguous function to be an extremely difficult one. He tried to fight against this amputation of the president's powers, which brought the already cumbersome administrative machinery of Brasilia virtually to a standstill.

But the worsening of the economic situation, the continual rise in the cost of living and fall in the value of the *cruzeiro* resulted, in June 1962, in serious disturbances in Rio, where crowds tried to break into the food shops. The resignation of Tancredo Neves's cabinet was obviously not going to improve the general situation, and it became clear that the internecine rivalries among political parties and personalities which had made up the essence of Brazilian political life during the past ten years really no longer mattered.

Jânio Quadros was beaten in the election of October 1962, even in his own São Paulo. The industrial bourgeoisie of this Brazilian Chicago had lauded him to the skies, for his apostolate of austerity, but he now departed ingloriously. Such an episode would be enough to condemn once for all any political man in any other country, but Brazil is different. The first clear sign that the 'Janiste' phenomenon might once again appear in future elections appeared in March 1965, when General Faria Lima, an official protégé of Quadros, won a triumphant victory as Mayor of São Paulo, and in doing so crushed the candidate supported by the ageing Adhemar de Barros – whose pontificating and somewhat aggressive rediscovery of religion made little impression on the middle class of the city.

After the elections of October 1962 Kubitschek demanded a referendum to give Brazil back its old form of presidential rule. 'Brazil,' he said, 'needs a leader with real power. As things are now, one third of the orders are given by President Goulart, another third by the Ministers, and yet another third by the leader of the governing party. If we don't have a return to presidential rule, Brazil will only enter a new crisis, and there may even be a revolution.'

Prophetic words they were! The referendum took place on 6 January 1963 and by a vast majority the Brazilians decided to bring the old system back into force. The president of the Council, Hermes Lima, handed in his resignation on 22

January and the President, Goulart, got all his powers back intact the next day. But it was not to be for long.

*

The ides of March 1964 brought Goulart's downfall. It had been clear to the least well informed observer from the beginning of the year that the most violent storm ever to have broken on Brazil was on its way. An important segment of both conservatives and the armed forces had never forgiven Goulart for his success in becoming president, remaining president, and then getting back the full powers he needed to fulfil his dream of succeeding Vargas.

It is rare for the son of a great king to live up to his father's reputation. Vargas had made his mark on Brazil for a quarter of a century, and what is today known as 'Getulism' is perfectly adapted to a particular political style of great value to a country not yet ready for the type of political struggle we have in Europe. João Goulart, a large landowner with still larger ambition, born to privilege and supported by it, was none the less vain, weak, and quite without that marvellous intuition which brought Getúlio so close to the people; he could thus hardly hope to open a second Getulist type of reign. Vargas had governed with extraordinary skill and a sympathy that spread to everyone. Quadros let himself be influenced far too easily by his innumerable advisers; it was certainly to his credit that he surrounded himself with such valuable and sincere men as Celso Furtado, the young economist who directed the SUDENE; but he also made the serious mistake of allowing complete freedom to a left-wing radicalism which was verbose, ineffective and pointlessly provocative. As I have said, Goulart was in China when the crisis broke in 1961 : he now tried to restore the foreign policies of Quadros: intensifying relationships with socialist bloc countries, and extending the hand of friendship to the neutralist countries of Africa and Asia. But – whether you call it skill or Machiavellianism – this policy of Quadros's went hand in hand with a social and economic policy at home which did not fundamentally undermine the larger interests of Brazilian capital. A close study of Goulart's agrarian reform shows that it was unadventurous, and quite inadequate to the real needs of the federation – yet that, and several other similar moves he made, were enough to label him an out and out left-winger. In the weeks preceding his fall, he made such enormous mistakes that one is tempted to wonder whether, like Quadros three years earlier, he was not trying to swing right over to the left so as to improve his chances of an eventual comeback.

At the beginning of March there were numerous incidents involving landowners and peasant workers. In the state of Paraíba one peasant leader was shot, and another in the state of Goiás. In Minas a group of rich *fazendeiros* set about organizing their own militia to deal with the 'Jacobin' threat whose shadow seemed to be moving down from the north east to the centre of the country. So it was in a peculiarly explosive atmosphere that Goulart decided to speed up the steps planned by the Supra (Supervisory Body for Agrarian Reform) while Congress was still discussing ways and means of indemnifying the expropriated landowners.

The threat to expropriate all uncultivated land along the arterial roads, the railways, and the dams up to a depth of ten kilometres aroused the rage and fear of the landowners. There was a certain charm about the idea that Brazilian agrarian reform might begin to be put into effect by the labours of a president who was a large landowner himself; but that charming possibility was quickly reduced to no more than a daring speculation by the concerted action of the conservatives and a section of the army. The report published in the U.S. in mid-March on 'the significant gains by the communist party in Brazil' caused barely a stir in Brasilia. Yet it was a signal that would have provided a warning light to anyone less immersed in the marvels he might achieve, and more aware of the real powers at work, than Goulart was. The parliamentary opposition worked hard to win over new supporters, even within Kubitschek's own Social Democratic Party so many of whom had connections with the wealthy rural middle class. The real beginning of the dramatic crisis that was to end two weeks later with the fall of the president was the announcement of a large public meeting in Rio de Janeiro (where Carlos Lacerda ruled supreme). Goulart was proposing, symbolically, to sign his decree on agrarian reform during that meeting. Two hundred thousand *cariocas* attended this revolutionary gathering, supervised by detachments of troops. Leonel Brizola, Goulart's brother-in-law, and also governor of Pernambuco, and Miguel Arraes, the leader of the moderate left, demanded the formation of a 'popular government'. The meeting took place on 13 March and on 24 March the government decided to increase the salaries of civil servants by 100 per cent. But two days later Rio became a 'red' city, with the mutiny of 1,500 quartermasters and seamen of the navy. Goulart temporized, and seemed to have no intention of meting out any very severe punishment for this breach of discipline. He refused to accept the resignation of Admiral Silvio Mota; and the trial of strength thus produced between the Admiralty, that bastion of aristocracy, and the government, could only serve to reinforce the fears of the conservatives, and provide an excuse for those who wanted a putsch. Seven hundred naval officers signed a motion 'deploring the government's lamentable decision to grant amnesty to the mutineers'. Certainly Goulart would have had a hard time disowning a sailors' rebellion based on the Popular Front he himself supported – but in any case the die was cast. Those in both army and conservative circles who were so impatiently waiting for D-Day decided to act.

*

The rebellion began in the name of 'God and country'. Looking back now, it may seem odd that Goulart and those loyal to him failed to recognize the indications of the approaching storm. But the fact is that when the state of Minas rose against the federal government on 31 March the whole of the president's entourage was taken completely by surprise. The *pronunciamiento* of the civil governor of Minas, Magalhães Pinto – made in the best Latin American tradition – was at once approved and followed by the states of Guanabara (Rio de Janeiro), São Paulo, and Rio Grande do Sul. 'Rich' Brazil was setting itself up against the Federation. The military leaders demanded that Goulart disown his left-wing and trade-unionist friends. In his palatial Rio residence, only a few hundred yards from the residence of his enemy Goulart, Carlos Lacerda was briefly the *deus ex machina* in the conspiracy. But it did not really depend on him. Goulart should have realized that to pursue his policies he needed the total support of the mass of the people and the trades unions, and might mean a confrontation, leading to bloodshed, with the forces of reaction. Now it is clear that no such left-wing front existed in Brazil at that time. Though the Goulart reforms naturally aroused great enthusiasm among the peasant classes who had for so long been exploited, and also the approval of left-wing intellectuals, the people as such were not organized for fighting. Juan Domingo Perón had been faced with the same problem in almost identical terms in September 1955 : the Argentine dictator also had to choose between resignation and civil war; he chose the former, and Goulart did the same.

Goulart's departure to exile in Uruguay was greeted with tremendous demonstrations of excitement in Rio and São Paulo. The demonstrators were mainly middle-class men and women who had been disturbed by repeated warnings of the 'communist peril', and who were perhaps affected more than any other group by the rising cost of living. In São Paulo, Adhemar de Barros went dashing round the town, urging on the communist witch-hunt. Zealous and almost illiterate soldiers went into the public libraries where they took out such books as Stendhal's *Le Rouge et le Noir* (chosen purely for its title!) and John XXIII's *Pacem in Terris* (for the comical reason that it was bound in red leather). There were thousands of arrests in Rio, São Paulo and also Recife – the north-eastern capital which was the nightmare of the forces behind the 'April movement'. The governor of Pernambuco, Miguel Arraes, was deported to the island of Fernando de Noronha – some 400 kilometres from the Brazilian coast – and Meneghetti, governor of Rio Grande do Sul, returned in triumph to Porte Alegre, his own capital, where for a time it had looked as though Leonel Brizola would organize the same kind of resistance as during the summer of 1961.

The repressive regime of Goulart's vanquishers was not bloody, apart from a few isolated cases in the north east – and in this it followed an old-established Brazilian rule – but it was at times inconsistent. Notorious communist leaders, for instance, could sometimes escape the rigours of the special military tribunals, whereas ordinary people and quite minor officials might be most harshly dealt with. By virtue of articles 7 and 10 of the institutional act which legalized the coup of 1 April 1964, almost 400 major figures in Brazil (among them the former presidents Goulart, Kubitschek and Quadros, governor Miguel Arraes, Celso Furtado, Josué de Castro, Oscar Niemeyer) were deprived of all civil rights for ten years, and almost 3,000 civil servants removed from office. Nor did well-known generals and admirals escape the vengeful axe of the new leaders, in their determination to cut off all the heads of the 'communist hydra' they saw spreading everywhere. The April revolution also declared itself a 'battle against corruption and waste'. But the officers applied this praiseworthy principle with a certain politic care, since ex-president Kubitschek, the builder of Brasilia, was only struck down a few days before the date they had set as a limit, while

Governor Adhemar de Barros, whose tanglings with justice were common knowledge all over the country, escaped altogether.

*

On 3 April Washington congratulated the provisional president Ranieri Mazzili on the success of the revolution, and this indiscreet haste on their part gave added credence to rumours that the CIA had played a major part in preparing and carrying out the coup. By 5 April Marshal Castello Branco, a man of soldierly discipline and rigidity, had been put forward as the 'candidate of the revolution' for the presidency of the Republic, and by 12 April his election had taken place. It was evident that most of the armed forces, the conservatives and the middle class were delighted by the fall of Goulart, and moral weight was added to their position when twenty-four Brazilian bishops made a public statement that 'the country had been saved from the abyss it had been heading for'.

But as the weeks passed it became clear that the new regime was receiving its inspiration from two major sources: pro-American technocrats, and the military. The leader of the first group was the new Minister for Planning, Roberto Campos, a young, intelligent, dynamic and highly competent man, but one who had spent far too much of his life outside the country. His objective was a simple one: he wanted to prevent the present galloping inflation, and get the economy back on to a sound footing. To do this he leant heavily, and of set purpose, on the U.S., and this policy resulted in an unprecedented in-pouring of dollars to Castello Branco's Brazil. During the eight years before Goulart's fall, Brazil had already received more than two thousand million dollars, but in 1965 alone, the splendid sum of 450 million dollars was brought into Brasilia by various banking firms in New York in the form of loans. But it was not long before the reverse side of the coin became apparent: a succession of agreements, like one with the Hanna Mining Corporation for the right to develop the fantastic iron ore reserves in Minas Gerais, made it clear that Roberto Campos was neglecting that other rule so dear to the hearts of the military nationalists : to give none of Brazil's wealth away. It looked in 1965 as though the battle for iron would lead to dissensions within the core of the new ruling group. More and more voices spoke up from among both the military and conservatives in criticism of the 'methods Roberto Campos is using against inflation'. Carlos Lacerda, the Cassandra of approaching storms, made Campos, who was his own immediate rival for the favour of the powers that be, his major target. The Minister of Planning thus under fire was hotly and consistently defended by Castello Branco. The history of the last ten years in Brazil had proved that in the end the chief polemicist of the Federation always defeated whoever he had decided to attack. But Lacerda's object was a little more ambitious : he had sworn he would become president of Brazil, and would certainly, with all his cleverness and energy, never give up until he had used every scrap of ammunition at his disposal.

The economic and financial policies of Campos were also viewed with some alarm in the military academy of Rio – of which all those who had joined to destroy Goulart were graduates. In March 1965 a group of colonels who belonged to the Council of National Security handed in their resignations to Castello Branco, and the important families in São Paulo were not unmoved. The fact that General Faria Lima was elected Mayor of São Paulo in March might be interpreted in various ways, but it certainly showed a certain disenchantment among the local bourgeoisie.

Paradoxically, Castello Branco found supporters in the federal Congress from among the ranks of Goulart's workers' party, and Kubitschek's Social Democrats. Obviously this was partly due to the fear inspired by the thunderbolts of a regime which could simply dismiss forty deputies from their posts in April – but not wholly so. In effect a great many people who represented parties falsely thought to be left-wing were in fact connected with the landowning and industrial upper middle class. In November 1964 the government had got an amendment passed to the Constitution that would allow of an agrarian reform whereby the responsibilities of the *municipios* were transferred to the federal authorities; but in December the pressure of the *latifundiarios* of Minas resulted in this particular fiscal measure proposed by Campos being abandoned as his most effective weapon against the great landed proprietors. When they seized power, the military had claimed that they would actually effect the reforms which Goulart could only hope for. But on this question of agrarian reform the parliamentary battle that took place provides a perfect illustration of the fact that it is impossible to put socialist policies into effect if you depend on a right-wing electorate.

More than a year after the revolution it would have been hard to claim that Castello Branco was secure in his position. But it would also have been Utopian to imagine that Brazil could possibly get back on to the road of representative democracy in a short time. Nor was it certain that the military extremists, who supported the *linha dura,** could defeat the 'legalist' moderates now supporting Castello Branco. But one thing was absolutely certain : the Brazilian army, which had for so long been so rightly proud of its respect for the laws of democracy, was beginning to be more like the Argentine army which it had so often blamed for its excessive political activity. From 1955 to 1968 Argentina's officers had continually argued among themselves as to the best tactics to fight neo-Peronism. Now, from April 1964 onwards, the Brazilian officers, divided into moderates and hard-liners, were in a similar situation : how could they prevent a return to some form of Getulism?

* Hard line.

For instance, it is impossible not to compare the crisis that rocked the Brazilian army after the gubernatorial elections of October 1965 with the rage of the Argentine military when faced with the continual threats of a resurgence of Peronism. In Buenos Aires, the response to a Peronist landslide in the elections was a direct seizure of power. In Brasilia the relative success of the opposition in the October elections (they won in 5 states out of 11) led to a rattling of swords in an army suddenly afraid of having to question one of their most basic axioms: 'the revolution is irreversible'. Even the president's authority was threatened, and it needed all the diplomatic skill of the Minister of War, Marshal Costa e Silva, to preserve unity among the armed forces. The 'institutional acts' published in October 1965 directed towards limiting the few freedoms the new regime had allowed in political matters were simply an expression of the army's panic: reinforcing the central power, limiting the authority of the governors, hastening forward the procedure of passing laws, giving military courts the power to hear cases against civilians accused of crimes against the security of the state, the election of the president of the Republic by indirect voting.

A totally authoritarian regime had been established, and the supposedly moderate tendency of what we may call early Castellism was gradually crushed between November 1965 and November 1966. With the complicity of a number of members of parliament who belonged theoretically to the opposition (i.e. Workers or Social Democrats), two new groups were formed: the Arena (National Renewal Alliance) and the MDB (Brazilian Democratic Movement). Arena was made up of supporters of the new regime, and the MDB, as a precaution that would provide a parliamentary opposition, thus making democracy a reality, was the 'opposition' in which all the most troublesome elements were, as far as possible, 'marginalized'. Of course the whole thing was artificially done, but at the same time it would have been impossible without the help of those same people who had proclaimed aloud their hostility to the April 1964 coup all over Brasilia. One humorist gave a neat but cruel definition of the situation: 'We now have a Yes party, and a Yes Sir party ...'

The election of the president by indirect voting should in theory have made the transition undramatic. Marshal Costa e Silva's candidature as successor to Castello Branco was caught in a web of palace intrigues, and the lack of enthusiasm shown by Castello Branco himself led to a diplomatic 'War Game' for several weeks in the amphitheatres of the military academy. It was evident that Castello did not think Costa e Silva – whose political role in the April conspiracy had been spasmodic – the best possible successor, if indeed such a creature existed in the tormented mind of one of the best thinkers the military academy had ever produced.

The two men were basically very different: Castello Branco, a north-easterner, had a certain severity, austerity even, about him, a silence, a secrecy, thoughtfulness and suspicion which contrasted with Costa e Silva's extrovert and friendly ways, his generosity, love of parties and good living – indeed all his southern qualities which tended more to action than reflection. He had the nerve to put himself forward at the beginning of 1966. As he was later to explain, 'It was the little people who wanted me to ...' The 'little people' were the junior officers. Castello Branco made the best of a bad job and yielded six months later, publicly handing over to his Minister of War. He left office amid almost universal unpopularity: this silent and not specially handsome soldier had not learnt how to touch the hearts of the people, though it would perhaps have taken only one generous gesture, one word said at the right time. He died in an accident in the north east in the same year as Costa e Silva came to power, and there were few to regret it.

One of the traits that most marked the Castello Branco regime was the fantastic speed with which American power in Brazil had advanced. Determined to fight Communism and Castroism, Castello Branco and his advisers – especially Roberto Campos, Minister of Planning – were resolutely pro-American, and made no attempt to moderate the greed of private investors. Campos certainly professed his theory that 'private foreign capital is welcome, because we shall always keep some of it'. In March 1968, Gama e Silva, the Minister of Justice, himself stated in parliament that one fifth of Brazilian territory – in other words 160 thousand million square metres – had in fact been sold to foreigners; he added that the mouth of the Amazon and all the land bordering on the Belém–Brasilia highway belonged to foreigners, mainly North Americans. The ever-increasing interference of the U.S. in Brazilian affairs was pointed out yet again by intellectual groups who spoke out against the plan for university reform approved by the Brazilian Minister of Education, and financed by USAID: this was a plan to restructure higher education in Brazil in a way that would be of assistance to the economic and political systems defended by the U.S. That agreement, reviewed by the government, became for those in the universities the very symbol of 'Brazil's enslavement to American interests' and was the starting point of a student revolt which culminated between March and July 1968 in violent rioting which the police could not control. (Other examples of American cultural, political or economic interference were denounced not only by the left-wing opposition who have no mass means of expression at their command, but also in the most modern circles of the leadership: agreements for military cooperation and the training of special anti-guerrilla forces, the handing over of the iron mines in Minas Gerais to Hanna Mining Corporation, raiding parties organized by the agents of American companies to get hold of precious metals and stones in the Mato Grosso or Minas or Amazonas, interference by missionaries with their birth control campaigns in Amazonas, plans for forming an artificial sea in Amazonas, linked with other huge-scale projects suggested by the Hudson Institute in order to achieve a 'rational' development of all the wealth of the soil and sub-soil of the virgin lands in the centre of the South American continent; and so on.)

From his exile in Algiers ex-Governor Miguel Arraes wrote a philippic attacking the situation of dependence, and making clear his own view of the plans for political re-grouping of the centre and left which had led to the formation in 1968 of a 'broadened' opposition front. 'Development,' he declared, 'cannot be contemplated except in direct relation to social problems. It is incomprehensible that the riches of a country should be exploited to suit the needs of a minority. The case of Brazil is even more shocking since there we find all the elements needed for development: a large population, a huge territory with all the resources that will ensure material progress. Unlike a great many other under-developed countries, Brazil already has a significant number of technologists, but the lack of national plans enables foreign interests to interfere in a lot of sectors that are basic to our economy. We have seen analysis of the harm done to under-developed countries during the past twenty years by the fall in the price of raw materials; to this one may add the fact of capital being taken out of the country. Though there have been investments and loans from abroad to Brazil to the tune of 1,815 million dollars, one must take into consideration the fact that North American companies sent 2,460 million dollars out of the country and more than 1,020 million in the guise of services between 1947 and 1960. In such a situation the term "international aid" hardly seems appropriate. There can be no development where there is economic dependence . . .'

In one sense the formation of Costa e Silva's government in March 1967 was the expression of an awareness of that excessive dependence by sections of the industrial bourgeoisie and nationalist finance groups. Magalhães Pinto, the Minister of Foreign Affairs, and a native of Minas, was a fairly typical example of this concern – a concern felt by that element in Brazilian opinion most easily moved by nationalist ideology. Pinto, ex-bank-director of Belo Horizonte, a close friend of Kubitschek, once a middle-of-the-road deputy from Minas and later governor of that state, was to do all that lay in his power to foster a return to the democratic norm that was undoubtedly wanted by the vast majority of Brazilians.

He was – privately at least – to give approval to that 'broadened front' in which the fallen presidents Goulart and Kubitschek had joined forces with Carlos Lacerda, ex-governor of Guanabara. There is no doubt that he hoped that in thus drawing together all the opposition, both the moderate left and orthodox communists, it would be possible to advance along the arduous road to the rebirth of a genuinely democratic Brazil.

But he was probably too late. For all its good will, Costa e Silva's government hardly achieved anything. The smiling chattiness of the president had led a lot of Brazilians to believe, over-hastily perhaps, that there would be a complete reversal of the rigid military regime. But they did not allow for the demands of the economy and the power of political alliances. The army's *linha dura* had no intention of yielding on essentials, and the 'gains of the April revolution' were to be maintained come what might. In fact, four years after the fall of Goulart it was hard to see any sign of hope, nor even quite what Goulart's vanquishers still obstinately called 'revolution'. The coup against the legislature on 13 December 1968 fully justified every such apprehension.*

Brazil in 1968 was certainly not a total dictatorship. The traditional parties had disappeared, but there was little to regret in that, and a semblance of parliamentary life was still going on in Brasilia where a few of the more courageous deputies, like Hermano Alves, publicly spoke out against the 'forces against democracy'. The left-wing and ultra left-wing

* Since October 1969 Emilio Garrastazu Medice has been president.

press had ceased to function – apart from *Ultima Hora* – but the major daily papers, like the *Jornal do Brasil*, the *Correioda Manhã*, or the conservative, *O Estado de São Paulo*, still had considerable freedom of expression. The leader-writers of these – which are among the best of all Latin American papers both for serious journalism and good news coverage – did not hesitate to castigate the excesses or errors of the regime. Despite everything there was some freedom of speech. But this was due more to the courage and individualism of certain people than to any lack of attempts to coerce on the part of the new establishment. The same may be said of all elections organized, or tolerated, since 1964. The Brazilian military, more concerned than their Argentine colleagues to respect the outward trappings of democracy, have been tempted several times since Goulart's fall to put to the test the popularity they feel so sure of. The measures adopted during the early days of Castellism justified their conviction. But later completely arbitrary restrictions undid the effects of these measures; thus, all 'undesirable' candidates since April 1964 have been systematically removed from the official lists, and thousands of people who were deprived of their rights as citizens or sent into exile abroad never even had a chance to offer themselves for election.

Last, and most important of all, it was clear in 1968 that the economic and social structures of the country had not been touched. Agrarian reform (the key reform that would indicate any genuine will to reconsider the structures under attack from all the most dynamic members of society and the Church) was not even being considered. The 'cadastral survey' ordered by Castello Branco's 'law of the land' seemed primarily intended by the Costa e Silva government to increase the revenue from income tax. In 1968 there were only three million Brazilians actually paying tax because the survey was not yet complete. Brazilian leaders undoubtedly thought that reform was no longer needed, since the mechan-

ization of agriculture and industrialization would make it
irrelevant. Yet anyone travelling through the countryside
could see that the population explosion was gradually making
nonsense of the very faint progress achieved by a hopelessly
inadequate 'development'. Ever greater crowds of landless
peasants and workless young people were rushing to the
city centres, and filling up the shanty towns where living
conditions are, to quote Archbishop Helder Camara of Recife,
'subhuman'.

Political parties banned, the 'peasant leagues' dissolved,
hundreds of leading Brazilians deprived of their citizenship
rights, the National Union of Students abolished, officers
gradually given all the really key posts (a general replaced a
civilian at the head of SUDENE in 1967, for instance), an
economic situation wholly dominated by the fight against inflation, a continual increase of foreign capital and foreign exploitation, fundamental reforms shelved indefinitely : this was
more or less what four years of this 'revolutionary' regime
had achieved. It was hardly surprising to find that it was the
intellectuals – more aware than anyone else of this paradox
of a country with such vast potentialities being paralysed
by its own antiquated structures – who were the leading
protesters and demonstrators. The student riots of spring
1968 showed the regime how unpopular it was. The army
had to be called in to assist the police, who were completely
overwhelmed by the demonstrations – demonstrations involving not only students, but the whole population. A
considerable part of the Church, especially from among the
lower clergy, also began to take a clearer stand against the
military regime, and a real crisis between the two began that
spring – a crisis whose consequences could hardly be over-
estimated, for condemnations by the bishops provided one of
the most important elements in the 'revolutionary awareness' developing everywhere.

Yet it was hard to see how the military rulers could

quickly resign from their 'mission'. The alliances, whether temporary or more permanent, between the former political leaders – Kubitschek, Goulart, Quadros, Lacerda – could not really have been made to work, even in the unlikely case of the army letting them try, except by returning to a botched-up version of the situation as it was before April 1964. Democracy might be restored in theory, but there would be little likelihood of the basic problems facing modern Brazil being any nearer solution. On the left, the April 1964 coup had led to a certain increase in maturity both of the men and their ideologies; but the grave divisions among the genuinely revolutionary forces, and the lack of leaders who could effectively take over were still major obstacles. The communists were divided among at least four rival factions in 1968, and the orthodox line urged by Prestes called for the 'restoration of democratic freedom' and an alliance with the leaders of the 'broadened front' that had been banned in April 1968. The 'cavalier of Hope' had aged; the revolutionary intellectuals were subjected to contradictory influences from Havana and Peking. Two men, both well-known exiles, still had some hope for the future. Leonel Brizola, formerly the governor of Rio Grande do Sul, seemed in 1968 to have given up the 'policy of insurrection' he had preached in 1965, and may have been thinking in terms of coming home. Miguel Arraes, the former governor of Recife, contemplated the long-term prospects for revolution from his retreat in Algiers. He was too clear-sighted to feel any great hopes, and no political leader can afford to be away from the scene for too long; but if Arraes were to return it would in fact mean a total reversal of the whole situation in Brazil . . .

CHAPTER 2

Argentina

STATISTICS

Area: 1,070,000 square miles
Estimated population in 1966: 22,691,000
Population density: 21 people per square mile
Annual rate of population increase: 1·57 per cent
Annual increase in average per capita *income from 1960 to 1966:*
    1·2 per cent.

PRINCIPAL PRODUCTS

Wheat, flax (the world's second largest producer), maize, cotton.
Sixth largest cattle population in the world; fourth largest sheep
    population.

Buenos Aires, like Rio de Janeiro, arose out of a mistake. The
'River January' existed only in the imaginations of Portuguese mariners : similarly, the favourable winds which Don
Pedro de Mendoza thought he had discovered on the right
bank of the estuary of the Río de la Plata never blew over the
vast capital of the Argentine republic. In point of fact, when
Don Pedro sailed up the Plata in search of gold and landed
on its flat shores to found the little colony of Santísima
Trinidad, his chief wish was to pay homage to Our Lady of
the Favouring Wind, patron of sailors. The climate of Latin
America's premier metropolis is indeed anything but temperate. The town was rebuilt three hundred kilometres from

the sea, and is exposed not only to the *pampero* * from the south, but also to the subtropical sea squalls that drive across the estuary, and to the icy winds from the Antarctic. There are constant storms, and sharp and unpleasant changes of temperature. From December to March – the hot, damp southern summer – there can be a mist lying constantly over the estuary and covering the whole town with its dank mantle. However, Buenos Aires is at an equivalent latitude in the south to that of North Africa in the north, and what it is like most of the time is a sun-drenched Mediterranean port. There is a delicious scent from the orange and lemon trees on the islands. In the residential districts, which extend almost to the Tigre delta, great masses of roses and English-style lawns surround elegant villas. On Sundays, the white sails from the Yacht Club regatta can be seen across the grassy, flowered banks of the Tigre less than thirty kilometres away from the dramatic and magnetic vastness of the *pampa*.

*

Buenos Aires is a proud city. The *porteños* † themselves feel it and share its pride. Apart from the outer harbour of La Boca, which is a cross between Barcelona and the docklands of Marseilles, the whole city is a harmony of concrete, stone, long vistas, marvellous diagonals, and skyscrapers. It certainly has not got Rio's romance and charm, but it makes up for that by its fantastic dynamism. At the end of the seventeenth century Buenos Aires, continually under attack from Indian tribes, had barely more than 4,000 inhabitants, less than a thousand of whom were white – the rest being made up of negro or Indian slaves brought in by the first Spaniards. Stock-breeding was almost the only source of revenue. The horses brought by the conquistadors multiplied rapidly, for the climate was just right for this rich and well watered

* Wind blowing from the *pampa*.
† Name for the inhabitants of Buenos Aires.

pastureland. But when the first census was made in Buenos
Aires at the end of the eighteenth century, though herds of
wild horses had been running free in the *pampa* for several
decades, the human population of the town was still only
16,000. It was just at that time that the Creoles recognized
their own strength, and felt the wish to create a real nation,
just as the pioneers of North America had done. What is
noteworthy about that period – and is still characteristic of
Argentina – is that there soon came to be a definite, struc-
tured society, with its artisans, its wealthy businessmen, its
officials, its doctors and its clergy. The pace of progress
accelerated and by 1869 there were 177,000 people in Buenos
Aires. In 1962, with over six million, it had become the largest
city in all South America, and fifth largest in the whole world
– surpassed only by Tokyo, New York, London and Paris. In
1966, out of a total estimated population of 22,691,000,
Buenos Aires, covering only 1 per cent of the land area of the
country, held 36 per cent of its population – 7,592,146 people.

One's first impression is disappointing. It is a town which,
because of its vast size, does not reveal itself all at once. Of
the picturesque there is almost nothing – one sees signs only
of work. The port, with all its buildings and machinery, extends for more than seven kilometres, and the docks themselves for twenty kilometres on either side of the harbour.
Spread out as it is, Buenos Aires has an ultra-modern motorway to its airport. From whichever direction you approach it,
the city gives an appearance of having sacrificed almost
everything to business, work and efficiency. It is more like a
warehouse, a bank, or a business office than an ordinary town
where one may wander round discovering the layers of
memory left by each century. There seems no softness anywhere – only right angles; the long straight roads are crossed
regularly every hundred metres, and an acute or obtuse angle
is something of an anomaly – certainly a surprise. The wide
avenues of Córdoba, Corrientes and Santa Fé are so flooded

with traffic as to force pedestrians into an anonymous huddle at the sides; but Florida, Buenos Aires's fashionable shopping street, is at times completely closed to traffic and there pedestrians come into their own, evincing the animation – though it is relatively restricted – of a town in which southern exuberance and love of idle wandering have long been relegated to the shelves of the antique shop by modern Argentinians whose one idea is making money. Everything converges on the business area, the heart of the city, and indeed of the country. The thirty kilometres of underground railway form a kind of spider's web round it. And the city's position, at the extreme end of the undulating *pampa*, has for long made it effectively the only centre of communication between the interior and the coast.

Buenos Aires is most certainly not the whole of Argentina. But it does absorb practically all the vitality of the country – and it is a country which cannot be judged by European rules or standards. It is five times the size of France – 1,214 kilometres at its widest, from the Andes to the Atlantic, and 3,693 from the tropical forests of the north to the icy loneliness of Tierra del Fuego. It seems as if this immense body has far too much of itself concentrated in its head : one out of every three Argentinians lives in the capital, nor is this disproportion of recent date. In 1947 the huge city already contained 29 per cent of the population, with 2,500 inhabitants per square kilometre. Such an imbalance is not peculiar to Argentina, but it does present problems more serious than it might elsewhere. Paradoxically Argentina as it is today is primarily a country that lives off the land, and its urban population continues to grow at the expense of those in the country. It has been said that it is a country without any villages, and this is becoming more and more the case. City-dwellers now represent more than 70 per cent of the population; Argentina, with no hamlets, hardly a village steeple anywhere, is a nation dominated by towns, and mainly big ones. Santa Fé, Córdoba, Rosario, Mendoza, Avellanoda, Mar del Plata are all competing with the capital in this race to urbanize, although the population growth in Argentina is the slowest anywhere in Latin America. The massive immigration of the late nineteenth century slowed down considerably afterwards (1,120,170 immigrants from 1901 to 1910; 882,631 from 1947 to 1956). Between 1963 and 1965 more people left the country (professionals, technicians and intellectuals) than came into it. But as recently as 1960 there were more than two and a half million foreigners – 770,000 of them Spanish, and almost 800,000 Italian.

*

Yet Buenos Aires has its past too; the Creoles fought the English, and there are squares with names like Reconquista and Defensa to commemorate the battles of the nineteenth century. Independence, however, was won more easily there than in many places. The Viceroyalty of Río de la Plata, which Charles III of Spain established in 1776 as a buffer against Portuguese pressure, comprised what are now Bolivia, Paraguay and Uruguay; this kingdom even had access to the Pacific from its centre in Potosí (in Bolivia). Leadership of this over-large area fell to Buenos Aires, which was too far away and lacked the power to pit itself with any chance of success against the struggles of the emancipation movement which shook South America in the early nineteenth century. Paraguay in 1811, Bolivia in 1825, and Uruguay in 1828, broke away without too much trouble. In 1810 the people of Buenos Aires heard that Seville had been captured by Napoleon's armies, and urged their own viceroy and his family to leave for the Canaries. This peaceful revolution which marked the beginning of Argentina's independence was achieved by people who still hesitated to break all links with the metropolitan country, and it finally took San Martín to dot the last 'i'; his objurgations finally won the day, and on 9 July 1816, Congress declared the independence of the 'United Provinces of South America'. In point of fact those provinces remained *dis*united for a very long time. Every town, with its local oligarchy, made itself a principality. Argentina's independence opened with a battle between the 'federalists' of the provinces, and the 'unitarists' of the capital. Up to the twentieth century, Mendoza, Santa Fé or Bahía Blanca marked the furthest limits of white conquest. But independence certainly did not mean that Argentina had won either its unity or real control of its own wealth. Indeed this latter battle is not over yet.

There could be little doubt that Buenos Aires had to be given all the attributes of a real capital city, with real power over the vast and tapering land that lay behind it; and the need to do this gives Argentinians a special character. The spirit of the first pioneers is still alive on the banks of the Plata, and ultimately the average modern Argentinian is far more like a North American than a European, despite successive waves of European immigration. Straightforwardness, the cult of virility, fondness for comfort, a certain reserve – all these are typically Argentinian traits. The *porteños* really dislike the untidiness and *dolce far niente* of Mediterranean peoples; in the fashionable shops you can seldom distinguish middle-class women from working-class ones, all are elegantly and carefully dressed; there is an almost Teutonic discipline among the queues at bus stops; pedestrians look serious, even unhappy. There remain a few wooden houses in La Boca which have miraculously escaped the demolition men; there are snack-bars selling chips at the foot of the shrine of Our Lady of Pompeii; but such fragments of Italy are lost in the faceless immensity of the spreading, dreary suburbs, where gangs of youths are forever playing football. The game is quite as popular in Argentina as it is in Brazil or Uruguay, and Sundays are filled with the roars of the spectators cheering their local teams. Almost no women are to be seen in the giant stadiums where the *porteños* express their pent-up violence for a few hours, their lively dialogues punctuated with the traditional 'Che' – an untranslatable word, meaning 'Hi', or 'You there', but in a special Argentinian tone, far softer than the severe Spanish of the Castilian.

*

Geographers in general will divide the vast area of Argentina into four natural sectors: the Andes, the North, the *pampa*, and Patagonia. Near the Bolivian border the train that chugs slowly up to the high plateaux goes through a landscape reminiscent of the *puna brava* of the cold lands in Bolivia and Peru. Herds of llamas run from the approaching train among sparse, not-very-leafy-trees. Near Tucamán the Incas had a fortress which enabled them to keep an eye on the Indian peoples moving down from the higher lands. The first road built by the Spaniards passed near this disused bastion, and the first business dealings between the plains and the Andean areas of the north west were only made possible by the intensive use of mules, since they were the only creatures that could safely follow the terrifyingly exposed trails of the outer Andean ranges. Rosario, Córdoba and Santa Fé first came into existence because of the need to provide staging posts on this long journey from Buenos Aires to Salta and Jujuy. The first centres of population in the north west later grew up round the camp-fires of the *gauchos* who tended semi-wild herds. The other products which brought wealth to the north west, especially sugar cane and alfalfa (lucerne), were only developed later on. Lower down, around Mendoza, the last town before the Uspallata Pass road, the finest of all the Argentine orchards have gradually extended over the plains where herds had previously roamed.

The vast *pampa* of Argentina spreads under an apparently infinite sky from the Uruguay river up to the eastern spurs of the Andes. It is as flat as your hand, totally bare, apart

from the occasional poplar tree someone has planted, and no
streams twist their way through the rich grass, no rocks
stand out. Any water there is is stagnant, in the depths of this
desert which was for so long totally uninhabited until it
became the background for galloping herds of horses. In early
days, the *gauchos* were satisfied with picking at random from
among those herds that belonged to no one, and whose numbers were impossible to estimate. The whole *gaucho* myth
which plays such a large part in Argentine life was born
then. The man on horseback, with his *bombachas* * and his
wide belt decorated with coins, is still a symbol of the free man
who cares nothing for social prejudice or convention. He
does not wear the wide Mexican sombrero as some North
American and European artists persist in thinking; his
brother is the violent and legendary *macho* † of the Jalisco
or Guadalajara mountains of Mexico. It is something of a
paradox that the Argentine people who, of all southern
American peoples, are those whose life-style is most like that
of modern Europe or North America, should have chosen as
their national hero this Robin Hood who was the champion
of independence, and is still the champion of the natural life.
There are no *gauchos* nowadays; all you find today are the
paisanos, who tend their herds, are paid wages and live a relatively domesticated life – a far cry from those magnificent
wild men who lived more or less outside the law right up to
the end of the nineteenth century. But Argentinians, who
for the most part live immured in the towns, still feel a
nostalgia for those who rode the wide prairies. As in Uruguay, the *gauchos* were finally destroyed by barbed wire;
they were entangled, so to say, in the fences built by the ever
more numerous immigrants who came from 1850 onwards,
wanting more and more quick returns, and anxious to own
properties that could be identified by their fences and carefully numbered herds. In this new world of figures, land-

---

* Wide trousers gathered at the ankle.   † Literally, 'male'.

marks and wire netting, there was no room for the *gaucho*. His way had been to kill animals, first for food, and then to sell the skins, or use them in exchange for other goods.

In effect the sixty million hectares of green *pampa* (roughly bounded by a strip of some 600 kilometres around Buenos Aires, and comprising land of a kind exceptionally fertile for anything that grows in a temperate climate) were never really developed until after independence. Up to then the north west had been the only part of the country to be really properly settled, providing stopping points on the route to Peru. Buenos Aires was unknown. Thus the transformation of the economy had an equally violent effect on population patterns. The moist *pampa* is ideal soil for cereals, and it is noteworthy that cereals still represent 45 per cent of the country's total exports. From 1900 up to the present, cereals and meat have remained the two products upon which the country's productivity is based.

It was in fact around the turn of the century that the Argentinians began the industry of killing their meat for export. Giant abattoirs and refrigerated ships began to appear in the Plata estuary. It was a turning-point in Argentina's economy, and the meat industry soon overtook leather and wool, with the *frigorficos* of San Nicolás and La Plata becoming a household word the world over. Argentina was not only the prime meat supplier, but also Europe's wheat granary – and the latter especially in relation to Great Britain, its most traditional customer.

*

Though the *pampa* has remained the chief centre of Argentina's agricultural wealth, Patagonia is on the way to becoming the Far West of the southern hemisphere, and could well tip the scales of the country's natural centre of gravity. The first thing to note about Patagonia is the wind, which sweeps from end to end of this land which was for so long unfriendly, a stony desert where there were rumours of fabulous fortresses left over from ancient cities, though none were ever found. It was long ago that the last of the Tehuelche Indians abandoned the stormy banks of Lake Nahuel Huapi – now a tourist centre and a developers' paradise. It is only comparatively recently that Patagonia has really been conquered – barely a hundred years. The first settlers followed the military detachments sent out from the government in Buenos Aires to protect their southern markets upon which many people were casting greedy eyes.

Crossing the Andes could only be done by using mules. While horses and cattle ran wild in the *pampa*, it was sheep who won Patagonia. Today, something in the region of forty million sheep wander in compact flocks along the pebbly plateaux, under stormy skies – and this remains the standard picture of an area whose means of communication with the rest of the republic are still hopelessly inadequate. There is no major road from Buenos Aires to this distant and long-unknown province. One railway line crosses the central plains, but it ends by Lake Nahuel Huapi. Thus it would be more logical to consider Bariloche as an Andean rather than a Patagonian village. Patagonia proper is sharply divided from the north by its height, and by the fast-flowing rivers which the state is trying to control and exploit by building giant dams. The foundations of the steel industry laid by the Perón regime were built up further by the Frondizi government. The petro-chemical industry naturally has a major place in the plans for industrializing Patagonia. But all such plans presuppose the cheap production of electric power. The Chocón dam, on the Limay river, should produce over 700,000 kilowatts per hour, and also make possible the irrigation of some 100,000 hectares of land. In this way it should soon be possible to work the coal and iron deposits in Patagonia. It was in 1957 that iron deposits were discovered in the Sierra

Grande, less than 199 kilometres from Puerto Madryn on the Atlantic seaboard. Mineral reserves there are estimated at 200 million tons, divided among three veins, all of them not very deep and therefore easily accessible. Since 1952 the coal from the Río Turbio has been mined by modern methods. In 1962 production had reached 200 million tons, but Argentinian experts considered that this figure could easily be doubled if only a satisfactory answer could be found to the problem of transport. And finally, of course, there is petroleum. The first well bored and brought into operation in 1910 on Comodoro Rivadavia yielded oil of a very high quality. Since then, despite the grimness of the area, the innumerable difficulties of everyday human living, the problem of communications, the *Yacimientos Petrolíferos Fiscales* (YPF) have set up a number of new installations. But progress has been relatively slow there. It is thirty years since the Argentine leaders recognized the importance of systematically working the oil reserves of Patagonia, but the lack of capital and of technicians has often forced them to get help from abroad, or sign agreements with the big Anglo-Saxon petroleum companies. Though not as important as it is in Brazil, for instance, the question of oil has given rise to quite a number of political storms. 'Our oil is ours,' echoing the famous *O petroleo e nosso* of Brazil, can be heard in Buenos Aires in nationalist circles, or from the military who have often made it the excuse for their risings. One of the reasons for the fall of Perón was his abandonment of a principle that had been so often proclaimed – the determination not to let foreign companies get control over the oil in Patagonia and Tierra del Fuego.

YPF, uninterested in such minor points of principle, has for the past few years systematically carried on its exploitation and drilling for oil. Three quarters of Argentine oil comes from Patagonia now. There is a development plan allowing for the drilling of 8,000 wells, which will mean the arrival of enormous numbers of technicians, office staff and manual workers. But there is plenty of room for them all. It is an area of 700,000 square kilometres with only 600,000 inhabitants. The Argentine Republic is perseveringly extending the frontiers of its exploration of its own territory. Barely a century back, an Argentinian could not go much further than Comodoro Rivadavia. Yet today the world's southernmost city is in Argentina – Ushuaia, which is both a naval base and fishing port for Tierra del Fuego, that falsely named land of ice and snow almost indistinguishable from the icy waters around it. When the first Spaniards landed on its inhospitable shores, the terrified Indians lit enormous fires in the hope of frightening off the invaders – and it was those fires that gave the land its name. It is often covered in thick fogs which all the gusty winds from the Straits of Magellan can scarcely blow away. At times its snow-tipped peaks, over 3,000 metres high, seem to be floating above an ocean of fog which hides the promontory the southern hemisphere directs towards the ice of the South Pole.

But Patagonia will undoubtedly remain for many years no more than a glorious and alluring hope. For Argentina, the conquest of Patagonia is what the conquest of Amazonia is for Brazil, or the tropical lands of the east for Peru or Bolivia. One can detect certain traces of movement and change among the population, but the real development of the wealth of the area must wait for time, money and men.

The possibilities of Patagonia should not lead us to ignore the development – since 1960 so very rapid – of the four north-western provinces, of which Mendoza forms the natural capital : rich lands, protected by the nearby wall of the Andes, with marvellously fertile soil, especially for fruit trees. The wealthy and profitable Argentina of the eighteenth century is now, in the twentieth century, under-developed Argentina. For reasons similar to those which brought about the crisis in the sugar industry on the north-eastern seaboard of Brazil, the region of Tucumán presents the government of Buenos Aires with a major problem. The failure of the large estates to modernize, the crisis in production, and the presence of a desperately poor agricultural proletariat combine to make Tucumán the most explosive part of a country whose industrial development is nowhere adequate or fast enough.

*

From 1815 to 1830 Argentina was a liberal country, tending to the ideals of the French revolution; that is from the glorious days of independence up till the time of the military leader, Rosas. Under Rosas it was conservative and indeed reactionary, but once again from 1850 to 1890 it became liberal, with men ruling who took their inspiration from Saint-Simon and Auguste Comte. The return to power of the conservatives in 1890 coincided with Argentina's integration into the international economy as Great Britain's best client. The need for the expanding middle classes to struggle against the conservatives with their British influence explains the rise of the radicalism which won the day for the first time in 1916. Then once again Argentina became conservative in 1930, and remained so up to the morning of 4 June 1943. From 1945 to 1955 it was Peronist; since then one can only say it has been post-Peronist. Undoubtedly Frondizi's election to the presidency in 1958 was a triumph, but one gained only with the support of the Peronists. He had promised to put in order a house which had become somewhat dilapidated in the confusion of the judicialist struggles. To do so he set up a plan of economic recovery which included appealing for enormous foreign loans. Frondizi wanted thus to try to draw together a mass of Peronist supporters, who, despite the inglorious fall of their idol, still represented almost a quarter of the electorate. But the General Workers' Federation (CGT), still enormously influenced by Peronism, has since 1958 fought against all the government attempts to de-nationalize. Torn between the conflicting pressures of the army which refused any collaboration, even at a tactical level, with the Peronists, and the Unions which still bewailed the loss of the Eva Perón Social Foundation, Frondizi became ever more the prisoner of his own armed forces. From 1959 to 1962 there was a fantastically rapid and disturbing succession of vetoes, ultimatums and demands by the army. The most serious and significant crisis broke in March 1962, after the Peronist landslide in the general elections. Frondizi, though himself a liberal and a democrat, was subject to new pressure from the army, and forced to annul the election results in five (out of nine) provinces, where the post of governor had been won by a Peronist. From 1958 to 1962 Peronists were not allowed to stand for office, and yet it was clear that at least 25 per cent of the electorate handed in blank ballot papers; in 1962, free for the first time to vote for Peronist candidates, the 'justicialists', now a new Union of the Left, won 35 per cent of the votes. In June 1966 the officers who took over direct control of power thought they could dispose of this troublesome problem by banning political parties and parliamentary life altogether. But the leaders of the rising which sent Dr Illia into relative obscurity had prepared their coup in coordination with some of the Peronist union leaders. In 1968 direct or indirect pressure from Peronism, resulting from the appearance of a 'rebel' CGT under the leadership of Ongaro, was still influencing political developments. However one looks at it, therefore, the political life of Argentina has been dominated since 1945 by the Peronist factor, and it is not something one can possibly ignore or underestimate.

The oligarchy of the large landed proprietors, whose power was taken from them briefly by the representatives of a daring and dynamic industrial middle class, was forced into opposition in 1943 by an authoritarian regime officially supported by the working class in both towns and countryside. In each case, in 1916 as in 1930, 1943, 1955, 1962 or 1966, it was the army that stepped in. Clearly, Argentina is less easy than any other Latin American country to govern against its will.

At first, Peronism appeared in the guise of an attempt to establish social democracy. It was only later on that its errors, its compromises and its mystifications became evident. But in 1943 it appeared as a new idea in Latin America. Only Mexico had had a victorious popular revolution, and that had been essentially agrarian, and bloody in the extreme, nor was it until Cárdenas came to power that the achievements of the revolution were actually put into effect.

The novelty in Argentina was the appearance and continual strengthening of a working class. In 1943, on the eve of the coup by the young officials of the GOU (*Grupo de Oficiales Unidos*) there were 60,000 industrial establishments, with almost a million Argentinians working in factories. On the other hand, the *pampa*, where the living conditions of the *peones* were clearly appalling, was continuing to lose its population. This mass of workers, mainly made up of descendants of highly politicized European immigrants, and non-specialized agricultural workers, provided what could be a most useful electorate, and Perón was quick to recognize the fact.

Peronism set about winning over this working-class clientele and the incident of the *descamisados** was followed with passionate interest by the masses who had never had any kind of political power. At last by his boldness – verbal at any rate – against the U.S., Perón and his ideology achieved considerable prestige in a continent where the *gringo* was so widely hated.

Liberals at once condemned the whole thing. They feared the persuasive powers of a totalitarianism whose violence of language was decidedly disturbing. But these liberals, who had sent some of the most eminent jurists and economists in the world to international conferences, were often thinking in terms of an ideal democracy, based on the north American or

* Literally, 'the shirtless'; see pp. 143 ff.

European pattern. Seldom did they put their humanitarian concepts to work on reality. The socialist opposition seemed more serious: the Argentine Socialist Party had been founded in Buenos Aires in 1894, but the academic approach of its leaders, successive divisions within it, the difficulty of penetrating country areas, had all up till then prevented its becoming a determining force in Argentina's politics.

The place was more or less ready, and was soon filled. When Perón declared that he had been given the confidence of the majority of the Argentine people, the figures bore him out. He was elected president in February 1946 by 1,478,372 votes as against 1,211,666 for his opponent from the Democratic Union. In November 1951 he was re-elected (something rare indeed in Latin America) by 4,652,000 votes to 2,348,000. The women, who were voting for the first time, gave their vote to Perón, thus, incidentally, following the advice of the Church. But even allowing for a certain amount of gerrymandering and the fact that the opposition did not have complete freedom of expression, it was still a significant margin.

Why it was so is another matter. Peronism apparently involved a need to wrap itself up in a doctrine of the most obscure phraseology. That doctrine was codified, commented upon with enthusiasm by the faithful, and expressed with a floweriness and wealth of superlatives which quite overwhelmed the foreigner unused to South American eloquence. Yet Peronism claimed to provide a model not merely for the American continent, but for the whole world.

It certainly included a number of themes traditional to South America; first of all, that of revolution: 'The Argentine revolution is not a political revolution, but a moral and national revolution'; that of the nation whose 'primacy must be recognized in every sphere'; the key notion of independence, especially economic independence, for 'Argentina, a great nation, can manage without foreign help'. Rejecting both communism and capitalism, Peronism claimed neutrality as between the U.S. and the U.S.S.R. And, finally, the crowning point of the whole system was *justicialismo* – 'the mean between spiritualism and materialism, a new word which will extend from Argentina to the whole world, and reawaken hope everywhere.'

*

Perón's brilliance – or luck – was his having taken the comparatively humble position of Secretary of State for Labour and Social Planning in the government formed after the revolution of 4 June 1943. He was as yet unknown. He had indeed taken part in the somewhat pro-Nazi coup by the armed forces but had not been among the organizers. He had just returned from a visit to Europe, where he had studied the art of mountain warfare with Mussolini's troops, and was filled with admiration by the tremendous victories of Nazi Germany. The new government brought in measure after measure in favour of the workers: a rise in wages, shorter working hours, instituting the *aguinaldo* (the obligation of employers to pay an extra month's salary as a bonus each year). The workers' standard of living did not improve at once, because the rises in salary automatically meant an increase in the cost of living. But in the suburbs of Buenos Aires there was a young woman with a raucous and impassioned voice who spoke glowingly on Radio Belgrano of Perón's social policies. She was Evita Duarte, and it was she who saved a still hesitating Peronism on 17 October 1945 – a memorable day whose events were tolerated, and indeed in part organized, by the police. For the army was beginning to be anxious over Perón's increasing popularity, and he was arrested. The *descamisados* invaded the streets and on that extraordinary day the army yielded before the threat of a workers' rising, and hurriedly called Perón back. Workers' leaders still speak about it with emotion – October is warm in Buenos Aires. The southern spring is short, and the damp heat of summer comes all too soon after the last agonies of winter. The first demonstrators reached Buenos Aires at nightfall, having come on foot from La Plata, 50 kilometres away, and outlying areas which extend for 30 kilometres. Some carried children on their shoulders; all were jacketless, marching in shirtsleeves. They formed a human torrent, uttering the single cry, 'Perón!' The most exhausted among them stopped by fountains to take off their shoes and cool their feet in the pools. The middle class in the city thought they were witnessing an Argentine version of the burning of the Bastille. But once Perón had been set free, the crowd withdrew fairly quickly from the centre of the city. The date 17 October 1945 still represents the greatest victory ever won in the minds of the workers. One of the papers in Buenos Aires published a photo of *descamisados* stripped to the waist; the Peronists seized upon this, and made the term their own : 'Yes, we, the shirtless, demand justice.' After that Evita never made a speech that did not begin with the phrase : 'My dear *descamisados . . .*'

General Perón's election as president of the Republic marked the beginning of the first phase of Peronism, that of triumphant autarchy. It was to last three years, from 1946 to 1949, with support from both internal and external events peculiarly favourable to it. His accession to power in fact coincided with an unprecedented wave of economic prosperity to the country. In 1945 alone the excess in the balance of payments rose to 1,671 million pesos. At the end of the Second World War foreign commercial missions vied with one another to buy wheat and meat from a country which had for so long been 'the agricultural preserve of Great Britain'.

Hitler's Germany had its Dr Schacht. Perón's Argentina had Dr Miranda, Don Miguel Miranda, a clever industrialist but a poor prophet, wielded what amounted to an economic dictatorship of the country for three years. He was in the confidence of Evita, who had married the general and was thus the first lady of Argentina. He was a self-made man, Catalan in origin, once a manual worker. In his youth he had fought in the socialist ranks; he considered, not without justification, that any real improvement in the standard of living of the masses must essentially depend on speeding up the industrialization of the country. However, Don Miguel's theories rested on a somewhat shaky basis : he believed that Argentina would always be able to sell its agricultural products to the highest foreign bidder. Ways and means must be found to buy the equipment needed for industrialization, and in May 1946 he formed the IAPI. The IAPI bought from the producers and re-sold to the monopolies which were in control of distribution and marketing. This intervention by the State as intermediary made it possible to sell the produce abroad for three or four times the price paid to the producers. In this way the government was able to buy back the English and French railways, the Gas and Telephone Companies (which latter belonged to the Bell company of North America). Though all these operations responded to the wish for nationalization, not all of them were economically advantageous.

The Central Bank was nationalized in March of that same year, and began directing credit towards operations 'useful to society as a whole'. Nationalized enterprises (*Empresas Nacionales del Estado*, ENDE) proliferated. The first five-year plan was launched (1947–51) for great public works and industrialization. And on 9 July 1947, Perón solemnly declared in Tucumán that Argentina had at last won its economic independence.

The incredible activity of early-style Peronism was no less frenzied in the social sphere. This was the preserve of Evita, the Madonna of the *descamisados*. The Evita story is surely one of the most curious in present-day history. Like Perón, her origins were humble, and for this it seemed that the aristocratic society of Buenos Aires could never forgive her.

With great energy she shook up the old-fashioned ways of the ladies of that *sociedad*, who had always felt the delicate monopoly of 'charity' to be theirs. Evita organized it on a gigantic scale. The Eva Perón Foundation, which replaced the old Society of Beneficence, had large sums of money at its disposal. It was quite obvious that they could not simply be the fruit of voluntary – or even 'suggested' – contributions, but also must be drawing on public funds. At the same time, a new plan of social security was brought into effect, first of all to help industrial workers, then for all business employees, absorbing the old retirement funds which had previously existed only to benefit officials, the military, railway and bank workers. The cost of social benefits rose to almost 50 per cent of the salary payments of all firms. From 1943 to 1949 the budget for retirement funds rose from 198 million pesos to 3,000 million. But because Argentina was becoming so much richer all the time, the mounting inflation was not immediately transposed into a rise in the cost of living. There was a real improvement in workers' pay packets, which rose by 30 per cent between 1943 and 1948.

Evita Perón seemed to have a lot in common with Encarnación Ezcurra, the wife of Juan Manuel Rosas who had been dictator of Argentina for twenty years in the nineteenth century. Rosas, who quite simply proclaimed himself as 'the leading *gaucho* of Argentina', governed with red as his colour and with the most effective help from his wife. Up to 17 October 1945, Evita was simply a second-rate actress and a radio announcer; after that date she became the first lady of Argentina. Her trip to Europe in 1947 was the event of the year. She visited Franco, who overwhelmed her with gifts in the name of *hispanidad*, and the Pope who received her most cordially. However, this spoiled child of South American politics had less success in Switzerland, where her arrival caused various disturbances, in England where she was ignored altogether by the royal family, and even in Brazil where she was unable to deliver the 'justicialist' speech she had prepared. Her meteoric rise was certainly not as easy as may now appear. There were a great many noisy protests from the armed forces, especially from military and naval cadets, the sons of the conservative middle class. All her life she was an anti-communist and a practising Catholic. Her tangles with the army, the mouthpiece of the recalcitrant bourgeoisie, largely explain the 'rebel' influence she had on Perón (with the workers as against the armed forces). But no kind of ideology ever interfered with her basic convictions. Perón made her the director of the Social Foundation; after that she was seen in factories, hospitals, working-class districts, making speeches in praise of President Perón. She had the same welcoming smile for the thousands who came to ask for favours. In the elections of 1951 she offered herself as a candidate for the vice-presidency, but the army vetoed it, and this was her first setback. She announced on the radio that she was submitting to the will of the people, but in fact she already knew that she was shortly to die : cancer was defeating her, and her doctors had told her that she only had a few months left to live. The frivolous, impatient, interfering Evita had often been quite intolerable; but her coming death transformed her completely. Week by week her face grew thinner, and her pallor became frightening. But as she spoke from platforms and addressed meetings, she was a true *Pasionaria*; a new Evita seemed to be standing there, burning to do something for the poorest of her fellow-citizens before she left them. She died on 27 July 1952, when she was just over thirty.

*

Perón declared : 'We shall create a fascism that is careful to avoid all the errors of Mussolini.' What he in fact created was a mixture of the military leadership inspired by Juan Manuel Rosas, and Mussolini-style totalitarianism.

The first lorries that drove out of a new factory were justicialist. Teaching in the schools was justicialist. The Argentine code of police repression was represented by the Director General of Prisons as 'a juridicial creation of justicialism'. And when the Argentinian champion parachutist Abrama beat a world record by jumping 120 times in ten hours and thirty-six minutes, it was obviously to the justicialist government of Perón that he dedicated his exploit. But just what is justicialism? Even now no one seems to have succeeded in giving a precise definition of it. The more severe foreign observers considered it, and still consider it, a meaningless pretence. And the explanations given by the Argentine government and Perón himself were always vague in the extreme. 'What we want,' said Perón, 'is to do away completely with all exploitation, under whatever guise ...' But how? Though the letter was unclear, the spirit was absolutely clear, and there were actions to put it into effect. After the 'colonel of the people' came to power, the standard of living of the *peones* in the *pampa*, of the factory workers, and generally of all labourers, was really improved. Whether or no it was a pretence, justicialism thus offered, alongside its useless and costly spectacular achievements, a series of other achievements that undoubtedly were of enormous benefit to the working class. They were effected at a price that in fact determined the length of his survival. But it remains true that this was a policy intended to favour the least favoured of the mass of the people. It rested on the support of what we should call the left wing of the electorate. General Perón may have begun his government in disfavour with that electorate. He could not govern against its interests, unless he either went back on his word or simply held power for its own sake. Such does not seem to have been his intention. 'I shall go before I am driven out,' he declared, during a public meeting on 15 April 1955 in the Plaza de Mayo.

His troubles began in 1949. Exports failed, there was suddenly a deficit in the balance of payments, and the country's reserves of foreign currency gradually diminished. International financial developments gave the lie to Miranda's optimistic prognoses, and he was removed from power in the spring of 1949. The IAPI, as might have been expected, had discouraged producers without producing any structural reforms. Should such reforms be undertaken, as the spirit of Peronism would seem to imply, or must the country be resigned to having a dependent economy? The Peronist government never made a definite choice between the two alternatives. The real value of salaries was reduced, and important concessions made to the oil trusts. Yet the government still refused to accept all the consequences of a dependent economy. The result of this policy was total confusion and a condemnation of this central period of Peronism.

Twice the peso was devalued – in October 1949 and August 1950 – to try to boost exports. In 1950 the government asked for, and got, a loan of 125 million dollars from the U.S. – a grievous shock after the intransigent declarations of independence Perón had made six months earlier : 'I would rather cut off my arm than accept a loan.'

In point of fact Perón had realized by 1948 that Miranda's financial policy was leading to disaster. He replaced him by a young official from the Ministry of Commerce, Dr Gómez Morales. The attempts to achieve an economic policy of deflation and austerity made by Gómez Morales indicated a certain courage, for the unions might well prove refractory; all the more so in that 1951 and 1952 were disastrous years for the Argentine economy. Extraordinary droughts resulted in poor harvests, and the worst level of exports since the beginning of the century. Inflation mounted and the cost of living in Buenos Aires rocketed, while the continual multiplication of industrial undertakings there continued to draw the *peones* in from the countryside, thus contributing to an increase in the urban proletariat. Finally Perón decided to freeze wages :

'Everyone knows that I am not in favour of low salaries. I have raised them as high as is possible in view of the economic situation of the country. We must now for a time stop at the level we have reached. We cannot reach the higher standard of living I had hoped for for all our people until we have first increased production . . .'

This was the essential purpose of the second five-year plan (1953 to 1957), a plan more moderate than the first as to the objectives fixed for heavy industry, and more concerned with fostering the traditional forms of production by mechanizing agriculture. But it was clear from this point of view that Argentina must become free of the enormous burden it faced by having to import fuel. The YPF's oil production had increased by 50 per cent in ten years, but this was not enough. It became essential to call in foreign capital – and this meant in effect to appeal to Standard Oil of America (Esso), which already owned refineries in Argentina. The negotiations were long and laborious, and concluded finally in the signing of an agreement which put an end to Peronism's determination to fight against American investment.

*

The Peronism of June 1955 had hardly anything in common with the Peronism of 1947. Even the radicals who favoured collaboration with the U.S. accused Perón of 'selling Argentine oil to foreign firms . . .'

In fact Perón was careful to involve only the three key sectors already in the hands of foreign companies: petroleum (YPF, the national company, was weakened by over-bureaucratization by 1955), refrigeration (in which there was only one tiny Argentine company, the CAO) and electricity.

At home he continued to fulminate against the oligarchs, though in fact they were no longer the only wielders of economic power, nor alone in achieving that exploitation of man by man that so enraged justicialism. On the other hand,

Argentine big business was in agreement with Perón over the signing of the contract with Standard Oil, which so aroused the hostility of the middle class.

*

Argentina is in an exceptionally fortunate situation. Its natural wealth, the extent of its land, a hard-working and homogeneous population are advantages which could make it aspire to the leadership of South America. Peronism could hardly fail to make this one of its objectives. The fierce denunciation of 'foreign imperialism' was the *leitmotiv* of Peronist foreign policy. In 1945 American capital did not have the preponderant place in Argentina which it holds today. It was British investment that contributed to the country's economic expansion from 1880 to 1915, and this process, approved by the basically conservative landowning classes, was a paying proposition up to the beginning of the Second World War. So much so that one English ambassador actually said 'Argentina is our best colony'. The 'colony' declared its freedom in 1943, driving the pro-British oligarchy out of power, at least to some extent. Anti-British and anti-imperialist, Argentina under Perón also welcomed fascist and Nazi refugees from Europe after the defeat of the Axis powers (indeed some of them were given important jobs there). At the same time, the regime sought for a diplomatic and temporary friendship with Russia and the people's democracies. True, this latter attempt did not prevent Peronism from making use of the special means of repression against communism created in 1930. Indeed the success of such means in Latin America was extremely rapid.

Argentina under Perón tried hard to unite several other South American countries under its banner. The *tercera posición* * became one more thing to export. But the successes of Peronism abroad did not coincide with the period of suc-

*Third position.

cessful revolution at home. Its successes in the diplomatic field took place just at the moment when it was forced into adopting an NEP for internal consumption. There was a serious attempt to form an ABC bloc (Argentina, Brazil, Chile – later succeeded by Argentina, Bolivia and Chile). More friends or sympathizers of Perón came to power in 1952: Paz Estenssoro in Bolivia in April, Velasco Ibarra in Ecuador on 31 August, and General Ibáñez in Chile in September. In November that year the formation of the new Atlas trades union centre in Buenos Aires seemed to bring the prestige of Perón's regime to its highest point. Perón made an official visit to Chile in February 1953, and before leaving home declared that 'union with Chile would be the central nucleus of Latin American unity'. It was an ambitious project. Too much so indeed. The only thing that could ever hold a Latin American bloc together would be anti-Americanism, so Perón's appeal for foreign, and especially north American, investment caused a sudden sharp decline in his popularity in the rest of the sub-continent.

*

The first attack on the regime occurred quite suddenly on 16 June 1955 : it was an armed rising organized by members of the navy and air force, and shook Peronism to its roots. Perón had just been virtually excommunicated by the Pope, which added to his troubles, though it does not seem to have been instrumental in determining the rising. It was nothing like the epic march on Buenos Aires organized by the old General Menéndez in September 1951; even the terrorist disturbances of May 1953 and the bombs of the sons of the Argentine gentry were child's play in comparison. The young rebel officers spent three years preparing for their revolt of June 1955. The new battle between Church and government and the increasing extent of Catholic demonstrations had helped to generate an atmosphere of crisis highly favourable to the rising. The question is why Perón, with his sure political skill, should deliberately have pursued a systematic campaign against the Argentine clergy, even to the point of cavalierly expelling two of the highest Church dignitaries and putting them on the first plane to Rome; why there should have been this *Kulturkampf* in a country whose constitution – which Perón himself had revised in 1949 – stated clearly that 'the federal government supports the Catholic and apostolic Roman Church'? There were several reasons : pressures from those around him, among whom numbers of freemasons had risen to several important positions; the need to give pledges to the Unions (divorce legislation, equality of rights for the numerous illegitimate children in the poorest sections of society, for instance) just at a time when the new economic policy made it impossible to improve the material conditions of the workers; the fear of seeing more and more Catholic Actionists infiltrating into Peronist and trade union organizations.

André Siegfried described the Argentina of 1930 as centred on the land, feudal, Catholic, romantic and colonial. The Argentina of 1955 was industrial, sports-loving, realistic, and the old feudal systems were having to face the rising power of the proletariat. Argentina's Catholicism is far less religious than that in Brazil, Colombia or Peru; indeed, the secularist traditions of Argentina are perhaps the oldest and most deep-rooted of any in Latin America. The Argentine clergy is an urban clergy, with almost a quarter of all priests living in Buenos Aires, while vast stretches of the country remain untouched. The dearth of priests, and vast size of rural parishes (two perennial problems in Latin America, despite the fact that more than a third of all the Catholics in the world live there) hamper the Church's work, and it has furthermore to face a tremendous attack from Protestantism – Methodists, United Brethren of America, the Bible Society, and so on.

The Church faces two other serious obstacles : first, the

de-Christianization of the mass of the working class concentrated in Buenos Aires; and second, the fact that for so long the Church in Argentina has given the impression of being ready to cooperate with any political power, and above all with Peronism.

Perón granted more favours to the Church, at least during his early years, than conservative or radical governments had ever done previously. In the presidential elections of 1946 the clergy boycotted Dr Tamberini, the Democratic Union candidate standing against Perón – not because they specially liked Perón – who was quite popular enough without any help from them in any case – but because the Democratic Union was supported by the socialists and communists, adversaries they knew far better and feared far more than the ill-defined doctrines of Peronism. And Cardinal Copello, the Primate, banned the daily paper *Estrada*, produced by a progressive group of Catholics moving towards collaboration with the Democratic Union.

*

The Church's flirtation with Peronism continued until at least 1950 – not without considerable advantage to the Church, which reaped from it a full return to the prestige and privilege it was in serious danger of losing. Catholicism is the official religion in Argentina : but the rise to power of the radical middle class was accompanied by a wave of anti-clericalism. Under Perón religious instruction once more became mandatory in schools and in the army. Before 1945 some religious orders were allowed to award certificates of education, but after 1945 the number of colleges permitted to do so doubled, thanks to the intervention of the Catholic ministers, Martínez Zuvirría and Ivanissevitch. State inspection, which had in the past been far stricter than in secular schools, was virtually stopped. State aid to the free schools (which accounted for about half of all secondary pupils) increased enormously. The Ministry of Education established a 'general department for religious instruction'; thus, for the first time, the Church in Argentina was in a position to train the young with the complicity and help of the State.

In the second presidential elections, in 1951, the Church indirectly supported Perón through the massive feminine vote. But that was the last manifestation of a collaboration between Church and State that was becoming gradually more and more difficult. In 1952 the first signs of coolness appeared. Perón decided that, all in all, it was better for the regime itself to take over the education of the young, and Peronist instruction became part of the second five-year plan launched in 1952. 'Where education is concerned, the basic objective is to effect the moral, intellectual and physical unification of the people according to the principles of Peronist teaching.' But this desire to rule people's minds was held in check for as long as the FUA (Federation of Argentine Universities) and the students who were for the most part hostile to Peronism, were able to resist. The suppression of the FUA, decreed before the opening of hostilities between Church and State, was the starting point for student unrest which increased up to the autumn of 1954.

Peronism, though it tolerated a radical but powerless parliamentary opposition, needed to prevent any possible internal disturbances, and was therefore obliged to limit freedom of expression and association. The fortunate discovery in September 1948 of a conspiracy had made it possible to get rid of Cipriano Reyes, a highly influential trade union leader; after the putsch of September 1954 the army itself was rigorously purged. Following the disturbances of May 1953 radicals and socialists were persecuted. *La Prensa*, representing the liberal press, and thought to be the best daily anywhere in Latin America, was seized in 1951 by the CGT, who turned it into their official organ. Then came the turn of the universities, where young socialists and Catholic actionists were stirring up trouble: the *Juventud Obrera Católica* (Young Christian Workers) was banned by the government. Though all university teachers and students were forced to join the CGU (General University Confederation, a body founded in 1950 to undermine the FUA, and legally linked with the CGT in 1953), it was never very successful. More and more students were arrested. The atmosphere was such that when the Catholic university leaders met in Córdoba in hopes of launching a Christian Democratic Movement, it precipitated a crisis. To start with, their choice of Córdoba was significant. It was the third largest city in the country, and its university was the oldest in Latin America apart from San Marcos in Lima, so clerical influence was very strong there. Furthermore, it was in Córdoba in 1918 that the Manifesto for university reform had come, the starting point for a movement that was profoundly to affect all the universities of the sub-continent, and contribute to the birth of a number of reformist parties, in particular the APRA in Peru.

Perón reacted violently; the logic of battle led him to take ever harsher measures, and in eight months he took away almost every favour he had given the Church since 1946. But the resultant Catholic disquiet made it possible for the opposition to re-form, so that oddly enough anti-clerical liberals and Catholics made common cause. The army hesitated; it still helped Perón to put down the revolt of naval and air force officers, but it looked as if the army was beginning to have its revenge for what had happened on 17 October 1945. Now, ten years after the triumph of the *descamisados*, the army still mistrusted the trades unions. It was uncertain whether the troops themselves were behind those of the higher officers who were hostile to Peronism. But the officers took the risk, and the second revolt in September ended with victory in four days. The generals involved in the anti-Perón uprising, like Lonardi or Balaguer, were in effect closer to the Catholics in the middle class than to its left-wing fringe. But the navy stepped in. Its officers had preserved intact their aristocratic traditions. Most of the army n.c.o.s had become Peronists, either from conviction or for advancement. When Rear Admiral Rojas brought the fleet at sea on to the rebel side, he left the 5,000 men under his command free to make their own choice. Only a hundred refused to join him. The ordinary people, the *petits bourgeois* thronging round the Casa Rosada after the revolution expressed their sympathy by repeating again and again '*La marina, es otra categoría ...*'

*

The Ministries of the Navy and of War stood only a few hundred metres apart in Buenos Aires, between the río de la Plata and the Plaza de Mayo. The Ministry of War is majestic, massive, classical; the Ministry of the Navy is more elegant and modern, with its huge glazed bays. In June, each Ministry was discreetly observing the other from its windows. By September they were exchanging signs of friendliness and cooperation. Perón's fate was sealed. The putsch of 16 September 1955 brought into action a group Perón himself had created similar to the American marines: the two regiments of marine fusiliers. Prepared to fight with them were cadets from the Naval Academy, and pupils of the Almirante Brown school based at Río Santiago, near La Plata. Finally 'Pocho' – the mocking nickname given to Perón – was defeated almost as much by ridicule as by his own mistakes and demagogy, and his ever mounting repressiveness. In short, Perón collapsed amid the jeers of the opposition. The Peronist government was probably no more corrupt than any other Latin American government; but it was corrupt enough to make the descriptions of the wealth left behind by the *Líder* in his flight, and the revelations of those close to him about his scandalous compromises, arouse the indignation of Catholics and bourgeoisie alike. Undoubtedly they were already aware that it was a corrupt regime, but they had not grasped the full extent of that corruption. It is quite clear that the buying and selling of influence, and the bribery permitted and indeed favoured by the Peronist regime accounted largely for its fall. The Argentine people have a sense of humour and a sense of the ridiculous. They do not drink because it is degrading to be drunk in public; they are immensely polite to foreigners, but their reserved attitude is quite different from the excessive familiarity or the agonizing obsequiousness you find among other Latin American peoples. They are disciplined – except perhaps when they are at the wheels of their cars, in which case their natural dignity prevents their ever slowing down too suddenly, but they trust to their reflexes which are, in fact, normally extremely good.

You have to know this in order to understand how Argentina was ever able to accept that unlikely Peronist law of the *desacato*, or lack of respect. Dated 24 October 1949, that law stipulated that no one 'guilty of *desacato* could give evidence as to the truth or falsity of actions or characteristics attributed to an offended party'. The nickname 'Pocho' is untranslatable : it means an effeminate man – its nearest equivalent is perhaps the *maricón* of the Mexicans and Cubans, who have a similar cult of virility. Perón, the ageing dictator, liked presenting himself as a sportsman, as a breaker of athletic records; he often wore an American baseball cap, and enjoyed riding a scooter. In Buenos Aires scooters have ever since been known as *pochonetas*. Perón also loved appearing in company with girl students from the UES (Union of Secondary Students), to whom he had presented his house in Olivos, a northern suburb of the city. It was near a most luxurious yacht club and sports ground, and there was, so it was rumoured, an underground passage which made it possible for the president to visit the UES girls' chalets. This picture of a decadent and corrupt 'court' was the last straw in bringing out the latent resentment of the middle class against

Peronism. The corruption now brought to light disgusted the aristocracy and the rapidly growing middle class. We cannot even yet be sure to what extent that disgust was shared by the masses of workers and the *peones*. Before Peronism there was little to look back to, apart perhaps from a few leaders of anarchist tendency who had come from Europe at the end of the nineteenth century.

Once in Argentina the immigrants tried to adapt themselves to their new community, and moved forward so rapidly that they were soon more Argentine than the Creoles themselves. The *peones* of the *pampa* or the poor areas in the north (around El Chaco), attracted by the cities with their growing industrialization, had no professional training of any kind, and very little class consciousness. As for the mass of rural workers in the country, it was made up of those known as the *golondrinas* (swallows), the nomad and desperately poor *peones*, who would hire their labour out for a minute wage as it might suit the needs of harvest or industry: their living conditions were barely less precarious than those of the *caboclos* of the Brazilian interior. Work was insecure and subject to all the ups and downs of the landlords' determination to manage with as little help as they could (averaging 150 days a year). The pitiless law of supply and demand was of advantage to the *estancieros*,* who were enabled by it to ignore any decisions made in Buenos Aires. The only thing the *peón* could claim was the right to a minimum of three hundred days' work a year. It is upon the shoulders of those *peones* that the vast and rich edifice of Argentine latifundism is built. The *peón* lives in a hovel; he sleeps on a mat that rolls up in the daytime, and his children, legitimate or otherwise (for marriage is a mere formality), are in rags. But radio and television are never far away; and for ten years the Argentine radio had been repeating Perón's proclamations of social justice. So it was hard to dissipate the

* Wealthy farmers.

myth of Peronism either in the working-class city areas or among the country labourers – the more especially since the prestige of the *gaucho*, the strong man, the *caudillo*, still worked in favour of Perón. The *gaucho* was the image above all others in the gallery of Argentinian national heroes: it gave inspiration to the poets. From 1835 to 1862 Rosas, first of the political *gauchos*, ruled the country as a tyrant, revelling in his own appalling cruelty. But he did begin to bring about the political unity of Argentina. Later when the *pampa* became marked out with barbed wire, so that the herds could be properly tended and selected, and large areas given over to the cultivation of cereals, the *gaucho* was driven away by the advent of the tractor. But the legend of virile and pitiless force surrounding him has never totally disappeared. So, ultimately, it mattered little to the Argentine proletariat whether or not Perón had made himself extremely rich during his time in power. As we know, Eva's fantastic collections of dresses and jewels, far from shocking the *descamisados*, made them very proud. Revelations about Perón's private bunker, his millions of dollars and his young mistresses, did nothing to lessen the dictator's popularity. After all, Peronism had undoubtedly improved the living conditions of the workers and the *peones*, for his new laws, even though not always enforced, certainly represented an enormous advance on anything that had existed hitherto. Wage increases were real up to 1949, and then only slowly eaten away by inflation up to 1955; and the social benefits remained – social security, increase in retirement pensions for almost all workers, hospitals, regular holidays, decent housing settlements for workers. One important innovation was the setting up of work tribunals. Up to 1943 legislation covering work was quite inadequately enforced, mainly due to the dearth of lawyers and judges trained for the work. The workers of Argentina realized after Perón how powerful a force the unions could be if only they could achieve unity. The way in which politics developed from 1955 to 1968 could only serve to strengthen that realization.

*

The same square was planted with the same rather stunted palm trees. It looked as though nothing had changed. More and more waves of people poured in, coming up from the Baseo Colón or flowing out of the Avenida de Mayo, and losing themselés in the vast and noisy crowd standing with the sun in their eyes facing the Casa Rosada.

There were perhaps half a million of them, and more kept coming. The banners of the last groups could be seen waving above heads at the top of Calle Maipú. In the Plaza de Mayo trees and lamp-posts had for some time borne the weight of waving clusters of people. Dark silhouettes stood out against the pale sky on the Banco Hipotecario and the tops of the blocks of flats from where they looked down on to the square: 500,000 Argentinians were present at the funeral rites of Peronism just where it had known its greatest triumphs.

The crowd roared and thousands of hands waved white handkerchiefs. A man had just come out on to the balcony of the Casa Rosada, closely surrounded by some half dozen officers; he wore an olive green uniform and had that slightly disconcerted, absent look you always see in men suddenly thrust into the limelight of the Capitol.

General Lonardi put on huge tortoise-shell glasses to read his speech, which gave him even more of the air of a serious, self-effacing professor. He spoke with great care; at times he would hesitate, and each hesitation was mercilessly amplified by the microphones in every corner of a square which had for ten years resounded with the gusts of laughter and bursts of rage of Juan Domingo Perón. But what he had to say was eminently reasonable, and he said it calmly: 'Mi gobierno actuará. . . . My government will act.'

No longer was the ragged group of *descamisados* there,

continually interrupting, and yet enthralled by the heady eloquence of Perón who was trying to re-create in his own country the thrill of Mussolini-style meetings. This was a happy and well-behaved crowd, still slightly surprised by the fact that a regime that looked eternal had suddenly vanished. Buenos Aires was in a state of high excitement. Late that night, despite the curfew still in force, tense groups were locked in discussion. The clock had been put back eleven years. Paris was free. People cried in the streets. Women were kissing the sailors, who smiled back at them. The war was over. Perón had fallen. He was almost forgotten, though he had taken refuge less than three kilometres out to sea, in a Paraguayan warship.

*

The fall of Peronism was a victory for the Argentine middle class, a class whose moving spirit lies in the universities, whose critical attitude and willingness to entertain progressive social ideas – whether from conviction or taste – has always made them resolutely hostile to any form of authoritarianism. But its political expression lies in the army. Students might continue to harass the Perón regime during the last months of its existence, but it was the army, and even more the navy, who brought to bear that decisive force without which student agitation might have continued almost indefinitely as little more than a pinprick to Perón.

The middle class first achieved power in Argentina in 1916, with the radicals. At that time it was they above all who represented the new industrial bourgeoisie, with their hostility to domination by foreign capital, and consequently also to the great landed proprietors with their conservative and Anglophile traditions. In 1930 the conservatives came once again to the fore. It is still said in Buenos Aires that the 1930 revolution smelt of oil. . . . But the conservatives either could not or would not learn anything from their period in opposition. They managed to annoy everyone, and the putsch of 4 June 1943 drove them out again. At that stage it was clear that the middle class was something very different from what it had been twenty-seven years earlier. Apart from anything else, it had become considerably proletarianized, widened to include a mass of small businessmen, officials and white-collar workers. Even in 1900 the business sector was the most important part of Argentine society. This fact became gradually more evident and explains some of the new difficulties the country has had to face from 1960 onwards (difficulties similar to those of Uruguay where that sector is also the most important).

The wealth of the great landed proprietors of Argentina dates back to the post-colonial era. Anarchy followed the departure of the Spanish : each province had its own *caudillo* who governed in his own way. Then one day Rosas, who needed money, decreed the first great public sale of land. There had always been enough land for everyone, and in those days to be rich meant to have large herds and thousands of hectares of ground. It was an ideal position to be in, for the political and economic development of the country went hand in hand with an astronomical rise in the value of land. Thus, latifundism gave rise to a class of rich *estancieros* who for many years dominated political life and had every reason to expect their supremacy to continue for a long time. At the turn of the century Argentina had virtually become an agricultural appendage to industrial England.

Then it began to manufacture some of the products which it had previously bought from those who bought its wheat and meat, and gradually the real economic power of the country changed hands. The defeat of the conservatives by the radicals in 1916 was no more than the political expression of a developing economic process. A modern society grew up in Argentina between the wars, long before most other South American countries, though there undoubtedly was at the bottom an enormous mass of the very poor who still represented the vast reservoir of manpower needed to exploit the country's agricultural wealth. The expansion of industrialization continued to bring country labourers into Buenos Aires and the surrounding area. The middle classes spread wider. And the aristocracy at the peak of the social pyramid no longer consisted only of the landowners. Vast estates had been divided up among the children of the first owners. Daughters and sons of aristocrats tended more and more to marry among the industrial class, or even to go into business themselves. Though only a few decades back it was usual to talk of the 2,000 wealthy families of Argentina, specialization and the wish to escape death duties or income tax, together with the formation of huge syndicates to manage the really big estates devoted to raising either crops or herds, combined to change all the social structures of the past. The new industrial middle class – with their textiles, canning, metallurgy, glass-works, sugar refineries – was not strong enough when Perón came on the scene to be other than delighted with a regime that made so explicit its intention to rid the country's economy of the control of foreign capital.

After Perón one might have thought that the traditional parties would return to their former function and influence; one might in particular have expected the Argentine left to be ready to denounce the ambiguity of Peronism and provide an alternative. But in fact the establishment of the Peronist myth among the mass of working people forced the left-wing leaders to form a coalition with the Peronists. In 1962 it was a combination of Peronism, of the left, and of Castroism which inflicted so spectacular a defeat on the Frondizi government. In 1968, two years after the establishment of the military regime of Onganía and the fascist elements of the right wing in the government, a considerable party of that Argentine 'left' could see no solution other than yet another military coup to 'liberate' the country. The same old illusion yet again.

*

The socialists have certainly never had much real influence in Argentina, and such as they have had has been limited to a few groups. At the end of the nineteenth century there was a moment when they gave the impression of being able to lead the workers' movement. Among them were French émigrés, refugees from the Commune, like Emile Dumas who founded the paper *El Trabajador*; there came also Spaniards, Germans (the *Vorwärts* group) and Italians. These people, whom the middle class scornfully labelled the 'internationals', were extremely active, and in 1890 formed the first workers' federation – but it was short-lived. From 1900 until the arrival of Perón the socialists took refuge in a romantic and humanitarian attitude, inspired by Palacios, the hero of half a dozen duels, a deputy in 1914, later a senator, and the Rector of Buenos Aires University. Argentine socialism then faded into the most uninspired reformism under the leadership of J. B. Justo who mistrusted all Marxists. Though he had splendid theories on the kind of agricultural reform that was needed, Justo restricted his action to minority groups and never managed to affect the mass of agricultural workers. It was clear in 1955 that the socialists, weakened by continual splits, and too academic to be really effective, would find it hard going to recapture the following they had had between the wars. One must face the fact that they have never succeeded.

The new Christian Democrat movement, whose activity against Peronism had been extremely significant, also gave rise to great hopes. At the start of this century there were already a number of ideas of a Christian social kind going around, and in about 1912 there was even an attempt to form a big popular Christian party. But though a brave attempt, it was condemned to fail so long as the Catholic Church remained the faithful ally of the landed proprietors and the upper middle class. The 1955 model of the Christian Democrat party appeared at least as badly divided as the socialists. Its greatest weakness was its presenting itself as a 'popular' movement, and its denying, despite all the evidence, the religious aspects of its programme.

The anarchists were a small group. The anarchist FORA (Argentine Regional Workers' Federation) was founded in 1901 and fought a long battle with the socialist-inspired UGT (General Workers' Union). The anarchists, who believed in direct action, mainly drew their support from the European proletariat. In November 1909 the chief of police in Buenos Aires was killed by a libertarian terrorist. The government reacted with some severity: a law was passed forbidding all militant anarchists entry into the country. Yet at the end of the First World War the FORA could still congratulate itself on having quite a number of supporters. However the systematic persecution to which it had been subjected since 1930, after the restoration by the military of a conservative government, was a heavy blow. All its leaders were deported to Patagonia.

In theory, of course, the major beneficiaries of Perón's fall should have been the communists. They were awaiting its occurrence with great impatience, though their tactic had for a long time been one of support for the regime – in which they were only following the example of a number of other Latin American Communist Parties, who could always collaborate with military dictatorships so long as they adopted an 'objectively' anti-American policy. The Argentine CP, which had grown out of a split in the *Partide socialista internacional*, was subject, of course, to conflicting tendencies within the party, battles with Trotskyism (though the Trotskyists in Argentina never succeeded in dominating the orthodox communists as they did in Bolivia), and crises of conscience. They supported Perón, when he displayed overt anti-Americanism, but did not commit themselves for the future. It was a difficult position to support in a country where the proletariat were not yet sufficiently politically aware to understand such subtleties, but knew very well which side their bread was buttered on. In addition the communists in Argentina constantly suffered the disadvantage of having middle-class leaders – though this was true of most socialist leaders as well. The CP at that time did gain a hearing from the intellectuals, both in the universities and the cooperative movements. Though a workers' party, it had a certain support from the middle class. Its leaders had for years lived under the threat of being banned, and their debates constantly turned upon the theme: 'Should we be stronger or weaker if we were forced to become a secret organization?'

After 1959 the influence of Castroism naturally forced them, as it did all the Latin American communist parties, to make a serious revision of their tactics. Up to 1964 Argentine communists followed the same line as the other orthodox communist parties, in particular sending delegates to the tricontinental conference in Havana in January 1966. But they were among the first to withdraw and to condemn the approach of the 'armed struggle' as defended by the Cubans and practised by Che Guevara. Yet Guevara was an Argentinian by birth, and paradoxically his death aroused great emotion in Buenos Aires – even among the military leadership.

Neither communists, nor socialists, nor Christian Democrats, who had all claimed in their different ways to represent the left, had managed to achieve success in 1966. There remained only the radicals. In Argentina radicalism is not a political party, but a state of mind. The electorate upon whom they depended was heterogeneous in the extreme. The personality of their leaders counted for more than their platform, and those leaders were so quick to fight among themselves that the radical camp was split into at least five major groups. Ricardo Balbín, the leader of the right wing, was curiously like Mirabeau (though he was commonly known in Buenos Aires as *el Chino*). His dynamism and authoritarianism were not unlike the traditional qualities of the *caudillo*.

Dr Frondizi, a lawyer, leader of the hard-line group, was thought by the pontificators of unionist radicalism to have been much influenced by Marxism. They, on the other hand, were strongly rooted in the provinces of Entre Ríos and Mendoza, and their lieutenants were on very good terms with the conservatives of the traditional landowning oligarchy.

The hero, if not the master-mind, of Argentine radicalism was called Irigoyen. He was twice president of the republic. Driven out of power by the conservative revolution of 1930, Irigoyen joined the supreme court in 1916 after the first genuinely free elections ever held in Argentina. Irigoyen was a man of integrity, modesty and few words. He was known as *el mudo*, the dumb man, but his discretion and honesty were by no means shared by most of the radicals around him. At first their intentions seemed very good, and because there was a highly favourable economic situation due to Argentina's neutrality during the First World War, they were able to achieve a modest measure of social reform. But all too soon personal struggles, an over-centralized policy, obvious paternalism and increasing corruption, combined to lose them their popularity; and when Alvear followed Irigoyen in 1922 the decline of radicalism was accentuated. Argentinians adore nicknames, and they found a rather picturesque one for the men surrounding Alvear : *galeritas*, because they wore black bowler hats with curly brims. In fact this bourgeois symbol expressed a profound reality : for these Anglophiles established a parliamentary rule which, though it respected the forms, was in fact completely authoritarian, and is known to this day as the *dictablanda*,* a dictatorship quite as corrupt as any of the others. When Alvear's term ended in 1928 Irigoyen was returned to power, for his personal incorruptibility seemed to promise reform. But he had aged; in fact he was eighty-four and could do nothing to prevent the State's money being drained by his supporters. No longer was he called *el mudo*, but *el peludo* – the difference here being that the *peludo* is a small hairy type of armadillo, hidden and impregnable in its burrow. When the great depression of 1930 swept across Latin America, officers, unknown to the people, took the Casa Rosada without a shot being fired, and a wild crowd broke into the home of the austere Irigoyen and took everything they could lay hands on.

Once more radicalism was in opposition, and remained so until 1955. By then its audience was far wider (it almost won a majority in Buenos Aires in the 1951 elections, despite all the pressures of the Peronists), and the 'young Turks' of radicalism, especially numerous and influential in the university, seemed capable of widening the far too bourgeois base of the party by attracting numbers of working-class groups.

In 1955 socialists and radicals had one great hope in common – to reconvert a working class whom they felt, with some justification, to have been grossly deceived by Peronism. Now, as in 1962, it can only be said once again that they have failed.

*

* Dictatorship is *dictadura*, *dura* meaning hard, while *blanda* means soft.

Perón heard the news of his supporters' victory in the 1962 elections in his Madrid apartment. Before finding refuge in Spain he had stayed in turn in Paraguay, Panama, the Dominican Republic and Venezuela. The revolution in Caracas in January 1958 then forced him to put the width of the Atlantic between himself and so unstable a continent.

But he was too vain to change his habits. The day after the votes had been counted he left to ski – his favourite sport – in the Guadarrama mountains, fifty kilometres from Madrid. He then waited with apparent patience for the promised visit of several Argentine trades union leaders. 'Now', he said, 'we must get ready to win the presidential elections of 1964.' Though by now sixty-six, Perón still stood straight and proud, his dark hair only touched with grey, his figure athletic. He received the friends who came to congratulate him in company with his third wife, Isabelle, a woman of twenty-seven, as blond as Evita had been.

From September 1955 to May 1958 the successive military and civil governments in Buenos Aires had tried to make it possible to return to normality. But it was far from simple. The weaknesses left in the country's economy by ten years of dictatorship could not be repaired in a matter of months, and only an all-embracing plan could possibly put matters right. Politically the working classes, convinced that they had been humiliated and defeated in 1955, remained extremely discontented. In the suburbs of Buenos Aires busts of Eva Perón were still decked with flowers by her unknown but still faithful admirers; and all over the city there were still walls daubed with the words: '*Perón volvera*'.* In the course of the various electoral battles from 1946 to 1955, the Radical Civic Union came to represent the whole of the opposition to Perón, and in 1951, it fought against Perón's re-election by putting up its own candidates for the presidency and vice-presidency, Ricardo Balbín and Arturo Fron-

*Perón will return.

dizi. In 1958 these two leaders had diverged because of their profound ideological differences, and they became the focal points of the opposing tendencies in traditional radicalism: Frondizi represented the hard-line radical Union, and Balbín the popular radical Union. The two therefore ran against one another, and Frondizi the 'hard-liner', won by a comfortable majority. On 10 May 1958, General Aramburu, who was presiding over the provisional government, solemnly handed over his powers to Dr Frondizi, who dealt with the Peronists as Louis Philippe had dealt with the Bonapartists; in return for the far-from-negligible support of their votes, he promised to remove the ban that forbade their taking any part in political life.

General Aramburu had vetoed any activity on the part of the Peronist leaders and given the General Workers' Confederation a new head whose very name was symbolic: Patrón.

Frondizi offered relatively important jobs to some of the Peronist leaders, while leaving out the more intransigent among them. Tall, thin, narrow-shouldered, his bony face hidden behind vast tortoiseshell glasses, Frondizi was the incarnation of the studious, absent-minded professor. He was no public speaker, and even less of a lawyer. The Argentinians were struck, not to say disconcerted, by the contrast between this pursed-up and austere character and Perón, with his overflowing vitality. Frondizi's parents were Italian by birth; he was one of a large family – he had five sisters and nine brothers – who moved from Umbria to the Argentine *pampa* in about 1892. The frankly Machiavellian policies he tried to carry out during his four years in power could do no more than delay the intervention of the genuinely 'hard-line' military, it certainly could not be delayed for ever. On 6 December 1930 Frondizi had just qualified as a lawyer (he was twenty-one), when President Irigoyen was driven out by a *coup d'état*. A member, like his father, of Irigoyen's radical party, Frondizi was certainly over-violent in expressing his anger and disapproval at hearing of the military putsch and for the first time in his life he found himself in a prison cell. This baptism of fire turned him into a confirmed militant. He refused out of bravado to accept his lawyer's diploma 'from a government established by force and maintained in power by the army'. In 1946 he was elected a deputy and during the Peronist period he divided his time between his legal work and his activities in the radical party. The man who was really behind his victory in 1958 was Rogelio Frigerio, an active and subtle businessman, once a communist sympathizer and a fellow-supporter of Perón's; he was the first to realize that the mass of Peronist supporters could decisively affect the balance of power. He visited Perón in exile and got him to promise to tell his supporters to vote for Frondizi. This in fact became a debt which Frondizi was never able to pay off. He would have been able to enter at once on the inevitable trial of strength with the army had he demonstrated from the first clearly marked leniency towards the Peronists and the CGT leaders. He preferred to dissemble. 'My one object,' he declared, 'is to build a modern nation. To do that I shall avoid all personal considerations.' The heritage of Peronism was a heavy burden and Aramburu had only taken temporary measures. In 1958 Argentina was still desperately short of electrical power and oil, and its steel production was minute. The balance-of-payments deficit was estimated at 300 million dollars a year. Thousands of officials, doing nothing but given jobs to please the Peronist leaders, encumbered and indeed virtually paralysed an overburdened administration. When Perón came to power four Argentine pesos were worth a dollar; in 1958 it was forty pesos to the dollar. Frondizi's economic plan was simple and could be summed up in the single word: austerity. Hardly a popular slogan. The meat-eating Argentinians had been condemned to two beefless days a week during the last months of Perón's rule:

Frondizi brought this back into force, thus reminding the *porteños* of the darkest days of a world war they had watched from afar. Two hundred thousand officials were dismissed from one day to the next, and he began to try to lower the chronic deficit of the railways by closing minor or purely local lines.

All these measures were undoubtedly necessary to raise the value of the peso and make it possible to establish an economic system firm enough to withstand crises. But the majority of the people simply could not understand them. One of their most ineradicable certainties is that Argentina is a paradise of inexhaustible wealth. As Clémenceau exclaimed after his voyage in the Plata estuary, 'What a rich country this must be if its politicians haven't yet managed to ruin it ! . . . .'

Frondizi's next consideration was oil. During the little free time he enjoyed while working as a lawyer and also being involved in the political world of Buenos Aires, before he became president, he had written a voluminous (500-page) work on *Petroleum and Politics*. The publisher had added an explanatory subtitle : 'A contribution to the study of Argentine economic history and the relationship between imperialism and the nation's political life.' This long study, in which Frondizi fiercely attacked the business trusts and 'reactionary sectors of Argentina' was also a profession of faith. Conservatives and military alike concluded that the new president must be a Marxist. Frondizi, leader of a radical party he hoped to reform, believed that Argentine oil belonged first and foremost to the Argentine people, and that any genuinely national oil policy must take as its first principle the need to fight against the great North American companies. Like so many other presidents, he resolved to be realistic and was prepared to compromise : but he was careful to appeal not only to American businesses. He asked advice and help of the Mattei group and other international consortia. He left the YPF, the national company, alone to deal as it chose with foreign enterprises. Perón had done the same during the last few months of his rule, but, champion demagogue that he was, continued to declaim his hatred of 'Yankee imperialism' at the top of his voice. Frondizi explained the reasons for this kind of prudent collaboration in simple terms. Foreign capital responded favourably and in three years 387 million dollars had been invested in the Argentine petroleum industry. In 1958 Argentina was producing barely five million tons of petroleum; in 1961 production had grown to 17 million. The exploitation of natural gas began to provide energy that was especially valuable in a country with almost no coal. Foreign investment also flowed in to expand the automobile industry, and in 1962 there were twenty factories producing 150,000 vehicles a year. Following oil, gas, and steel, Frondizi went on to try to modernize transport. Austerity, rationing, the cutting down of staff in government departments, had all continued to lose him the sympathy of ordinary people. The agreements made with American oil companies enraged the ultra-nationalist armed forces as well as the chauvinist bourgeoisie. Now the attempt to rationalize the railways also infuriated one of the most powerful workers' unions, and here Frondizi made a tactical error, for the railway unions were not wholly under Peronist control. His government's attack on the obvious dishonesty being practised in a public service with a chronic deficit had the result of uniting the alliance of free trades unions with the group of the sixty-two Peronist unions, and thus indirectly of making possible the formation of that Union of the Left which gave a peculiarly spectacular character to the tidal wave of Peronism which took place on 18 March 1962.

*

Frondizi might have done something to stem his growing unpopularity had he adopted real reforms to help the *peones* and effectively preserve the workers' standard of living. Perón used to give with one hand what he took from public funds with the other. Frondizi proposed agrarian reform; Parliament accepted it. Its terms were that estates which employed more than four managers be expropriated, given to the men who worked them, and provided with modern equipment by means of twenty-five-year loans. The big landowners, supported by the armed forces, expressed their horror. The army vetoed the reform. This was one of the thirty-eight crises Frondizi had to deal with in three and a half years of power, and the law of agrarian reform remained a dead letter. He froze wages, but the cost of living continued to rise. During 1961 the economic situation grew rapidly worse. The money in circulation rose from 80 to 127 thousands of millions of *pesos*, and the Central Bank had to raise 127 million out of its own reserves to protect the *peso*, which had been held steady since 1951 at a rate of 83 to the dollar.

The great plan for reforming and modernizing the econ-omic structure of Argentina was not yet sufficiently advanced to have much effect on everyday life. In 1962 the country was like a modernized building, reinforced with solid steel girders, but with the kitchens and bathrooms unaltered. It was a policy that could offer only a mediocre present while promising better things for the future as it were pulling down the façade in order to strengthen the walls, before ordering the washing machines and television sets. On the whole it benefited the landowning classes more than ordinary people. Frondizi wanted to remain in power and he would undoubtedly have succeeded in doing so had he not also tried to make promises to the left to balance his liberal economy.

The spectacular reception Quadros gave Che Guevara in Brasilia was not an unimportant element in provoking the crisis of August 1961 which led to the Brazilian president's downfall. Similarly, Guevara's visit to Buenos Aires pushed the military leaders there slightly further against Frondizi.

They were waiting for him to make a major mistake and he did so when he allowed the Peronists to offer themselves for office in the partial elections of March 1962. Though he had refused to vote for the resolution expelling Cuba from the OAS, as demanded by Washington at the Punta del Este conference, Frondizi yielded once again to the military by finally breaking off diplomatic relations with Havana. To counterbalance this he gave the justicialists leave to go ahead, which was dangerous on any count. There was no lack of warning signals. One important indication came in June 1961 and showed the rising power of the Peronists in the municipal elections held in one town in the Santiago del Estero province. In 1960 the socialist party had polled 180 votes as against 2,000 blank ballot papers supposed by everyone to represent Peronists. The Peronist party decided in 1961 to vote for the socialist candidate and he polled over 2,800 votes, whereas the government candidate only got 2,500. Most leaders, however, assured the military that the Peronist votes would gradually disperse – this was a view particularly strongly held by Alfredo Roque Vitolio, the Minister of the Interior. Perón, on hearing that the ban on his party had been lifted, summoned to Madrid Framini, a man of forty-seven, leader of the powerful textiles trades union, with 146,000 members. Framini, who had been arrested after Perón's fall, stood as candidate for the post of Governor of Buenos Aires province, the most important job in the country after the presidency itself. And on returning from Madrid he announced that 'the candidate for the vice-governorship is Perón ...' Perón's candidature was turned down because 'Pocho' was still wanted by the police for 'inciting girls under age to debauchery', but Framini won a triumphant victory. He was more than 400,000 votes ahead of his leading adversary. In all the Peronists picked up 2,538,000 votes – which amounted to 30·9 per cent of the total. President Frondizi's hard-line radicals got 2,038,000 votes, and Ricardo Balbín's popular radicals only 1,659,000. In other words, about one third of the electorate was still as faithful to Perón as it had been in 1955, 1958 or 1960; in effect, an alliance between the two rival radicalist parties would have been large enough to put the Peronists into second place, a place more representative of their true strength. But they won 44 of the 86 seats in the Chamber of Deputies, and Frondizi's party lost control of five out of the nine provinces. In Jujuy the Peronists formed an alliance with the Christian Democrats. The first victim of the Peronist victory was Vitolio, the Minister of the Interior. He was summoned to the Ministry of the Navy to face a furious and implacable tribunal of officers: when he left three hours later he had lost his job. The second victim was Frondizi himself. He had managed, with luck and skill, to live through thirty-seven crises, but the thirty-eighth was his undoing. Though he was a lawyer who enjoyed working quietly at his desk, he also liked travelling. Between 1958 and 1962 he had made visits to Europe, America and Asia. In February 1962 he went in turn to Canada, Greece, India, Siam and Japan – more or less a world tour in fact, and one which aroused some criticism at home. It was thought especially inopportune only a few weeks before the general elections, elections about which the government insisted on remaining far too calm. Frondizi had underestimated both the real force of the Peronist movement and the power of an armed force 150,000 strong, with at least forty generals and ten admirals. He was to pay for these two errors of judgement by being forced to allow the elections of 18 March to be declared null and void in those provinces where the Peronists had won them. For a moment it looked as though this might yet save him. But the military leaders, uneasy over the tactical alliance between the Peronist bloc and the Castroist extreme left, decided that they must have a closer control themselves of the presidency. 'Castro,' said Frondizi, 'will be driven out of power in Havana, just as Perón has from

Buenos Aires. History is not on his side . . .' Yet it was one of history's bitter ironies that it should be the immense shadow of Castro which rubbed out the faint silhouette of our professor of political economy; it was a further irony of fate that Frondizi, having been deposed by the army, was imprisoned in the island fortress of Martín García, in the Plata estuary, where Perón had been taken by the same group of officers in October 1945. But Perón had been got out two days later, borne aloft like a matador by his *descamisados*, whereas Frondizi's fall was received with almost total indifference by everyone. The investiture as president of Guido, president of the Senate, and Frondizi's legitimate successor, looked simply like a ministerial re-shuffle.

The general elections of the 14 March 1965 were yet another undeniable success for the Peronists. After three years, almost to the day, the counting of the votes once again demonstrated the persistence of a phenomenon which infuriated the military and greatly worried the political leaders. One in every three Argentinians still voted Peronist, and the body which more or less demanded justicalism amounted to something like 30 per cent of the electorate.

The Peronists had managed to defeat the popular radical civic union, led by the president of the Republic, Arturo Illia. In Buenos Aires province (which included such working-class suburbs as Avellaneda and Quilmes) the Peronist Front candidates defeated those of the radical party by something like 400,000 votes. In Buenos Aires itself the government only barely scraped in, and they had to give up Córdoba, a traditional fief of conservatism and militant right-wing Catholicism.

*

This about-face was easy enough to explain in terms of the industrial advance since 1960 in the noble and middle-class city of Córdoba, and the consequent settlement there of a large working-class population. But it must also be admitted that the Illia government, which had been in power since July 1963, had been no more successful than the Frondizi government before it. The elections of 14 March were also a complete rout for such small parties as the progressive Democrats, the socialists, and above all for the Christian Democrats who were quite incapable of following the example of their opposite numbers in Chile. Within a week the Christian Democrat party, thought by all observers to be a fast developing movement in Latin America, triumphed in Santiago but was badly beaten in Buenos Aires.

One reason for the difference was that in Chile an intelligent and dynamic clergy had recognized the need for urgent social reforms and supported the programme of President Eduardo Frei. In Argentina, on the other hand, Church and clergy were still, in the eyes of most people, suffering from a long reactionary past, and from the support they had given the conservatives and military in September 1955 in their fight against Perón.

At first the Peronist victory had no obvious or serious consequences. All it meant for the electors was that half of the Chamber of Deputies was filled with new faces. The number of deputies claiming to belong to the Popular Union (the name given for the moment to the Peronists and their allies) had grown from 15 to 51, which ensured a far more effective possibility of action on the part of the opposition. But the government bloc still had a comfortable majority, and the increase in the number of votes won by the popular radicals in Buenos Aires itself was enough to satisfy the leadership. Yet in fact, after the election, Argentina appeared to be divided into two more or less equal power blocs. The danger here lay in the fact that the division corresponded to a social and economic cleavage. On the one hand were the mass of the people, shouting for Peronism with all the undertones and possible developments suggested in the term; on the other the lower and upper middle classes and the armed forces. The duel, begun in 1955 between the trades unions and the army (and its allies), thus continued to dominate the Argentine political scene.

However, there was one vital difference between the 1962 and the 1965 elections. The Peronist victory of 1962 had brought about the fall of President Frondizi because the army blamed him for having made it possible for the Peronists to give this show of force legally; even the results of that election were rejected by the anti-Frondizi putsch. In 1965, on the other hand, though the success of Peronism was impressive, it did not seem to disturb the military leaders unduly. In fact, during the weeks before the election, a number of officers had declared themselves no longer basically opposed to action along 'justicialist' lines. But statements of this kind were certainly not enough to explain the apparent and surprising moderation shown afterwards by armed forces well known for their intransigence and their desire to give orders to civilians whom they tended to think of as ineffective and lacking in dynamism.

Since Perón's fall, all of Argentine politics really consisted in the continual to-ing and fro-ing of the army between direct interventions and well-planned behind-the-scene pressures, both with the single object of preventing any resurgence of Peronism. There are few Latin American countries where the military pressure group plays so determining or consistent a part as in Argentina. Yet one must distinguish certain subtle differences actually without the armed forces. The navy, because of its aristocratic traditions, is firmly and almost 100 per cent anti-Peronist. Vice-Admiral Isaac Rojas, one of those responsible for the coup against Perón in September 1955, is perhaps most symbolic of this attitude. When, on 2 April 1963, a significant part of the Argentine navy rose against the Guido government (Frondizi's successor), it was yet again in the name of 'democratic principles' and to 'counter a government plan to let the Peronists come back'. The revolt was led by Vice-Admiral Julio Palma. But the air force opted to support the armoured troops in assisting the legal government, and by the next day the revolt had petered out. It was not that the air or land forces had become any less anti-Peronist in 1963 than they had been in 1955; but it was clear that the great debate going on among the armed forces as to the best way to combat justicialism had acquired some new elements. In 1965 it could be said that the forces were divided into two major groups: one wanted a return to constitutional normality, with a direct or indirect ban on Peronism, while the other favoured a reform of the economic and social structures – thus supporting some aspects of Peronism. The publication in May 1963 of part of the encyclical *Pacem in Terris* in the military bulletin was perhaps a first noteworthy indication of the altered state of mind among some of the officers. Even by then there were a number of young officers and n.c.o.s who had come to feel – as was only to become clearer and more definitely the case later – that Argentina could not be sheltered from the wind of change blowing through the world at large.

*

A parallel development was clearly taking place within the Church from 1963 onwards. It was a Church with a long history of compromise with the powers that be, including the power of Perón in its heyday from 1945 to 1950. But voices, though still only rare and isolated, began to be raised against the clergy's silence in face of the poverty of the masses. The bishop of Morón, Bishop Raspanti, wrote a pastoral letter in which he denounced the 'profound moral crisis, and the prevalence of corruption'. 'We look,' he added, 'to the leaders of industry, to ask them to work for solidarity and justice.'

Thus the Argentina of 1965 was not quite the same as the Argentina of 1955. Though there were still the two major blocs in the electorate and in Parliament, there were a number of things to indicate that new awarenesses were coming to the surface. The elections of March 1965 proved to the working class that they still had a position of considerable power, as long as they did not fall into the trap, so common among Mediterranean-descended people, of fragmenting their political movements. Such fragmentation worked in favour of the preponderance of economic pressure-groups, chief among them the ACIEL (Action for Coordinating Free Institutions).

In the autumn of 1964 two influential unionists, Andrés Framini and Augusto Vandor, set about trying to stage a 'Perón comeback'. Perón himself, in Madrid, had been receiving visits from delegates and politicians from Buenos Aires ever since his supporters' victory in 1962, but such furtive meetings could hardly be considered serious breaches in the agreement he had made with his Spanish hosts – they being anxious not to annoy the leadership in Buenos Aires, in payment of a debt dating back to the end of the Second World War when Argentina had refused to join in the United Nations' sanctions against France. The fact that five important Argentinians stayed in Madrid for six weeks (Framini, Vandor, Lascane, Iturbe, and Sra de Parodi) might suggest that a trial of force was soon to take place in Buenos Aires. Endless discussions took place in the villa of *Puerta de Hierre* among the 'Comeback committee', Perón, and the Argentine financier, Jorge Antonio, who had played such an important role during Perón's time in power. In effect, though it was apparently a united group with the single aim of getting Perón back into power, there were actually several divergent tendencies: there was a difference of perspective between Vandor, the magnate, who had considerable friendships among the powerful North American unions, and Framini, who was more attracted to the idea of a single action with the most left-wing groups in the Argentine CGT. While some members of the committee, such as the fiery Sra de Parodi, really did want to see Perón back on the balcony of the Casa Rosada, the personal motives which were influencing a man like Vandor, whose real popularity would gain nothing from a confrontation between the military leaders and the former leader of the *descamisados*, are open to question. It was clear that Perón, who though still athletic was by now somewhat stout, was not enormously enthusiastic towards the uncertain struggle proposed to him by the cleverest advocates of the 'Comeback committee'. Gradually, however, as the weeks passed, the former glories of his triumphal days at the Casa Rosada and that fever which politicians never wholly lose, came to the fore, and transformed the peaceful tourist of the '*quinta* of the 17th of October'.* He began to speak with more conviction of his 'forthcoming return'.

*

The attempt was made on 2 December. In the utmost secrecy Perón and his staff boarded an ordinary Spanish flight going to Ascunción by way of Rio de Janeiro. Whether they realized it or not, this was an error that was to precipitate the failure of 'Operation Comeback'. When they landed in Rio the Brazilian authorities, waiving some of the legal regulations governing air traffic, firmly refused to let Perón continue his journey. The next day Perón was back on Spanish soil, in Seville, where the government in Madrid had decided to keep him safe from the curiosity of journalists, while considering the possibility of a new place of political

* *Quinta* means 'class of', and, of course, 17 October was the date of Perón's triumph.

asylum. He settled down in the Hotel Andalucía, well-guarded, in a room he had had in January 1960. But this time he was a man whose political career seemed finally finished, though he remained something of a celebrity. Despite the assurances of those around him, it seemed most unlikely that Perón could ever hope to make a spectacular return to the banks of the Plata. He still declared that he had not changed his mind, and thought of settling in Havana, where Castro had offered him asylum, or perhaps Algiers. But as weeks, and then months, went by, Perón once again became the quiet man who had for so long obeyed the careful rules of political inaction in Spain. It was significant that the Peronist success of March 1965 did not, as it had three years earlier, result in any rush of supporters and advisers to Perón's prison.

At the end of December 1964 the members of the 'Comeback committee' managed to get back to Buenos Aires. Framini was held by the police for twenty-four hours; they did not accuse him of having spent more than a month with Perón in Madrid and having incited him to 'try to overthrow the legal government', which was what he had in fact done: instead he was accused of having destroyed some furniture at a political meeting in a suburb of Buenos Aires during the summer of 1964! After this symbolic detention Framini got in touch with the other Peronist leaders, and they declared that 'Perón's return was only a matter of time'. But such statements deceived no one. The mortgage was paid off. Peronism without Perón could start afresh. The trades union leaders could enter the political arena with a clear mind and re-establish the contacts they had made earlier with various high-ranking officers. The day after the March 1965 elections one of Illia's popular radical party leaders declared: 'We aren't dealing with a phantom any more, but with a political reality.' The matter could hardly have been better put. After all, all the army really wanted to prevent was the return of another officer whom they saw as a usurper and a demagogue. It mattered little whether the working-class opposition re-formed, and was determined to re-form, under the banner of 'Justicialism', 'Neo-Peronism', or 'Popular Union'. The armed forces and the ruling classes felt powerful enough to keep this opposition in opposition, for they were still badly organ-ized, and their electoral support was evidently anything but politically astute. There was still antagonism. But in both camps everyone settled down into their established positions, and there was every indication that the fight would be a long and difficult one.

On 28 June 1966 the junta of commanders-in-chief dis-missed President Illia, dissolved Congress and all the political parties, and enforced the 'statute of the revolution'. Dr Illia tried in vain – and with great dignity – to get the rebel officers to return to legality, and only gave up trying when it became clear that resistance was useless. Since June 1943, if not longer, the army had kept a close watch on the political situation in the country. In June 1966 they intervened deliberately yet again, to take public affairs completely into their own hands. The 'statute of the revolution' gave ex-ecutive power, legislative authority, and even the power to appoint the state governors, to the president of the nation. That same day the junta appointed Lieutenant-General Juan Carlos Onganía president. In his investiture speech Onganía declared that 'the country could only return to democratic institutions when the economic and social situation had been put into order'. Neither the pretext nor the occasion was a new one.

In point of fact the officers had no special grudge against Illia's constitutional government, which had been in power since the 1963 elections – elections 'authorized' by the mili-tary themselves in an effort to solve the crisis produced by the overthrow of the Frondizi government. Thus, between 1958 and 1966, from Frondizi's victory until Illia's fall, two radical leaders were sent packing by the military. It can certainly be said that neither of them had succeeded in stopping the inflation created by ten years of Peronist spending. The chaotic printing of money had led to a continuing rise in the cost of living, and a gap between wages and prices which forced many of the *porteños* to supplement their income by taking a second job. But would anyone claim that any other politician, or even any of the officers themselves, could have done better? The whole Argentine economy, so badly set askew by Peronism (and also, it must be admitted, by an international situation that was far less favourable in 1966 than it had been in 1945) could not be put right without certain vital structural changes, starting with agrarian reform, the putting in order of sectors making really heavy losses, such as the railways, and a better organization for marketing raw materials.

The army could certainly not suspect Illia of *gauchism*, nor accuse him of demagogy or of having abused his power. 'Nor,' as the Argentine economist Moïse Ikonicoff so rightly said, 'could he be blamed for having achieved power as a result of Peronist votes, for his party was almost the only one to have made no kind of agreement with the former dictator's supporters. Furthermore, the outgoing government, despite the yearnings for independence it had indicated, had done nothing to arouse any mistrust in Washington, least of all in the State Department.'

In effect what the army was doing in 1966 was to yield to a long-standing temptation. The highest-ranking officers, convinced from the first of the value of authoritarianism and strong rule, had failed in 1930 because of the special circumstances prevailing at the time. They had failed again in 1943 because Perón, beneficiary of the coup, was a pragmatist and not a theorist. He only intended to remain faithful to the programme of the GOU officers in so far as that programme did nothing to hamper his own power and prestige.

Seen in this light, the coup of June 1966 was simply the third attempt in fifty years to put into practice a long-planned ideological programme.

The overthrow of the Illia government was made easier by the pro-Peronist trades unionists. From 1963 to 1966, they had become gradually disenchanted with the experiment of re-entering the democratic arena which Illia had tried to bring about, and were coming once more to see the armed forces as the only worthwhile people to deal with. The coup of June 1966 was also facilitated by the state of mind of other sections of society: the middle classes were worried over the worsening economic situation, and believed that a strong regime might find some solution; the old landed oligarchy were opposed to Illia for having cut down the profits they got from exporting crops and meat; the Catholic hierarchy remained basically integrist, despite mounting pressure from young priests and laymen who wanted to enforce the resolutions of Vatican II; and, finally, the industrial groups involved in international capital, badly affected by the annulment of their contracts for the exploitation of oil, were especially infuriated by the policies of the Illia government. Only the weakest of voices spoke up against the coup, and the working class was completely passive. The warnings from the universities, from a few intellectuals, liberals and progressives, went unheeded amid the general apathy.

Dr Illia took refuge in a dignified and critical attitude which he maintained to the last. It seemed that this honourable country doctor, whose promotion to power had resulted more from chance than anything else, was a greater man in adversity than Dr Frondizi, who ended by giving his approval to a 'revolution' which was to stamp out all the democratic principles he himself had so forcefully proclaimed. In March 1967 Dr Illia and his political allies mounted a campaign of 'banquets' intended to arouse public opinion as to 'the totalitarian direction the regime was taking' after the promulgation of its law on the civilian defence service. The campaign was banned by the authorities, but Dr Illia continued to protest against the erosion of the democratic system. A 'ten-year plan for military government' said to have been made by the army had been put out by the Argentine press a few days before the fall of the Illia government, and the first measures announced by Onganía showed that the officers did in fact seem to be planning on taking so long a time to get the economic situation back into good order, and consequently to 'return to democracy'. 'An ambitious but realistic plan': that was the brief given the planners in April 1967 for their 'ten-year plan for political, economic and social renewal'. The intention was to get rid of 'outworn economic and political structures', and, as the officers saw it, to 'found the nation afresh, and lead it towards the destiny every Argentinian desires for his country: to see it become a world power'.

The first Onganía government consisted wholly of civilians, technocrats and Catholics, but officers held such important posts as the leaders of the National Security Council (CONASE). However, it could be seen that General Onganía wanted to subordinate the armed forces to the government. He clearly distrusted the ambitions of men like General Alsogaray, the new army commander-in-chief, and the involvement of his supporters with a so-called 'liberal' economic policy – in other words a policy of collaborating with foreign capital interests. The dismissal of General Alsogaray in August 1968, shortly followed by his brother's being replaced as ambassador to Washington, seemed an indication that ultra-nationalist and even perhaps pro-fascist tendencies were triumphing within the government two years after the coup. Guillermo Borda, the Minister of the Interior, tried to establish in some provinces institutions directly inspired by fascist corporatism. It became questionable whether the 'liberal' experiment of the Minister of the Economy, Adalberto

Krieger-Vasena, who had held the post since 1966, was not also in danger. Krieger-Vasena, who wanted to use persuasion rather than force in his dealings with both management and the unions, had succeeded Salimei whose determination to manage everything himself had attracted much criticism. Krieger-Vasena put forward in January 1967 a 'plan for major transformation' – which was in effect a plan for stabilization not very different from the French and Spanish stabilization plans of 1958.

The battle against inflation was worked out in agreement with the International Monetary Fund, and the peso was once again devalued on 13 March 1967, while at the same time an almost totally free exchange was authorized. In return Argentina was given stand-by credit amounting to 400 million dollars (of which 150 came from the IMF and 100 from the U.S. treasury). Argentine capital which had been taken abroad was thus to be attracted back and foreign investment encouraged. In July 1967 a law was passed creating a 'service for the promotion of foreign investment'. Other contracts were made with private banks by Krieger-Vasena.

With these fresh resources, Argentina could certainly face paying off a considerable part of its foreign debts in 1967, and increase its quota of imports. A law governing fuel resources annulled the Illia government's provisions against foreign monopolies, which were once again given every facility. Finally a development plan to cover the period from 1968 to 1972 was entrusted to the CONADE (National Development Council), but the CONASE, 'as the body whose function is to work out the decisions necessary for the country's interior and exterior security', had a right to be consulted. The measures on which the Minister of the Economy decided were welcomed abroad with delight, and it is estimated that in 1968 stability was achieved as regards external finance. But the inflationary tension continued. From March 1967 to July 1968 prices increased by 30 per cent, and the situation became particularly disturbing in the employment field, where the CGT estimated that there were one and a half million men out of work. In 1968 Krieger-Vasena's balance sheet undoubtedly indicated an effort to restore the economy, and the re-establishment of a degree of confidence from foreign capital, but there still remained numerous problems to overcome.

In effect leading Argentine economists considered that it would be hard to reduce imports, since 80 per cent of these consisted of such necessary products as oil and raw materials for industry or such vital equipment as highly complicated machine tools. Exports were facing obstacles similar to those they had always had to contend with – for instance, frozen meat was having to compete more and more with meat being produced in Australia and New Zealand. Krieger-Vasena's fundamental idea was briefly to combat the internal factors that made for inflation by over-valuing the dollar and letting the State pocket the difference. It soon became clear that rising prices would have to be checked by legislation. The old oligarchy accepted the over-valuation of the dollar with an ill grace, and industrialists demanded a share in the duty being paid in order to enable them to compete with foreign business. Some of the country's industries were being directly threatened – textiles, motors, plastics, electrical goods – and the situation in the province of Tucumán grew ever more desperate. The crisis in the sugar industry there resulted in half a million people being out of jobs – in other words half of the nation's total of unemployed rural workers.

It would therefore have been hard to say that two years after the 1966 coup the first results of the ten-year plan were very outstanding. The deficit in the budget was still enormous (27,900 million pesos in the first three months of 1968). The loss made by the railways was still mounting, despite the enormous cutting back in staff which so enraged the unions that the enterprises had to be nationalized. Wages were frozen till the end of the year, and pressure from the workers forced the union leaders who had come to terms with the 1966 putsch to protest against the Onganía government's economic policies. The Peronist leaders of the golden age, Vander, Framini, Alonse and the rest, came to be forgotten more completely, and Ongaro, now a coming man, atetmpted with great difficulty to recreate a dynamic central party which he called the CGT *rebelde*.* A large number of the union leaders did in fact still owe their power over the rank and file to the use they made of the Peronist myth, though they continued from time to time to 'negotiate' with a government whose policies, though no doubt reasonable from the point of view of international finance, could not but conflict with the interests of the great mass of the workers at home.

Consequently the likclihood of any really effective movements among the proletariat remained remote in the extreme, especially since those on the 'left' – former communists, socialists or Peronists – could see no alternative to the Onganía military regime other than a further coup which would bring 'really revolutionary officers' into power. In Argentina, definitely the most right-wing country in South America, the 'left' would certainly have found it hard to undo the effects of over fifteen years of equivocation and disappointments.

The CP (which somewhat optimistically laid claim to 300,000 card-holding members), under the leadership of Vittorio Codovilla, decided on the pre-Soviet path of peaceful coexistence, and thus forbore from any undue criticism of the government's agreements with capitalist monopolies. The pro-Chinese and Trotskyist communists of the People's Revolutionary Party had to remain underground, and therefore were of as little importance as the left-wing independents of the MLN (National Liberation Movement) who still

* Rebel CGT.

fought the old Frondizi battles. Other groups, like that led by the Peronist Cooke, or the MRP (Revolutionary Peronist Movement), defended Castroist or Guevarist theses, but without much conviction. The Christian Democrats were growing stronger, but the Church remained for the most part steadfastly opposed to the new ideas proceeding from Vatican II. One small but revealing incident was the eviction of Bishop Podestá of Avellaneda, a working-class suburb. Podestá, often compared to the Brazilian Bishop Helder Camara of Recife, was forced to resign by the combined pressures of the government and the apostolic nuncio. 'I tremble,' he declared as he left, 'when I think of the future of Argentina.' There were other incidents in 1968 involving young priests who were shocked by the massive and increasing poverty of the rural working class in Tucumán.

The universities, deeply affected by the Onganía regime, remained the real bastion of the opposition. Hundreds of intellectuals, scholars and technologists left their homeland after the coup to escape attack and to get away altogether from the type of leadership which banned more and more activities and ordered its officials to burn books on Marxism – books actually published in Spain but thought in Buenos Aires to be 'subversive'. This was a revealing indication of the path chosen by an army which was itself torn apart by internal battles.

In Madrid, to an ever smaller group of visitors, Perón still talked complacently of his past, denouncing American imperialism, and declaring – whether from conviction or merely from demagogy is uncertain – that the only possible road for Argentina must be socialism.

CHAPTER 3

Uruguay

STATISTICS

Area: 72,172 square miles
Estimated population in 1966: 2,749,000
Population density: 38 per square mile
Annual rate of population increase: 1·5 per cent
Annual increase in average per capita income from 1960 to 1966: 0·3 per cent.

PRINCIPAL PRODUCTS

Wool, meat, leather.

The strip of beaches begins in the very middle of Montevideo. The first and the most popular, is Ramírez; then comes Pocitos, the most fashionable. But the sand is no softer nor more dazzlingly white there than it is at Buceo, at Malvín, the 'beach of the English', or at Carrasco, with its fringe of pine trees, tamarisks and eucalyptus, among which one glimpses charming villas, painted in pink or white. Then come the summer beaches, which are invaded by Argentinians who only have the stony shores of the south side of the Plata: Atlándida, Piriápolis, and above all Punta del Este, with its film festivals in the spring, and its pan-American conferences in the winter. From there to the Brazilian border, 200 kilometres to the north, is all simply one long beach, with a fine, well-made road alongside it.

Uruguay has no mountains, no deserts, nothing old. It barely has any Indians left, since the last few of the fierce and independent Charrúas were killed in 1832. But Uruguay does undoubtedly have finer beaches than anywhere else in the sub-continent except perhaps Rio.

In the business district of Montevideo, the shops are bursting with imported goods. The *cambios*, where currency can be changed, proliferate all along the main Avenida 18 de Julio. Every currency in the world could once be changed as easily here as in Geneva or Beirut. Only total stability makes it possible for any town or country to fill this difficult and envied role of international banker. South America's currency exchange centre until after the Second World War, Montevideo entered in 1957 upon an economic crisis so serious that by 1968 the country was on the verge of chaos. In less than ten years poor sales for the two basic products, wool and meat, resulted in a truly alarming situation, especially surprising in what had been for almost fifteen years South America's show window of prosperity. Certainly the Uruguayans are finding it hard to give up the customs of their happier days.

The building- and other workers of Montevideo, who are as remarkable for their immaculate working clothes as the Swiss or the Scandinavians, can still be seen at mealtimes grilling their pound of steak – and no steak is better anywhere – in the open air, *gaucho*-fashion. The carefree *gauchos* of Uruguay tend some of the most magnificent herds of cattle, horses and sheep in the world. There are no *gauchos* left in Argentina; one still finds a few in Brazil, in Rio Grande do Sul. But on large Uruguayan estates they are still there, usually at least fifteen together, though, as in Argentina, they have lost some of their importance and their freedom. Once it became necessary to mark out areas of 800 or so square metres, surrounding them with barbed wire and dividing them into *potreros**, in the estates which, in the north where the land is poor, might still extend over thousands of hectares, the number of *gauchos* obviously diminished. Instead of being merely a man who kept watch on the herds, the Uruguayan *gaucho* became a manager. Each estate, depending on the quality of the pasturage and the facility of communications, would be given over to young bulls, or cattle for beef, or horses, or calves, but the actual style of living was barely any different from that of a century before. The proprietor's house would be at the centre of an estate employing a number of agricultural labourers; on average, one *gaucho* would be enough to manage a 500-head herd.

Like the Argentine *pampa*, the Uruguayan countryside is still the centre of the country's wealth and stability; its grassy plains have become a kind of open-air factory where people manufacture meat, leather, and a particular wool which was up till recently one of the most popular in the world. As the Uruguayans say, 'we prefer fleecing the sheep to fleecing the tax-payer', and the fleecing of their vast flocks is really a quasi-industrial operation. It can take two or three months, with teams of specialists going from one estate to another filling sack after 150-kilo sack with the *capas* it takes only minutes to shear from the animals.

The special taxes received from importing and exporting represent the major resource of the state treasury. Though wool exports (65 per cent of the country's total exports) form the basis of the country's foreign currency reserves (54·9 million dollars in 1966), the only tax anyone really objects to is the one affecting Uruguayans going abroad. The authorities in Montevideo consider, with some justification that those citizens who can afford to spend their holidays in Europe or the U.S., are clearly the lucky ones. What

*Paddocks.

they receive in tax from 'long-term travellers' is put towards the help of the needy aged.

From 5 p.m. onwards the coffee-houses are full, and a merry though quite orderly crowd, well though not outstandingly fashionably dressed, devotes itself to comparing the quality of the refrigerators, television sets and cars which are to be seen in the show-windows of the luxury stores. The gentleness of Uruguay comes across very well in their accent which avoids the deep guttural qualities of Castilian Spanish. There is no doubt that the virtues most valued by the three million inhabitants of this eastern side of the Río de la Plata are individualism and the endeavour to achieve a life of contentment and comfort. Uruguay is also the most civic-minded of all South American states.

A gem of a country, it could well have been pressured out of existence between its two giant neighbours. Its land area is only one fifteenth that of Argentina, and a forty-fifth that of Brazil, but it is a smaller kind of country in other ways too. The first thing that strikes one in both people and things in Uruguay is their temperateness. The winters are never really cold – the only bad times coinciding with the *pampero*, the chilly breeze that blows across from Buenos Aires. It never snows, there is moderate rainfall and droughts are infrequent. The country has a long coastline yet the Uruguayans are not a nation of seafarers. They look inwards, like their rivers, and their real shoreline has always been the bank of the river Uruguay, from where the first immigrants, Spaniards hunting wild horses, and also some of their greatest dangers, have come. But in effect Uruguay's special distinction, up to 1966, was its political system.

The army had never up to then played any part in public life (unlike what was happening in Argentina or Brazil), nor given an impression of wishing to do so, though, as elsewhere, the country won its independence by the sword. In Brazil Getúlio Vargas from the Rio Grande do Sul ruled for twenty-five years. In Uruguay the *gauchos*, cousins of their Brazilian counterparts, could drive their herds to the abattoirs in the capital and go straight home again to the *estancias* without so much as a glance at the Chamber of Deputies.

At 9 per thousand, the infant mortality rate is the lowest in the whole of Latin America. The birth rate (20 per thousand) is low, and the population growth is not more than 1·5 per cent.

Primary, secondary and technical schools, and even universities, are open to everyone, and all teaching is free. The Workers' University alone comprises no fewer than seventy-four different professional training schools. You can find any book you want in the bookshops and especially, during the period of Peronism, all the political books which the Buenos Aires government had banned. This freedom also extended to the press up to the time when the crisis broke. The first daily paper appeared in Montevideo in 1807 : it was called *The Southern Star* and was edited and printed by the British. Its career was as short-lived as that of the settlers who had come from the fogs of London. But today there are 24 dailies in Uruguay, 8 of them in the capital. The two major political parties appear to have an equal number of papers at their disposal. There is a very well-known weekly of political comment, *Marcha*, edited by Dr Quijano, and a communist paper *El Popular* – which, it must be admitted, is no longer in the forefront of revolutionary comment since it, too, has adopted the relatively moderate line that prevails among all the pro-Soviet Latin American communist parties. Uruguay is a Catholic country but its people are religious in moderation and intolerance does not exist. There is even a breath of Jacobinism in the air. God is not written with a capital 'g'. Religious festivals were removed from the calendar in 1919, when the government decreed the separation of Church and State : 25 December is 'Family Day', and Holy Week is now known as 'Tourist Week', after a period when it was known as 'Creole Week'!

The divorce law is one of the most advanced in the world for it gives every advantage to the wives: it is the men who are called on to present a defence of themselves. Uruguay has regular diplomatic relations with the U.S.S.R., but does not have to cope with the problem found elsewhere of the existence of a powerful and well-organized communist party.

These noteworthy qualities which in themselves make Uruguay something quite special in a continent weakened by malnutrition and paralysed by illiteracy, are really unimportant details as compared with the way the Uruguayans have chosen to be governed. From 1917 to 1933, a collegial system modelled on the Swiss Federal Council continued unshaken amid the avalanche of *pronunciamientos* taking place all over the rest of South America. By the terms of Article 82 of the 1917 Constitution, the President of the Uruguayan Republic shared the executive power with a national administrative council of nine, a council in which minorities had to be represented. The President was elected for four years. He took over the running of the basically political ministerial departments: foreign affairs, war, the navy and the interior. The great economic crisis of 1929–30 also struck Uruguay, but not terribly forcefully, and President Gabriel Terra did no more than get rid of the national administrative council who were accused of delay and inefficiency at a moment when it was vital that dynamic action be taken. But after this brief interval, which one would hesitate to describe as really authoritarian, the determinedly democratic wishes of the Uruguayan leaders were expressed with more conviction than ever. The new Constitution of 1951 marked the definite triumph of the collegial system. From then until 1966 there was no President of the Republic. Executive power was in the hands of a national governing council of nine, elected directly by the people for a four-year term, three of whose members must belong to the opposition. This revolutionary innovation was only made possible because of the civic spirit of Andrés Martínez Trueba, a disciple of Batlle y Ordóñez who was the author of the 1917 Constitution. Appointed President on 1 March 1951, Martínez Trueba immediately got in touch with the chief opposition leader, Luis Alberto de Herrera. For the very first time in Latin American history a head of State agreed of his own accord to give up some of his own powers. Discussions between the *colorados* * in power and the *blancos* † in opposition resulted in an agreement to do away with the Presidency.

Obviously such an idyllic picture could not be without a shadow. The leaders of the *blanco* party accepted Martínez Trueba's proposals because they in fact represented their only possible chance of sharing in power after their shattering defeat in the 1950 elections. Their unexpected victory in the 1958 elections necessarily posed the question of the survival of the collegial system in force. On the other hand the electors had ratified the law of 1951 by only the tiniest margin – 232,000 in favour as against 198,000 against. In Montevideo itself the reform had been rejected by 100,000 votes to 78,000. Finally, and most important of all, only 37 per cent of the 1,150,000 electors qualified to vote actually did so. Clearly, then, there was a mass of people either indifferent or undecided, whose weight might easily swing the balance in either direction. The economic crisis which had been latent since 1957 and the terrific disturbance aroused by Castroism in Montevideo, as in all the other South American capitals, combined to cast doubt on the everlasting inviolability of the Uruguayan Utopia. They had declared that 'the Helvetization of our political system is far too advanced for collegiality ever to be brought into question, whatever may happen'.

* Reds (see page 202). † Whites.

But they were wrong. For reasons not unlike those which had once before forced them to give up their collegial system, the people of Uruguay decided in 1966 to revert to the presidential system, in the hope of being thus in a better position to resist the mounting economic crisis. The referendum of 27 November 1966 approved this policy by a large majority, though it was hoped that, as in 1930, the measure would prove a temporary one, since the form of government being abrogated, though not so well adapted to the needs of the moment, was far more satisfying to the spirit. After that about-face, Uruguay could no longer be the perfect example of South American democracy. But it had yet to face the upheavals, the state of siege, the suspension of constitutional rights, the barricades of students, and, even, that height of misfortune, rumours of a *coup d'état* – things which the Uruguayans had for so long thought only happened in other countries.

*

Yet, in fact, before becoming that exemplary democracy, Uruguay had passed through many vicissitudes, and indeed had had a long history of bloodshed and suffering. As in Argentina, no one in Uruguay had ever thought in the early years of colonization to stake any claim to the land: the herds belonged to whoever wanted them, and rival gangs of *gauchos* and shepherds would quarrel among themselves before agreeing to work for Spaniards or Portuguese, not caring which.

Montevideo was founded in 1728. The continual advance of the Portuguese coming down from the north forced the Spanish to find a suitable spot on the north bank of the Plata estuary and build a fortress there. The site chosen was an ideal one, and it has remained so. A belt of hills protects the sheltered port of Montevideo.

For a long time Uruguay was a buffer state between the

rival greeds of Brazil and Argentina. In 1810, just after the Argentine proclamation of independence, the Uruguayans embarked on what was to be a twenty-year struggle for the recognition of their rights by their too-powerful neighbours each of whom considered the Banda Oriental * an integral part of its territory. In 1811 Montevideo was occupied by Spanish troops whose job was to restore the authority of the metropolis on the rebel lands of La Plata. The city yielded, but the countryside rallied to the rebel banner of José Artigas, who launched the 'grito de Asencio'†. He was an ordinary militia officer whose task was limited to the modest duties of policing the countryside. In February 1811 Artigas collected a hundred or so militiamen and *gauchos*, soon to be reinforced by volunteers from every province. The first battle against royalist troops took place in May 1811 at Las Piedras. Artigas won, and suddenly found himself in the difficult role of *Libertador*. Having fought the Spanish with the help of the Argentinians, he now had to confront the latter, who certainly did not envisage the total breakaway of the Banda Oriental. Having repelled the Argentine moves, he then had to fight the claims of the Portuguese. This unwearying fighter was continually pressured from both sides; he hated half-measures and was anything but a diplomat. He was defeated and sought refuge in Paraguay where he lived in poverty for thirty years, to die forgotten and rejected. Modern Uruguay has rendered him belated justice.

Eight years after Artigas's departure for final exile, the Uruguayans at last won their political independence. But this was partly due to the intervention of Britain, which recommended that both Argentina and Brazil admit the existence of this indomitable nation. From 1843 to 1851

* Name of the territory comprising what is now Uruguay together with three of the southern provinces of Brazil: literally 'eastern strip'.
† Call to rise.

Montevideo was compared by European romantics to a latter-day Troy. The city had been besieged by the troops of the Argentine dictator Rosas, under the leadership of the Uruguayan General and President Oribe. Garibaldi was struck by this epic and landed in Uruguay with a legion of 600 men. In the end the Uruguayan Troy won the day, giving the lie to those who carried historical analogy too far. It was at that time that the rival political groups got their names : the besieged wore a red ribbon, and the besiegers a white one. Throughout the nineteenth century Uruguay in fact underwent a difficult development with wars of independence which provided an arena in which Argentina and Brazil could fight under the Spanish and Portuguese banners. Rivalry between France and Great Britain also gave rise to a lot of foreign interference. Thus the march towards genuine political freedom was slow and gradual in the extreme. It was out of this painful experience that the traditional parties were born in 1838, and the democratic institutions founded. In the end England won, and its influence remained the major one in the land round the Río de la Plata up to the time when the Americans came on the scene. The battle between the *blanco* and *colorado* parties continued, but it had become a civilized duel, and for more than fifty years now has been purely a verbal one. The fragmentation of the parties into differing directions (or, as they say in Montevideo, different lists), and the appearance of such classic movements as the socialist party have not seriously altered the basic background of Uruguayan political life. However, since 1958, the communists have concentrated their efforts on the unions and the university; and the defence of the Castro regime in Cuba is a rallying cry for a great many students and workers.

To everyone's surprise, the *blanco* party won the last elections in December 1958. The *colorado* party had been virtually in power for ninety-three years, and was obliged, for the first time in almost a century, to give up the six seats (out of nine) on the National Council reserved for the majority party. Increasing economic problems, rising cost of living, indications of administrative muddle, a totally uncharacteristic epidemic of strikes : these were so many unconvincing reasons given in 1958 to explain the sudden defeat of the *colorados* – even though there were fewer than a hundred thousand votes in it. In effect the change was less amazing than the Uruguayans appear to have thought. The *blancos* and *colorados* were mainly opposed by habit and tradition; undoubtedly the *blancos* were more conservative, and more opposed to economic planning, while the *colorados* were more ready to do business with the whole world, including the Russians. But there could be no question of the *blancos* repealing the remarkable social laws of the country, nor did they attempt to do anything of the kind. All in all, there is not much more difference between *blancos* and *colorados* in Uruguay than between Republicans and Democrats in the U.S.

This became abundantly clear in 1968 when President Pancheco Areco was faced with a wave of strikes and violent student demonstrations. Abandoned by the liberal wing of the *colorados*, he was supported by the conservative wing of the *blancos*. The return to a presidential system, and the giving up of the most equitable possible division of power between the two major parties obviously also involved Uruguay in a realignment of political movements within a classically European spectrum. The tactical, and clearly temporary, alliance achieved by Pacheco Areco may have split the *colorados* and *blancos* but also contributed to the formation both on the left and on the right of movements which had long been in the making.

One cannot understand Uruguay without remembering that it is a country with some sixty million cattle and twice as many sheep, one must also recall that it is crossed every day by hundreds of herds of animals from all the provinces being driven towards the one great port. Selling meat and exporting wool – these are the two bases of Uruguay's life. Benito Nardone, in 1963, began a policy of deflation intended to halt the crisis. Nardone had a far freer hand after the death of Herrera (the leader of the *blancos*) and the retirement for health reasons of Batlle Berres (leader of the *colorados*).

When Luis Giannattasio, who succeeded Nardone, welcomed General de Gaulle in 1964, the crisis grew. The continuing rise in the cost of living, unemployment (half the active population was jobless), terrible inflation, an increasing loss of importance for the money-changing firms, the continuous crisis in the meat and wool markets – all these were so many signs that this Utopia was in danger of being shaken by the same storms as its neighbours. For the first time there was even a possibility of a 'loss of morale' in the armed forces – a term that has so often been the prelude to a coup in South America. Giannattasio, an engineer, a genius in his own way and a civilian, worked energetically to renew the network of roads all over the country. He died of a heart attack only three weeks before the end of his term of office, and Washington Beltrán followed him as leader of the governing council.

'Uruguay consumes like a developed country, and produces like an under-developed one.' This description sums up perfectly the basic underlying causes of the Uruguayan crisis. The development of industry after the Second World War, and the establishment of a European-style 'consumer society' went hand in hand with increasing nationalization and de-centralization. In 1965 800,000 officials were directly or indirectly working with the State as their employer.

Out of an estimated population of 2,749,000 at the end of 1966, 79 per cent were city dwellers. Like Buenos Aires in Argentina, Montevideo is a head swollen out of all proportion to the body it rules. The rural population represents no more than 21 per cent of the whole, though the country's basic wealth continues to lie in its land. In other words, the entrepreneurial sector is developed out of all proportion: officials, office-workers, artisans, businessmen. The *per capita* income was still in 1965 one of the highest in Latin America (at 597 dollars) but even this was in danger. In 1966, the gross increase in production per head was lower than it had been in 1961.

The industrial sector could not make up for the weakening in the agricultural sector, for it had developed in a limited way, protected by tariffs, and even its development was held back from 1960 onwards by the limitations of the internal market. Furthermore, industrial exports in 1967 represented no more than 3 per cent of total exports. Out of a total export income of 181·1 million dollars, wool came first (54·9 million), followed by meat (45·1 million) – though meat sales were facing the same difficulties here as in Argentina – and leather (17·6 million). The decline in exports naturally produced a twofold deficit, in the balance of payments and in the balance of trade, as well as the reduction of the country's gold and dollar reserves.

As long as there appeared to be general prosperity, it may not have looked as though any fiscal reforms were needed. Now the attempt to establish direct income tax has been fought tooth and nail by the wealthy and tax evasion is general. Uruguay is now having its turn in experiencing the cycle of selfishness, violence, repression, and the control caused by budget deficits. The index of the cost of living, taking 100 as its basis, was 439 in 1960, and by the end of 1965 had reached 1,995·9. The increasing gap between prices and wages led in 1965 to a positive avalanche of strikes.

A month before he died President Gestido, under strong pressure from the International Monetary Fund, devalued the peso. This draconian measure, dating from 6 November 1967, was accompanied by a plan foreseeing the freeing of imports and the freezing of wages – traditional and commonplace measures clearly expressing the uninspired mind of the IMF. Jorge Pacheco Areco who was to be President in December 1967 seems, as far as one can judge, to have accepted the IMF's advice with even fewer reservations than his predecessor. He got rid of such reformist ministers as Vasconcellos (a member of the left wing of the *colorados*) and handed all the key posts in the government over to representatives of the major economic groups, like Carlos Frick-Davies, spokesman for the cattle-breeders, and Jorge Peirano Faccio, the bankers' representative.

In June 1968 Pacheco Areco was to decree emergency security measures to deal with a wave of unprecedented student violence. He suspended constitutional rights. It was a minor revolution. Left-wing students and trades unionists responded to him with fresh orders to strike. Two newspapers were temporarily banned; union leaders were imprisoned, and this, together with the 'militarization' of officialdom, made it possible to mobilize the employees of the nationalized banks. 'What are we making of our country?' asked the weekly paper *Marcha* in August. 'A general prison? A huge concentration camp? A great barracks?' Those who admire Uruguay and its democratic traditions can only hope that the Banda Oriental may yet have time to escape the total military domination that has been the fate of its Argentine neighbour. But many of the fears expressed in *Marcha* do, alas, seem to have been realized.

CHAPTER 4

Paraguay

STATISTICS

Area: 57,000 square miles
Estimated population in 1967: 2,161,000
Population density: Just under 14 per square mile
Annual rate of population increase: 2·4 per cent
Annual increase in average per capita income from 1960 to 1966 0·7 per cent.

PRINCIPAL PRODUCTS

Cotton, wood, leather, *yerba mate*, meat, *quebrache* extract.

Paraguay is a country that has been bled white. By 1 March 1870 when the war known as the War of the Triple Alliance, in which it fought the combined forces of Brazil, Argentina and Uruguay, ended with the disastrous battle of Cerro Cora, almost a million Paraguayans had died. Most of them had died in the fighting but others had succumbed to the appalling cholera epidemic of 1867. There were barely 300,000 people left: the country was a heap of rubble in which epidemics could spread more rapidly than ever. This country which had for five years fought with incredible courage against far larger and better equipped armies, seemed almost on the point of death.

Yet, in 1967, the UN survey estimated the country's population as 2,161,000. A century after the 1870 disaster the

scars are still visible, and emigration from 1947 onwards led
to a further weakening. In 1968 almost half a million Paraguayans were living in Brazil, Uruguay, and above all Argentina. The causes of this massive emigration are both economic
and political, but what has made it more serious is that so
many of those who have left were the most skilled – doctors
or engineers who had studied in Brazil, and decided not to
come home. The departure of the best brains – a phenomenon
common to all of Latin America in the sixties – affected Paraguay more than most because its initial needs were greater.
Furthermore there was a massive exodus inside the country
from rural areas to Asunción (one of the few capital cities in
the world actually situated by a frontier river) and other
border cities like Encarnación or Puerto General Stroessner.
The Paraguayans seem to be looking outwards, and turning
their backs on the almost totally unexploited vastnesses of
the Chaco.

It was in 1865 that the young President, Francisco Solano
López, with the temerity of a *novillero*,* declared war on the
Argentine and Brazilian colossi. He had just succeeded his
father, who had guided the fate of the country for some
twenty years with the iron hand of a benevolent *caudillo*.
Solano López Junior was a hot-blooded man, a general and a
romantic, who also loved travelling. When visiting Paris,
shortly before he became president, he planted a willow on
the tomb of Alfred de Musset; but he was also obsessed by
the dream of giving his country pride of place in South
America. The Paraguayan army, 50,000 strong and marvellously trained, was certainly still the best at that time. But
when faced with the combined force of Brazil, Argentina and
Uruguay, resolved to put down what looked like becoming a
disturbing kind of South American Prussia, López could only
demonstrate his determination and the fantastic courage of
Paraguayans of both sexes in a succession of hopeless battles.

*Young bullfighter.

He inflicted terrible losses on the enemy, though he was out-numbered two to one; he had two generals and some of his finest lieutenants – including his own brother Benigno – shot for being responsible for what he saw as unforgivable defeats or unworthy retreats. The women, caught up in a patriotic fervour unparalleled anywhere in South America, relieved the men killed in the trenches and attacked the Brazilian troops with broken bottles. The last battle of all was the ultimate in systematic and unlimited extermination. López, ambushed with 500 men on the banks of the Aquidaban by a powerful allied army, died with his gun in his hand. His eldest son, vice president Sánchez, the Minister of War and all his officers died with him. There was one shocked and des-pairing survivor, Alice Lynch, a fair young Irishwoman whom López had brought with him from Paris, and who had stayed with him to the end.

*

Paraguay was totally devastated. All cultivation had been destroyed; the livestock, the country's main wealth, had vanished. The slow and difficult return to normal was continually hampered by sterile and underhand struggles between two groups – the *azules* (the blues), liberals and anti-clericals, and the *colorados* (the reds), conservatives and land-owners. In fact it was from that period that the creation of the vast *latifundios* dated. The agrarian structure prevailing at the end of the nineteenth century has hardly changed since. Despite the tiny population per square mile, present-day Paraguay still has its agrarian problem. History barely re-calls the names of the presidents who held office from 1870 to 1932 – probably because so few among them managed to survive the whole of their four-year term. Yet Paraguay was in fact beginning to come back to life again when a fresh blow struck it down – the infamous and horrible Chaco war.

The terrible bloodbath of 1870 had left the rest of the world almost unmoved. Yet the Chaco war affected the capitals of Europe, and the major daily papers of Paris, London and New York sent their best reporters to cover it; it lasted for three years, from 1932–5, in a country of desert, bush and swampland, infested with snakes, jaguars and mosquitoes. Though it might at first seem somewhat surprising, there was in fact good cause for this interest: in theory the combatants were Bolivians and Paraguayans fighting for the exact determination of their frontiers, but the real combatants were the huge oil companies. The dispute concerned land that was uncultivated and where only a few Indian tribes still lived, among them the Tobas, rightly considered the most fearsome in the whole continent. In point of fact this fight for the legal title to an ill-defined few hundred square kilometres of the northern Chaco had really been going on unofficially for a couple of centuries. No one really wanted to trouble to go to see at first hand what was happening in this green desert, where there were no villages or roads, and which had been chosen for its very isolation by a Mennonite colony from Canada to establish itself.

The whole thing began with the discovery by the Standard Oil company of an oilfield in the Santa Cruz district. Suddenly greed for this 'black gold' seized prospectors and political leaders alike. A further oilfield was found in the Paraguayan Chaco by a Spanish engineer of the Royal Dutch Co. Diplomats, lawyers and businessmen rushed to study maps which had hardly been altered since the far-off days of the Spanish conquest, when the Plata river was discovered by García, Sebastian Cabot, Pedro de Mendoza and Juan de Ayolas, whose lieutenant, Martínez de Irala, founded Nuestra Señora de la Asunción in 1537. To Bolivia's arguments based on the law and the statements of the Liberator, Simón Bolívar, Paraguay replied with other arguments equally well justified both legally and historically. However, any kind of gentleman's agreement seemed improbable in view of the fact that neither Standard Oil nor Royal Dutch, who were the real antagonists and organizers, wanted one. The first incident occurred on 5 December 1928. A group of Paraguayan soldiers ambushed and captured a Bolivian outpost on the Paraguay–Brazil border. The Bolivians responded by besieging several of the Paraguayan fortifications established along the Pilcomayo – a wayward river whose course would change each year during the rainy season, and which was only to be discovered after some half-dozen expeditions had vanished without trace along its muddy and shifting banks. This phoney war, reckoned in terms of miniature fortresses, long forgotten in the Andean foothills, seemed to be dying a natural death in the damp heat of the Chaco, so ill adapted for troop movements. There was even a period of peace, which excited no one but a few philatelists. By 1929 hostilities consisted solely in a battle of postage stamps : Bolivia put out a series of stamps in which the southern borders of the Chaco coincided with the river Paraguay; the Asunción government replied by publishing stamps showing the Chaco frontier extending beyond the first slopes of the Andes. After this philatelic interlude, however, the real war started, despite appeals from a pan-American arbitration conference for calm, and the platonic beseechings of a League of Nations already beginning to indicate its powerlessness to achieve anything.

*

The Paraguayans at once showed clearly in battle those amazingly warlike qualities which had made it possible for them to be militarily ahead of their more powerful neighbours. Of course they were men of mixed Guaraní and Spanish blood fighting on their own home ground. The Aymará Indians who had come down from their high Bolivian plateaux, used as they were to the rains and icy

winds of the *altiplano*,* found the intense unhealthy heat
of the Chaco very hard to cope with. It was a truly dreadful
war, in a jungle where soldiers half-mad with hunger, thirst
and fear, had to cut their way through with machetes. Bolivia
had an army of 80,000 men, commanded by a German,
General Kuntz. Every one of them was to travel 1,500 kilometres – only very little of it by rail – from La Paz to the
hellish battlefields of the Chaco. The transporting of food and
munitions used up Bolivia's resources far sooner than had
been expected by the experts in La Paz before the war began.
On the other hand the Paraguayan troops of General Estigarribia, a former Saint-Cyr cadet, were working near their bases
and their homes. There were incredible episodes, matched
perhaps only by things that happened in the Spanish civil
war or the jungle battles in the Pacific Islands during the
Second World War : whole columns of Bolivian soldiers were
lost in the thorny bush in the shadow of the great *palmas
negras*, and long after the war people found the remains of
skeletons dried out by the burning sun of the Chaco. The
Bolivian writer Augusto Céspedes, one of the group who
founded the National Revolutionary Movement after the
Chaco War, told the story of these lost patrols, battling as
much against the demon thirst as against the machine guns
of the *pilas*, as their enemies nicknamed the Paraguayan
troops. After a year of fighting the *pilas* had captured some
hundred cannon and two tanks – one of which is still enthroned in the central square of Asunción. Dysentery,
malaria and typhus added to the sufferings of the men; in
January 1935 Estigarribia was nearing Santa Cruz and threatening to invade Bolivia. Under contradictory pressures, and
with endless crises of conscience taking place behind the
scenes in Geneva, the League of Nations at last decided to step
in. Muffled echoes of the desperate battle began to reach

* Region of elevated plateaux.

Europe and the civilized world followed with growing horror this meaningless war which was quite obviously inspired by the oil companies alone. Things were complicated unexpectedly by the fact that the advance of the Paraguayan troops into the high valleys of Bolivia became a threat to the tin mines controlled by the Patino–Aramayo–Hochschild trio and their whole Anglo-American complex of interests. This made it vital to prevent Bolivia's total defeat. In the spring of 1935 an embargo was declared on all arms to Paraguay, and the unanimous pressure of the major powers enforced an armistice, signed on 12 June 1935, though the peace treaty was not actually ratified by the countries concerned until 1938. The northern Chaco, for which so much blood had been shed, was divided more or less equally between Bolivia and Paraguay, following an arbitration conference composed of the presidents of Argentina, Brazil, Chile, Peru, Uruguay and the U.S. Bolivia had lost 80,000 men and Paraguay over 50,000. By an added irony of history, the Asunción government was finally, in 1944, forced to grant prospecting rights for oil in the Chaco to a satellite company of Standard Oil, who had led the Bolivians into starting the war in the first place. After several years of prospecting and drilling, the oil men made a decision quite astonishing to the Paraguayans who had by now invested the Chaco with immense importance: the wells already drilled were filled up with cement, and the engineers of the Standard Oil Company of California coldly informed the Paraguayan government that there wasn't a drop of oil under the Chaco. Fifteen years too late, the descendants of the Guaranís discovered that they had fought one of the most foolish wars of the century.

It further seems that, after four hundred years, Paraguay has been left with the thankless role of South America's Cinderella; there is today no country south of the Rio Grande more abused, more unknown or more isolated. Yet Paraguay's natural resources should place it high among the few un-known Edens of the modern world. The climate is like Florida, marred only by occasional hurricanes; the great central plains, the *campos*, are ideal for stock-breeding; recent statistics indicate that the animal population of Paraguay amounts to four and a half million cattle, 650,000 pigs and 500,000 sheep. In 1546 a bull and seven cows were landed in Spanish wagons. In the Chaco there are still whole herds of wild animals awaiting domestication, and at least half a million skins are exported every year. The soil is such as to permit several harvests of maize, of cassava, of rice, of cotton or of tobacco. It is perhaps symbolic that one of Paraguay's principal exports is orange-flower essence; the *haciendas* lost in the vastnesses of the country, under spreading mauve jacarandas, suggest the kind of picture of peaceful, pastoral happiness so beloved of the eighteenth-century philosophers. Yet it must be admitted that the standard of life of the people in Paraguay is one of the lowest in the sub-continent. The purchasing power of a farm labourer is only half that of a Brazilian coffee worker, and a fifth of that of a Chilean copper worker. According to UN statistics, the national *per capita* income is one of the lowest, if not the very lowest, in all Latin America. Add to this that more than 60 per cent of the total population is still rural, though the land only belongs to a tiny handful. In fact here Paraguay is the holder of another record : it has the highest concentration of cultivated land in the hands of the fewest large landowners anywhere in Latin America. The most recent CEPAL figures indicate that 1,552 large landowners and large foreign businesses own 31·5 million hectares, while 250,000 families of the lowest peasants (probably about a million people all told) only own half a million hectares. The situation has in fact grown worse during the past twenty years. In 1946 a smallholder would have an average allotment of two hectares; in 1966 his holding would only be one hectare, because of the continually increasing population, and the consequent fragmentation of the smallholdings. At the other end of the social scale twenty-five families own 17 million hectares – almost half the country, in other words. One finds the same astounding percentages in livestock: a dozen breeders own 20,000 animals, while 30,300 small breeders have only 11 per cent of the total stock.

Foreign investments are especially large in agriculture: Argentine, English or American companies have bought up enormous areas. The American Coffee Corporation, for instance, owns a quarter of a million hectares, and the *yerba mate*,* that plant peculiar to Paraguay, is almost wholly the monopoly of foreign firms. One English firm, Industrial Paraguaya, has a concession of two million hectares, and the Argentine company, Compañía Yerbatera del Amanbay, one almost equal to that. The desperately poor *peones* in the lonely and magnificent countryside of Paraguay live in conditions scarcely better than those of the peasants in upper Peru or Ecuador, their situation is in practice one of serfdom, and they are exploited in the usual feudal manner.

*

The geographical situation of Paraguay, situated as it is at the centre of all the major southern lines of communication in Latin America, should in point of fact contribute to the development of the country. Asunción, the great airline centre, certainly holds an ideal position as a result of its geographical situation. But the advantages of this are limited to the capital and do nothing for the country as a whole. Transport problems are really one of the worst handicaps; the river is not the cure-all it looks like if one studies the astonishingly rich network of waterways which follow the twisting frontiers before debouching into the great Plata estuary. The trouble is that there is no point in Paraguay that is more than 500 metres high; consequently the rivers flow very slowly and there are

*Paraguay tea.

constant floods. Yet in spite of the poverty and inadequacy of this means of communication, it enabled Asunción, the capital, to communicate with the rest of the world right up to the beginning of this century. The first railway between Buenos Aires and Asunción was only built in 1913; but there are relatively few bridges, and the innumerable manoeuvres necessitated by the ferry-boats make the journey a maddeningly slow one. The end of the War of the Triple Alliance in 1870 also marked the beginning for Paraguay of a process of integrating the country into the business circuits of the world outside it through the Río de la Plata, but communications were not expanded to keep pace with that. A number of Paraguayan experts in fact dispute the suggestion that the lack of high land is any obstacle to river navigation and envisage a system of trains of river-barges which seem to them more profitable than ordinary boats.

However the recent political history of Paraguay is dominated by its unavoidable dependence on Argentina, because of the need for access to the sea. American historians consider that Paraguay has been navigating between Scylla and Charybdis ever since its independence was first proclaimed in 1811 – Charybdis being Buenos Aires and Scylla hell. Germán Arciniegas, in particular, considers that the very fact that Paraguay is still a nation proves that its people have opted for hell. However that may be it is evident that the pressure of Peronism in its years of triumph indirectly resulted in Federico Chaves coming to power in 1950. In Paraguay, as in most Latin American countries, the *colorado* party does not necessarily mean the more revolutionary party. The Paraguayan *colorados* called themselves republicans in the nineteenth century; in effect they would have been better described as pro-Brazilians, whereas the liberal *azules* tended more to favour Argentina. The liberals, who were in fact more free-thinkers than active anti-clericals, were chiefly concerned to escape the often stifling constraint of the Church. Politically they were attracted by the authoritarianism of the *caudillos*. Their methods of government, applied in a country that had not yet forgotten the rigorous religious discipline of the Jesuits, might well have looked fairly moderate at the time. But the real ideal of those who formed the liberal party at the end of the nineteenth century was a man called Rosas. The *gaucho* Rosas had been the absolute exemplar of the *caudillo* in Argentina from 1828 to 1852. He was an efficient man who wanted power for its own sake, cynical and skilful, but hard enough to stay in power for over a quarter of a century. It was only natural for some Paraguayans to have looked admiringly towards Buenos Aires in 1950, where Rosas had come back in the guise of Colonel Perón.

*

In Asunción the liberals were in power from 1904 to 1931, and returned to power again in 1937. But it would be wrong to infer that the early twentieth century was a period of peace in Paraguay. In effect, in thirty-one years there were no fewer than twenty-two presidents who led the people with varying degrees of success. One of them was no more than three weeks in the president's palace, another four and a half. During that peculiarly disturbed period the average presidential term was nineteen months.

For fourteen years there was more or less a state of siege. Those who came to power after the terrible Chaco war were hardly more democratic than their predecessors. The first of them was, perhaps prophetically, named Rafael Franco. He declared that his *coup d'état* was based on the same principles as those upon which the totalitarian states of Europe were founded, and it was certainly at just about the same time that Getúlio Vargas thought he was following the pattern of history in proclaiming the *Estado Novo* in Brazil, and Perón was undergoing his fascist apprenticeship in the Argentine military missions to Mussolini's Italy. There are, however, some Paraguayan historians who do not consider Franco's work to have been wholly negative; his regime, they say, tried to alter the feudal structures of rural society and create the foundations of an infra-structure for a modern State. He also promulgated a public health law. Colonel Franco had in fact come to power following a popular uprising supported by nationalist officers in February 1936; his party was called the National Revolutionary Union, and from it there was born the revolutionary *febrerista* party which in 1968 was working in coordination with revolutionary left-wing movements, and being actively persecuted by the regime of General Stroessner. It is not easy to pronounce an objective judgement on Colonel Franco : in fact his plan for agrarian reform never got beyond the discussion stage, and he never even began to put it into effect. On the other hand he did authorize the formation of the National Workers' Confederation of Paraguay (CNT), and sixty-six unions had a membership of 55,000 at the end of his presidency, but such an apparently progressive act soon alarmed the land-owning oligarchy. He was thrown out by a coup in 1937 and General Estigarribia, who had emerged covered with glory from the Chaco war, was put into office in 1939.

Estigarribia at once formed a Council of State to include officers, clerics, and representatives of industry and commerce, along lines inspired by fascist corporatism. A month after the new Constitution had been proclaimed, Estigarribia, by then a marshal, was killed in a plane crash. His Minister of War, General Morinigo, naturally moved up a step in the governmental hierarchy, and for seven years he ruled the country with an energy certainly never surpassed by any of his predecessors. He ordered a plebiscite on the 1940 constitution – the shortest of any in Latin America : its terms were that the president be elected for five years, being at the same time head of government, commander-in-chief of the armed forces, and both legal and religious head of the country. He also had the right of veto on any laws passed by the chamber of 50 deputies. In 1945 Morinigo decreed the dissolution of the unions; their leaders had decided to protest against a law that placed them under direct control by the government. From one day to the next the moderate trades unionist activity of Paraguay came to a stop. Yet in 1947 the dictator was faced with several uprisings, which seemed certain to fail, and developed in fact into real guerrilla warfare surviving for several months against trained troops. The repression following this was merciless, and no one yet knows for certain just how many people were killed. Morinigo established, for the first time and with incredible rapidity, concentration camps on the unfriendly plains of the Chaco, and he there deported hundreds of the students who had inspired, and at times actually led, the revolt. He then closed his file on 'repression', and opened a new one on 'public works'; for Morinigo was no exception to the passion shared by all Latin American dictators for setting up three-year or five-year plans and getting themselves remembered by means of monuments, dams, or railway lines. He also sensed how to make the best of the new wind blowing through Asunción; in effect, it was still only a slight breeze, making the *colorado* flag flutter. Morinigo considered it wise to foster this, and did nothing to oppose the election to the presidency of a courageous and talented *colorado* leader, the writer Natalicio Gonzáles. After Gonzáles's victory a mass of over 50,000 peasants poured into the flowery squares of Asunción, and danced and sang under the balconies of the presidential palace. It was quite an unheard-of phenomenon, but it was to be short-lived. Gonzáles was inaugurated on 15 August 1948, and overthrown on the following 20 January. He was an idealistic politician and a poet, and his great wish was to improve the lot of the *campesinos*,* and free his country from its virtual economic domination by Argentina.

* Peasants.

He promised agrarian reform and declared that a national merchant fleet would be constructed – in other words he declared war both on the wealthy landowners and the Peronists. Conspiracies against his government were formed on all sides, and in every one it was pretty clear that the major part was played by Peronist agents. The *coup de grâce* came in two sections : the first putsch failed, but the second succeeded, and Gonzáles was forced to hide in the Brazilian embassy, and beg for a safe-conduct to get out of his own country. When Federico Chaves, his successor, officially took up his position as president, the only foreign ambassador to come to the ceremony was the Argentine one.

Chaves embarked on a policy of developing closer ties with Perón's Argentina. He even made a ceremonial visit to Buenos Aires, to proclaim the virtues of justicialism and promise his allegiance to the then triumphant Perón and his wife. The lyricism with which Chaves spoke of Argentina began to flag at the point when Perón's star began its downward curve. But the Paraguayan army decided to step in without even waiting for the obviously imminent departure of Perón, and Chaves was overthrown by a *pronunciamiento* on 5 May 1954. It was a warning light for Perón, for the fall of his enthusiastic admirer in Asunción must herald his own defeat. Chaves was succeeded by a general, as yet unknown to most people – Alfredo Stroessner. It would be an overstatement to say that Stroessner was any better known as a person by 1968. It was convenient at first to lump him together with the dictators ruling elsewhere in the continent – Batista, Pérez Jiménez, Somoza, Trujillo; but the classic *caudillo* caste has diminished amazingly of recent years, and Stroessner achieved the unenviable title of being Latin America's one remaining *caudillo*. So isolated, however, is Paraguay, that the Stroessner regime could follow its course amid the almost total indifference of the world, and behind an impenetrable wall of silence.

*

Paraguay, a still unknown paradise, returned in 1954 into total isolation. It was a situation well known there, and explains the perplexity with which the world that begins almost opposite Asunción – on the opposite bank of the huge, slow-moving river – tries to disentangle the real meaning underlying the *pronunciamientos* which appear for a few hours or a few days to shake the capital out of its general apathy, rather like a sudden sandstorm blowing in from the *campo*. One thing that is quite clear is that the differences between *colorados* and *azules*, between presumed conservatives and declared liberals, generally have little meaning. The key to the inner tragedy of Paraguay is to be found elsewhere. With a land area thirteen times that of Belgium, and a population of only just over two million, it is equally clear that the standard of living of the Paraguayan people ought to be considerably higher than it was in 1968. The vast majority still stagnate in an abject poverty which the comparative ease of life in the tropics does little to mitigate. A tiny minority of Spanish-descended whites, perhaps 2 per cent of the total population, still control all the vital positions in the country's economic and political life.

There are few pure-blooded Indians left – except in the Chaco, where a group estimated at about 50,000 live a primitive life more like the stone age than the twentieth century. In the forests some twenty thousand Indians – Guayanas, Cainguas or Guayakis – still survive, and within the last thirty years, Professor Jean Vellard has discovered and written about the peaceful way of life of the honey-eating Guayaki Indians. The mass of the population of Paraguay thus consists of people of mixed Spanish and Guaraní blood. Foreign immigration has been minimal, apart from a large recent influx of Japanese, and has therefore done nothing to change the picture, despite a slight increase in the number of Italian families arriving in the past few years. It is therefore hardly surprising that the Guaraní language has survived several centuries of war, extermination and oppression, and still survives among the working class – so much so that it is a second national language alongside Spanish. It is probable, however, that Guaraní would have been totally forgotten during the various turmoils had not the Jesuits become established in the heart of the forest land in the central part of South America.

Jesuit missionaries, fervent priests and bold pioneers, have in fact been working since 1610 to protect the Indians against the inroads of the Spanish settlers. With the assent of the king of Spain they organized Indian communities, persuading them to abandon their nomadic life and live in a restricted area – hence the quite incorrect name given to these communities: 'reservations'. In a short time more than 100,000 Indians were gathered into some thirty different 'reservations' spread out over a wide area. This experiment was to develop in such an unusual way as to shape the whole way of life of the Paraguayan people.

Before the Spanish conquest the Guaranís were considered as being among the least civilized of south American peoples: with their copper skin, high cheekbones, narrow eyes and long straight hair, they were undoubtedly of Mongol descent. Professor Paul Rivet thought their early ancestors had probably come from Asia to America by way of the Bering strait. Historians of the conquest wrote pages of argument over the virtues and defects of these people; but one thing is certain: they must certainly be classed in the category of 'good' peaceful savages, and the language they spoke was the one factor that united the thousands of Indians who lived in that vast area where the Jesuits established their 'reservations'. At sunset the Guaranís would gather to listen to sad singing, and some Guaraní songs, more or less bastardized, can today be heard all over the world.

*

At first these 'reservations' undoubtedly had about them a

dubious suggestion of segregation; it certainly was a question of the Spanish authorities handing over to the Jesuits the control and organization of these hundreds of thousands of Guaranís, as yet by no means ready to accept it. Paraguayan historians at the time stressed the undeniable character of exploitation in the whole affair; Blas Garay especially made a point often forgotten in Europe, where admiration for the Jesuits' work in Paraguay had been idealized by quite a number of highly fictionalized accounts presented in the theatres. The Jesuits were allowed not to pay taxes, and they could export goods to great advantage without Paraguay getting a penny from their 'reservations'. These same historians also denied that the reservations were really autonomous, and declared that there was a very strong administrative centralization : 'Autonomy' was used simply to keep order internally in the reservations. Whether this was so or not, the experiment developed into one of the most extraordinary attempts ever made in community living. It would not be accurate to describe the reservations as communist republics; there were more than thirty of them around the mid-eighteenth century, not only in Paraguay itself but also in southern Brazil and northern Argentina. On the other hand, the rules governing them, which were stringent, very precise and dealt with the very smallest details of everyday life, both day and night, were socialist-inspired. The products of the community's work were distributed to everyone according to need; the old, the sick, and orphans were supported by the group, who shared their work, their struggles and their joys. Almost all the communities lived in the same way. The Church was the natural centre, and around it were grouped the hospital, shops for food and seeds, and further away the Indians' stone houses. A fortified wall surrounded the whole reservation, and from 1639 onwards armed forces were trained and equipped to confront any attempts by adventurers from São Paulo to make off with human beings as slaves. These community villages hummed with the noise of work, with blacksmiths, carpenters, shoemakers, clockmakers, and even printers. The Jesuits taught the Indians how to cultivate and dry *yerba mate*, and perhaps their greatest contribution was to give up running public affairs themselves, leaving that to an elected council, and remain in the background to give advice when asked.

The decline of these reservations was induced by jealousies from outside, intrigues by the local Spanish authorities, and the banning of the Jesuits. In 1768 Spain decreed the destruction of these communities in which the Indians had achieved something very close to the primitive Christian ideal. When the Jesuits were expelled from America the reservations were sacked and the Indians once again subjected to the will of the whites. The Jesuits who had tried to create the kingdom of God 'on earth as it is in heaven', left for Europe in the chains that symbolized criminality. A few of their charges managed to flee into the forests and there remain free; and in fact the preservation for almost two centuries of a fairly large Indian population explains a great deal about the present characteristics of Paraguay. And it is significant that writers as little likely to favour the Jesuits as Montesquieu, Voltaire, Elisée Reclus and Stefan Zweig, spoke in very similar terms of praise for the unequalled work done by them in South America. At San Ignacio Guazú giant grass grows over the old scattered stones of the mission; bushes grow through the windowless façades of the baroque church, and one can barely trace where the old mosaic paths used to be. In the crucifixion scene by Yaguarón (in fact not a Jesuit but a Franciscan), the Indian Christ is crucified between two white thieves; in Paraguay as in Haiti, Judas is the white man.

There is relatively little difference between Paraguay as it is today and Paraguay as it was under the dictator Francia who ruled from 1816 to 1840. Gaspar Rodríguez Francia was a strange, austere and secretive man. He studied in Córdoba university and became a lawyer who knew his theology as well as his jurisprudence – he was a kind of fiercely secularist Salazar. Paraguay owes its independence (proclaimed in 1811) to him, and also a quarter-century of almost total isolation. He would allow no Paraguayans to leave the country and no foreigners to come in, and anyone who protested against his tyranny was imprisoned or shot. One day he decreed that there must be no bachelors in Paraguay, and priests must be made to marry. Deception and theft were banned by the Constitution : Francia was obsessed by the thought that his country might be contaminated by the dark forces surrounding its borders. This obsession led him to commit two enormous blunders, which caused fury in the capitals of other countries. The French naturalist Bonpland came to do some research in Paraguay and Francia had him arrested and kept in a primitive village for eight years. He also imprisoned the hero of Uruguayan independence, Artigas, for twenty years. It is hard to conceive how anyone could behave in such an extraordinary way – yet his character can be seen clearly enough from a single incident : one of his sisters married without his permission, and he had both her husband and the priest who had married them shot. At the end of his life Francia became pathologically mistrustful; when he had to cross Asunción he insisted that all the streets must be empty, and his guards had orders to fire without warning on anyone who did not vanish the moment the presidential cortège was announced. He admired two men : Robespierre and Napoleon; he kept in his library the revolutionary speeches of 1789, and had himself made a jacket and hat like Napoleon's. He died at the age of seventy-four, and the Paraguayans were then given a new tyrant – less eccentric but equally authoritarian.

At this distance it is perhaps easier to see Francia's rule in its historical context. Indeed some Paraguayans can now even find it in his favour that he 'preserved his country by every possible means from interference by the Argentinians'. If this were the criterion, then Francia's dictatorship could well be justified as belonging to a 'special moment in history'; and his 'national-revolutionary' regime certainly made it possible to confiscate some of the enormous estates owned by the Church and the colonial oligarchy. The formation of 'national farms' further fostered an increase in agricultural production, and the liberation of a large number of peasants who had up till then been exploited by lay or religious landowners.

If one looks at it in this light – and, paradoxically, some young revolutionaries of today do – it must be admitted that General Stroessner's regime has not even attempted to interfere with the big estates still existing since colonial times. What he has done is to achieve a certain industrial advance since 1960.

When he came to power in 1954, Stroessner was in theory dependent on the *colorado* party, but in 1959 he had himself re-elected with complete disregard for political parties of either side, and of Parliament too, though he had rigged its membership himself. Opposition continued to grow and become stronger after that, and his re-election was criticized even in circles which had before favoured him. The opposition was led by students and such priests as Fr Talavera; a 'United Front for National Liberation' was formed, not dissimilar to the Venezuelan Democratic Front which, combining a great many political streams in Caracas, finally with the help of part of the army succeeded in getting rid of the Pérez Jiménez dictatorship in January 1958. This United Front included elements just as diverse as the *febreristas* (who still boasted of their success in February 1936 in getting Colonel Franco into power), a few active communists, the Catholics, dissident *colorados*, and even a number of dissatisfied officers who feared loss of support from Washington. For certainly the most serious threat to the Stroessner regime could only come from the U.S.: during the early years American support for him had been obvious.

In April 1960 Secretary of State Christian Herter could still express his satisfaction with 'the democratic regime in Paraguay'. Adlai Stevenson indicated a similar enthusiasm after visiting Asunción and promised a 15 million dollar aid grant, but only on condition 'that the internal situation becomes more stable'. In May 1961 President Kennedy sent a telegram to Stroessner on Paraguayan independence day, congratulating him on 'the democratic strengthening of his government'. Stroessner of course was skilful in playing the card played earlier by Trujillo and Tacho Somoza : he accused international communism and Fidel Castro of interfering in Paraguay's internal affairs. But doing that had not stopped Tacho Somoza from dying, nor prevented the fall of the Trujillo regime after the murder of General Trujillo himself; on the very day Kennedy's telegram landed on Stroessner's desk hundreds of students poured into the streets of Asunción.

On 12 December 1959 armed groups of emigrants crossed the frontiers of Paraguay; the rebels wore police berets in the colours of Paraguay, and arm-bands with the number '14' embroidered in red. The '14 May Movement', a pale imitation of Castro's '26 July Movement', had begun. There was another invasion in April 1960; the government responded with stringent and effective repressive measures. Stroessner had been in power since 1954, an extraordinarily long period in that part of the world; he could still depend on the support of a large section of the *colorado* party and on the 15,000 strong state police under the leadership of Colonel Duarte Vera. The armed forces had fine modern equipment, and since a third of the national budget was spent on them, they were especially privileged; it seems likely that most of the officers felt that their fate was closely bound up with that of the Stroessner regime, but it was significant that some rallied to the Liberation Front. To retain power Stroessner did what the Caribbean dictators had done before him : he promised genuine democratization of the country's political structures. But such pretences never succeeded in saving the cruel and outdated tyrannies in other places.

With this weapon of charm he succeeded, it is true, in convincing some liberals and some *febreristas*, and this made it possible to re-establish a Congress which was termed by those in exile a 'rump parliament'. The communists, though divided, like all the other communist parties in the sub-continent, into three main streams, remained firm in opposition, as did the young and dynamic Christian Democrat party. The latter, made up chiefly of intellectuals, was small, but its left wing, supported by a fast-developing movement among the lower clergy, was intensely revolutionary.

The other card Stroessner and his associates played with great skill was that of development. Paraguay, which certainly could not complain about the sums of money allotted to it in recent years by the BID, the U.S. Treasury and the Alliance for Progress, used its loans to create an infrastructure suited to modern needs. But the armed forces, many of whose officers completed their training in the U.S., continued at the same time to tighten their grip on the romantic and forgotten land of the Guaranís.

Stroessner still undoubtedly controlled the army in 1968, but he had partly lost the support of the Church; bishops had gone so far as to describe his constitution as 'personalist' and 'dictatorial' – an unheard-of thing in Paraguay. And Stroessner who, it is said, could manage with only a few hours' sleep, began to telephone in the night to divisional headquarters to make sure no one there was plotting against him.

CHAPTER 5

Mexico

STATISTICS

Area: 761,530 square miles
Estimated population in 1967: 45,671,000
Population density: 60 people per square mile
Annual rate of population increase: 3·2 per cent
Annual increase in average per capita income from 1960 to 1966:
2·8 per cent.

PRINCIPAL PRODUCTS

Cotton, maize, wheat, barley.
Silver (world's major producer), iron, sulphur, tin, copper, zinc, gold, manganese, lead, oil.

The moment you cross the Rio Grande – that deep, ochre-coloured depression which half a million Mexican 'wetbacks' used to cross every year up till quite recently to find work on the farms of the southern United States – everything seems quite different. The sky changes totally; the clouds are wilder, the ground rougher, the ravines deeper. Mexico is like no-where else. People who like finding comparisons have described it as a mixture of America, Japan, Spain and Corsica – but this odd cocktail of similarities does not satisfy those who really know. Mexico has a special fascination of its own, and it has exercised that fascination on people ever since Cortés gazed in astonishment on the cities, temples and palaces of the Aztec civilization, and of other kingdoms too, each with its own language, culture and religion. Spanish colonization here after the conquest was on a scale unknown elsewhere in the continent, yet it never wholly succeeded in stamping out the traces of those Indian civilizations. In Peru, Ecuador or Bolivia the names of the last great Indian leaders, Huascar or Atahualpa, have been expunged from the history books, if not from the memories of their descendants on the *sierra*. In Lima, remains said to be those of Pizarro are laid out for public veneration in the cathedral in a glass case, and a statue of the cruel conquistador stands in a city square. But in Mexico you will not find Herman Cortés in any of the squares, but Cuauhtemoc, the last hero of the battle against Spain, is enthroned in the centre of one of the finest squares on the Paseo de la Reforma. Unlike other American Indian nations, Mexico is proud of her past; you could not find a single Mexican who would suggest that Cortés was a greater man than Cuauhtemoc. In the south, in the mountains of the north west, and in parts of Michoacán state in the south west, there are still large populations of almost completely pure-blooded Indians: short people with coppery skin and fine features, who love the land, live peaceably and are in general quite satisfied with their modest standard of living. Almost three million Indians still speak the language of the old Aztec conquerors, or other Indian tongues, and know no Spanish at all, though that is the language spoken in the cities and recognized by the state. Like their cousins in Guatemala, they cling to the laws and customs of their local group, looking even on the mestizo shopkeepers who live in their villages as foreigners, and the inhabitants of the distant capital almost as people from another planet. If pressure from the mestizo businessmen becomes too great, so that eventually they take over the centre of the town, the colonial *zócalo*, inevitably flanked by the church and the town hall, the Indians will move out to the surrounding countryside.

Van orillando : they go quietly, without weeping or wailing, 'edging' into what still remains the outside world.

*

These large numbers of Indians are gradually learning to adapt to a settled agricultural way of life; but really integrating them into the modern economic and social structures of Mexico is a problem that is far from being solved. It is one of which the government is acutely aware, and in 1949, after a Congress held at Pátzcuaro in Michoacán, on the shores of the lake where fishermen still use nets shaped like butterflies, an Institute for Indian Affairs was established, under the direction of Alfonso Caso, one of Mexico's most brilliant anthropologists. The purpose of the Institute is twofold : to improve the living conditions of the as yet unassimilated mass of Indians, and to speed up their integration into the rest of society. Teams of anthropologists, doctors, agronomists and schoolteachers have been sent out; a coordinating centre was set up in Chiapas state, whose Indian communities are specially backward. Other centres have followed on the Huastec coast, in the valley of the Papaloapán, where the pungent dampness of the *tierras calientes** mingles with the smell from the oil refineries. They have also been set up among the Tarascos of Michoacán, the Tarahumaras of the north west – perhaps the most amazing of all Mexican Indians, with their ability to spend four, five or six days hunting deer in the *sierra*, and then killing the animal they have tracked with their traditional sharp stone knives; and also their ability to remain motionless for a whole day beside a lake to capture migrating birds. The results produced by Alfonso Caso's teams have certainly been widely disputed. Sociologists reckon that in many cases the effects of the Institute's action have been more theoretical than practical, and they

*Hot steamy coastal plains and mountain slopes below 3,000 ft.

also deplore a certain impoverishment of the 'Indian communities'. But it cannot be denied that the Institute and its promoters have as their first concern to integrate these Indians without doing anything to alter their unique personality, or undermine their traditions or their craftsmanship which date back to the far distant past.

*

The ancestral stones are next door to the modern city. Of Tenochtitlán's canals all that remains in the south are the shady banks of Xochimilco where *chenampas* (a type of small boat) modelled on those of the Aztecs slip alongside flowered gondolas from which the strains of guitar music can be heard. But the pyramids of Teotihuacán, which were already in ruins when the Aztecs arrived at Lake Texcoco in 1325 or thereabouts, still stand. Excavation has only uncovered part of the archaeological whole of Teotihuacán, and new discoveries are gradually revealing more of the hidden life of a city whose temples celebrate the mystical glories of Quetzalcoatl, the plumed serpent. The Peruvian Indians believed, on seeing Pizarro's bearded conquistadors, that Viracocha * had returned; it may well be that when the troops of Cortés first appeared the Indians of central Mexico believed they were witnessing the return of Quetzalcoatl from the east to which he had gone. Teotihuacán , 'the place where men became gods', is lost in the mists of the past. 'We know nothing,' says the Mexican archaeologist Covarrubias, quite rightly, 'of the origin or the identity of the men who created the so-called archaic cultures.' They seem to have come, fully formed, out of nowhere, and suddenly appeared over a vast area. It is a mystery how, from the beginning, the ancient Mexicans were evidently skilled farmers and sophisticated potters, whose perfect taste in this simple art form has

* The creator God.

a long tradition behind it. In effect, dating the cultures of the past is one of the unsolved problems for Mexican archaeology.

*

Every year thousands of tourists make the pilgrimage to Teotihuacán, half an hour's drive from Mexico City. Adventurers, poets and scholars set out to try to find the Toltecs, the Mixtecs, the Zapotecs or the mysterious peoples of the Gulf. Their efforts and enthusiasm are occasionally rewarded. At Palenque a royal tomb, after a thousand years of oblivion, yielded up an anonymous jade death mask, with eyes of volcanic glass – one of the most important archaeological discoveries of the last twenty years. As they saw the bracelets, the jewels, the jade plaques, and the little statues of the sun-god, archaeologists thought in terms of a kind of Mexican pharaoh. At Tajín, near the pyramid, the *voladores* perform their endless dizzying whirlwind opposite the steps of the monument: these aerial dancers, attached to cables fixed to a greased pole, somersault above the heads of the audience. Hanging by their feet, a team of five *voladores*, wearing loose red trousers, white shirts, and multicoloured ribbons on their heads, perform at least thirteen turns. This is an acrobatic exercise dating back to pre-Cortés times, both dangerous and spectacular, and of course a great attraction to tourists on their way down to Papantla.

In Palenque, which only a few years back was three days' journey by mule from San Cristóbal de las Casas, the temple stands out in its setting of virgin forest. Further on splendid names are dotted about the savanna of Yucatán with its sharp carpet of sisal needles – Uxmal, Chichén Itzá, Sayi Labna, Izamal, Tulum. The Maya civilization probably reached a high degree of development and refinement unequalled by any other pre-Cortés civilization. S. G. Morley, the American anthropologist whose work and study on the civilizations of this area are considered the most authoritative, thinks that the Mayas were first of all settled in the warm jungle of Peten, in what is now northern Guatemala. Alfonso Caso on his part thinks they lived south of Vera Cruz. But what is undisputed is that the Mayas, having been subjected successively to the varying influences of the Toltecs and the Aztecs, only yielded to the Spaniards in 1697 – almost two hundred years after the arrival of the first conquistadors. These, the Greeks of Central America, have left us a temple at Chichén Itzá of which the pyramid (the *castillo*) we now see was only the base, and the remains of other temples – fragments of truncated colonnades, and a games stadium decorated with bas-reliefs giving some notion of how the Mayas lived. Jaguars with jade eyes, eagles, *chacmools* (statues of reclining men), are reflected in the glassy mirrors of the *cenotes*: these are a kind of well still being explored – though in fact an American consul from Mérida has 'visited' them, and a good part of the wealth found there is now in the United States, where it is the subject of constant claims from the Mexican government. Systematic searching of the *cenotes* has been undertaken, for these formidable wells were used to receive the virgins offered in sacrifice to the gods by Maya priests, and also offerings of precious stones. Inestimable treasures are probably still lying deep down in them, and the Mexican National Institute of Anthropology and History set about excavating them in 1962. So far thousands of pieces of jade, copper, gold and pottery have been recovered. Every modern method is being used, with small derricks being brought to the edge of the wells, and frogmen from the Mexican Water Sports Club working in relays to bring to light the still hidden Maya treasures. Uxmal is 80 kilometres south of Mérida, the capital of Yucatán, near the old paved road which linked it with the fortified port of Campeche. The gaping mouth of the plumed serpent is turned on the visitor there, as it is at Chichén Itzá and Teotihuacán; and these two, probably once rival, towns now share the same sleep, disturbed only by the noises of the savanna that was once a forest.

, The people of Yucatán are perfect examples of miscegenation between Mayas and Spaniards (pure-blooded Mayas are now virtually only to be found in the jungles of Chiapas: the Lacandons). They are meticulously clean and neat, civilized and courteous; they wear plain white shirts over straight white trousers, while their wives are wrapped in *huipils* with borders richly embroidered in red, orange or blue. At night, when the silence around the ruins of Chichén Itzá is broken only by the monotonous and dreary croaking of toads, they meet together in the courtyards of their houses, in front of the church, under palm trees standing out motionless against the sky. It is thought today that the Maya civilization is one of the two major branches of pre-Columbian civilization – the other being the Nahuatl, to be found in such towns as Teotihuacán and Tula. The Aztecs who ruled Mexico and Central America at the time of the Spanish conquest had created and consolidated their empire in a relatively short time, for the foundation of Tenochtitlán (now Mexico City) only dates back to 1325, and the conquest was in 1521. But it was obvious that the Mayas and Nahuatls were only the heirs of civilizations dating back to 2000 B.C. The archaeological site of Cuicuilco in the Mexico Valley, for instance, is far older than the one at Teotihuacán, and its architecture was already remarkable. The appearance of advanced civilizations in the Mexico Valley was no sudden thing, but the fruit of a long period of development. The Aztecs, the last to arrive, were looked on by the other peoples on the Agusco plateau as 'people without faces', for though they too spoke the Nahuatl language, the Aztecs did not really have any culture of their own.

*

The fate of Mexico, and indeed of all Spanish America, almost took a different turn on the night of 1 July 1520, the famous *noche triste*.* Cortés and his troops, surrounded in Tenochtitlán, were beseiged by thousands of Aztecs, and only just managed to escape by following an unguarded path under the waterfalls to the bank of Lake Texcoco. Cortés lost half his men, and seemed certain of defeat. The planning of this successful counter-offensive was the work of one man – Cuauhtemoc, deputizing for the imprisoned emperor, Montezuma. In the whole history of the Spanish conquest it is the only instance of a serious and seemingly final defeat inflicted on the European soldiers. Cortés was paying dearly for the massacre his lieutenant Alvarado had inflicted on all the natives taking part in a ceremony in the great temple (*teocalli*) of the Aztec capital. It is easy to see why the name of Cuauhtemoc (whose ashes were thrown to the winds some years later by Cortés when he at last captured him) has come down the ages.

It was by way of Mexico that Spain really got its foothold in the American continent. Had Cortés failed, it would have marked the failure of the whole attempt at colonization. 'In the conquest of Mexico,' wrote Zabre, the historian, 'what is surprising is that this gigantic undertaking should have been successful given the very poor means at Cortés's disposal. Many explanations have been suggested for this quasi-miracle: the genius of Cortés, his talents as a conqueror, an organizer, a politician and a soldier all certainly played a part. But it must be admitted too that luck was on his side. Throughout his campaign Cortés seemed as though guided by a hand which led, protected and directed him along the safest paths.... He was among people who had the most profound fear of the supernatural and the unknown. And, finally, the weakness of Montezuma and the wars among the various local peoples were so many more factors in his favour...' Yet this 'storm which suddenly burst upon the new world' was

* Unhappy night.

very nearly stopped by the Aztec chiefs. But where Montezuma's wiliness was naïve, Cortés's was brutal. Having made
Montezuma his prisoner, Cortés had to leave Mexico again to
go and meet the Spanish troops of Velásquez whom he was
to defeat. When he got back to the Aztec capital Cortés had
an even more formidable adversary to face in the person of
Cuauhtemoc. After the weeping of the *noche triste* came the
victory of Otumba, the reconquest of Mexico, and the capture
and death of the indomitable Cuauhtemoc.

*

On the wide, rugged tableland lying between the eastern and
western Sierras Madre, the tiniest drop of water results in the
burgeoning of acacias and jujube trees, cactus and even
yuccas. The great mountain chains are difficult to cross, and
the rivers lose themselves in the loneliness without anyone
being able to see precisely where they go. The aridity is
almost total. It was the mines which first drew people here –
mines of silver, copper, iron, gold and lead. But San Luis
Potosí and Zacatecas have suffered somewhat the same fate as
the Brazilian cities of Minas Gerais, which became wealthy
and brilliant too quickly, and were almost destroyed before
finding the right balance. Monterrey, the biggest city in the
north, is an excellent example of this kind of spectacular
development: in twenty years its population trebled; before
long motels, garages, caravan sites, advertisement hoardings
and neon signs had attracted thousands of *gringo* tourists in
their rush to the south. Yet Saltillo is in fact the preferred
stopping place for tourists coming across the Rio Grande, for
though it has not the dynamism of Monterrey, it has far
more charm. Monterrey, on the other hand, has become industrialized very successfully, due to the proximity of the mines,
its own good geographical situation, the inflow of capital,
and most of all the hard work and determination of its people,
the 'Mexicans of the north'. Monterrey produces three

quarters of the country's iron and steel, and its cement works, glass-works, breweries, cigarette factories, and various food factories, make it one of the major industrial centres of Mexico. Six railway lines meet there, and its Technological Institute is as fine as any in the capital.

*

Vera Cruz, the wealthy town of the True Cross founded by Cortés, was for a long time the only port of entry to Mexico. The sixteenth-century Spaniards, Napoleon III's Frenchmen in 1862, and the Americans in 1847 and in 1917, all landed there with the same intentions, but very varying fortunes. From the low-lying, swampy and warm coast, they had to climb up the first line of hills before reaching the cold highlands and setting off to conquer Mexico. Few expeditions anywhere have been more laborious than these long and exhausting marches, on which the soldiers were totally disorientated by the wholly unexpected difficulties presented by this unknown terrain. Though centuries apart, Spanish conquerors and invaders from France and America all shared the belief that success was achieved once they came within sight of the capital. Yet that was only the beginning.

In the present century the Mexican government has tried – hitherto not very successfully – to achieve the opposite: to get those used to living on the high plateaux to settle in the warm lowlands. Other Latin American leaders have been trying to do the same thing, for the same reasons – the Bolivian government, whose problem here is similar to Mexico's, wants to foster the exodus of the Aymará peoples from the Andean highlands to the warm and fertile plains near Brazil; in both cases progress is very slow and uncertain, coming up against long-standing traditions and resistance of many kinds.

The *marcha al mar*, the move to the sea, was a slogan often heard in Mexico in the fifties, directed to settling people in the coastal areas, in the often marshy and unhealthy plains of the Huastec coast and the Pacific. The main problem of modern Mexico is in fact a simple and dramatic one. Though the population density per square mile is not a high one for Latin America, the growth rate of 3·2 per cent is considerable. The age-pyramid in Mexico is ominous: 41 per cent of the population is under fourteen. This racing birth-rate means solutions must soon be found, for such an increase in the younger generation is a two-edged weapon: it could make the Mexico of 1980 the leader of Latin America and one of the most powerful countries in the Third World; but if its government cannot create enough new jobs and raise the standards of living of the poorer classes, then it could make it one of the most deeply indebted and impoverished. To build dams and roads, to establish new industries, to diversify the economy, to increase and modernize agricultural production: all these demands are subsumed in the *marcha al mar*, and are an integral part of recent economic planning. During the past fifteen years some 30,000 kilometres of paved or asphalted roads have been laid. Mexico City now has either road or rail links with all the provinces, and the route from there to Oaxaca via Puebla is one of the finest pieces of acrobatic road-engineering in the world. A road which is perhaps the most beautiful of all Mexican roads goes from the great port of Vera Cruz to Yucatán, by way of Villahermosa and Ciudad del Carmen. In 1967 Mexico had over 50,000 kilometres of roads all told, and, more important still, 41,000 of them passable in all weathers. Communications gradually being established among the various once-isolated centres of population are making agricultural development easier. In the Michoacán, for instance, the villages have increased their potato production sevenfold since the road was built. The closed-circuit economy is slowly but surely emerging from the confines of the local market-town or commune. In 1946 a Ministry of Hydraulic Resources replaced the irrigation commission founded twenty years before. From Tampico to Vera Cruz the Huastec coast looks quite different now. Though the *marcha al mar*, of which so much was hoped, did not quite fulfil its promises, it is clear today that Mexico has finally emerged from the stage of under-development characteristic of so many other Latin American countries. Between 1951 and 1961 industrial production doubled. The targets set in 1952 for 1958 were not all reached, especially those relating to port development; but thanks to its infra-structure, thanks to an intelligent oil policy and rapid industrialization, Mexico now offers conditions for economic development which are quite exceptional for Latin America.

Furthermore we see in its economy a constant tendency towards 'Mexicanization'. Back in 1917 legislation already foresaw the nationalization of land, water and minerals. Oil concessions, the laying of railways, radio and television are all exclusively state-controlled too. The result of this strict control is that the most successful development plans have been those relating to communications. With 23,000 kilometres of railway lines, Mexico has third place in Latin America, and communications among the provinces are improving as more air routes are opened up. The public companies now have 202 aircraft among them, and there are over 2,000 private planes in use by farmers.

*

Around Poza Rica the oil wells throw up their metal derricks against a background of tropical forest. Oil has become one of the essential pillars of the economy. Pemex, a nationalized firm, has been responsible since 1938 for the extraction, sale and refining of the oil, and the development of its by-products. Though Mexican users are not always over-enthusiastic over the petrol Pemex distributes, oil production nevertheless represents an appreciable part of the nation's total consumption. In 1962 oil accounted for 90 per cent of

Mexico's power consumption, while coal consumption lagged far behind (in France, for instance, an average of 1,340 kilos of coal per head per year is consumed, whereas in Mexico the figure is only 45 kilos). By 1921 Mexico was already the world's second largest oil producer. When the industry was nationalized in 1938 there were four major production areas: Tampico-Panuco, Faja de Oro, Poza Rica and Tehuantepec. Other zones were prospected and gradually brought into production: the north east (mainly for gas), the northern belt of the Faja de Oro, Vera Cruz since 1953, and the Tabasco area where there are large deposits of gas. The heart of the oil industry remains Tampico. The first well was successfully drilled west of the town in 1901 and it was not long before the importance of these new oilfields was recognized by the American and English oil companies. Foreign capital poured in, mainly into two zones: the country behind Tampico, and the Tuxpan area 150 kilometres to the south. In 1904 Mexico exported 221,000 barrels, and in 1910, 13 million barrels. Before the 1914–18 war exports had risen to 25 million barrels, and then, after a slight fall, rose again until 1921, a record year, when they reached 193 million, 25 per cent of the entire world production. From 1921 onwards production and exports fell, and by 1929, Mexico was exporting less than 45 million barrels (Texas in that year produced 297 million). In 1931 Mexico was producing only 2.4 per cent of the world's total. One of the reasons for this decline was the behaviour of the foreign companies who were not anxious to continue exploiting areas as yet undeveloped. In 1938 the property of foreign firms was nationalized by the Mexican government of Lázaro Cárdenas. For years the oil companies had been uneasily watching the programme of social reform, and their hesitation in developing new oilfields was explained in terms of a fear that it would not pay them to do so. Social conflict became more and more frequent. In 1938 they agreed to increase wages at the government's insistence, but refused to allow the workers any share in the profits : this was the spark that led to nationalization.

Oil still held first place in the national economy, and since the formation of Pemex, it has been politically important as well. In 1961 Pemex had a turnover of 460 million dollars, and the firm's autonomous budget represented three quarters of that of the whole Mexican Federation. The refineries were processing 335,000 barrels a day (Tampico, Minatitlán, Mexico City, Poza Rica, and Mazatlan since 1960). During recent years Pemex has tried bit by bit to cut down on trade with the United States and make agreements with a number of other countries (the U.A.R., Germany, Italy, Japan). Agreements were also made with Bolivia, and in 1962 a programme of collaboration with Brazil, Peru and Venezuela was begun. Like Argentina, Brazil and now Venezuela, Mexico has set on foot a petro-chemicals industry, controlled and run by Pemex. In 1962 a credit of 100 million dollars was voted to permit the construction of twenty-eight new factories specializing in producing industrial nitrates, synthetic rubber, plastics, and sulphur derivates – Mexico being the world's second largest producer of sulphur.

*

The real heart of Mexico is still the same: the Aztecs' plateau of the Agusco. It begins south of the northern deserts, and extends to the steep 2,000-metre escarpments, wrapped in their layers of mist, that overhang the lowlands. For centuries it has been dominated by volcanoes, now dormant and softer in outline, but still with the same names given them by the Indians; the two most famous in eastern Mexico are close together : Popocatepetl (5,349 metres) the 'smoking mountain', and Ixtaccihuatl (5,286 metres) the 'white lady', whose names are tongue-twisters to the foreigners. This central area only accounts for 14 per cent of the country's territory, but nearly 50 per cent of the people live in it. Its rivers have formed well-defined valleys, and the variety of peoples, languages and cultures to be found there when the Spaniards came is only slowly disappearing. The American geographer Preston James distinguishes seven distinct zones of population on this central plateau, corresponding to seven river-basins: those of Mexico, Puebla, Toluca, Guanajuato, Jalisco, Aguescalientes and Morelos. Of all these, only the Mexico valley is without natural drainage to the sea. The old Aztec city of Tenochtitlán was built on an island in the centre of Lake Texcoco and linked with the mainland by causeways. The lake is almost completely dried up now, and the salt streaks give metallic gleams to this arid earth which the wind whirls in dust-storms towards the capital during the winter months. Mexican architects have to cope with ground which has been eroded and gradually the buildings are subsiding. The Fine Arts Palace, completed in 1935, has shifted a whole metre; in the city centre the old churches now stand askew; and of recent years it has been estimated that some apartment blocks have been slipping at a rate of 30 centimetres a year. To stop this disturbing process the new skyscrapers of glass, steel and concrete rising up from the Paseo de la Reforma, or the Avenida de los Insurgentes, have been built on vast jacks. Elsewhere water has been injected into the subsoil. But the only real solution is to move new districts out towards Pedregal, beyond the university centre. Pedregal at present consists mainly of luxury residences, whereas working-class housing is moving more to the north west, where the *Ciudad Satélite* looks like turning into a really spectacular development.

The magnificent university centre, thought at first to be over-ambitious, too enormous, unsuited to Mexico's true needs, is undoubtedly one of the most representative examples of modern Mexican architecture. This district between Pedregal and San Angel was covered in lava, and lava was used by the builders as their major material. The complex, housing 45,000 people – 30,000 students and 15,000 staff – in an area of some five square kilometres is, in fact, a veritable satellite town. Unlimited space was allowed for everything – including the parks and the gigantic Olympic stadium which seats 100,000 spectators. Through it runs the Avenida de los Insurgentes, and in the centre, dominating the whole bold complex, stands the ten-storey library, a gigantic, windowless cube, totally covered in brilliant mosaics.

*

Mexico City was founded in 1325 and still bears its original coat of arms: the eagle, serpent, cactus and rock. When Cortés came it must have looked very much like Venice, and was probably about the same size as Seville at that date. In 1900 it had half a million inhabitants but by 1968 the greater city area contained 6 million people. A seventh of the country's population live in the capital, and its rapid growth parallels that of the most dynamic cities in north America. The distance from the Zócalo to Chapultepec park is five kilometres – the same as from Notre Dame to the Arc de Triomphe in Paris, but the residential areas only begin past Chapultepec, out in the *lomas* * amid the hills and flowers. The Avenida de los Insurgentes, which crosses the city from north to south, branching off from the Laredo road and linking up with the road to Cuernavaca and Acapulco, is thirty kilometres long. At night, at its height of 2,300 metres, Mexico City is a glittering mass of neon lights.

The development of the capital is the most perfect and significant image of modern Mexico, a country whose expansion can be likened only to that of Japan. In 1964 the growth of the GNP in real terms reached the fantastic figure of 10 per cent. But the increase in population makes it necessary

*Low-lying hills.

to create 500,000 new jobs a year. A good sign, however, is that the average *per capita* income is over 400 dollars, there is little or no inflation, and the cost of living did not increase by more than 2·5 per cent a year between 1960 and 1965. Since 1967 twenty thousand men have been at work on the construction of an underground railway of 32 kilometres, which was opened to the public in 1970. The rolling stock is similar in type to that used in Paris and Montreal, and a contract was signed in August 1967 for three hundred carriages and locomotives to be built in France. This vast-scale operation had become absolutely imperative in a mush-room city, some areas of which still resembled gigantic build-ing sites. Mexico City already covers an area larger than Paris.

It certainly benefited from the dynamic impetus provided by 'Major' Uruchurtu, who ruled Mexico City for fourteen years as Chief of Department of the federal district. Active and enterprising, but determinedly austere, Uruchurtu ran a surgeon's knife through this city of which a great many areas still recalled the charms of colonial days. He built new avenues and widened old ones; squares were built and foun-tains put into them; lighting was modernized, and Chapul-tepec park became the object of an ambitious improvement scheme.

Old markets, picturesque undoubtedly but impractical in the extreme, were replaced by ultra-modern ones. Some remarkable museums were opened, the most spectacular of which is certainly the new national museum of anthropology in Chapultepec park, opened in 1964, as a 'monument erected by the Mexican people in honour of the magnificent cultures which flourished in the pre-Columbian epoch in places which are now part of our national territory'. There is no spot in Mexico City today more conducive to medita-tion than this: in the beautifully designed halls and court-yards of the national museum of anthropology, the two

Mexicos, old and new, come together in a perfect marrying of the treasures of pre-Columbian statuary with the bold lines of modern architecture.

'Major' Uruchurtu undoubtedly annoyed some people by closing certain late-night shows and a few discothèques. Under his watchful administration the old Tenampa and the Plaza Garibaldi where the orchestras of *mariachis** traditionally played were quite different, falling into total silence by midnight. But his fall in 1966 was ultimately a consequence of his excessive zeal and dynamism. To facilitate the building of the vast Aztec Stadium for the Olympic Games he had ordered the removal of certain tenements where squatters had settled – the usual patchwork of wooden planks and cardboard boxes, without any kind of sanitation. Some of the families thus expelled had been living there, near the university centre, for over twenty years, and since they had been paying rent, believed they had certain rights of ownership. The authorities confirmed that the land was government-owned, so the police moved in to evacuate these families by force. The whole affair caused great upheavals in the Chamber of Deputies, and 'Major' Uruchurtu was forced to resign, even though he was a member of the president's cabinet.

This incident astounded people who thought of Mexico as well-balanced politically, and ruled by an Institutional Revolutionary Party which ran on well-oiled wheels. Things were not, of course, quite so simple – in Mexico City or anywhere else – and Mexico is in any case a country abounding in paradoxes.

This dynamism, this orgy of functional architecture and brilliant frescoes, stands in contrast to the black spots in the city. The Paseo de la Reforma has its dark side; the Calzada del Niño Perdido† is well named. Though there are tens of square kilometres of beautiful *lomas*, there are an equal number of slum districts with crumbling roads which become

*See page 247.   † Street of the Lost Child.

fast-flowing canals when it rains. Mexico City shows the familiar contrast between immense wealth and immense poverty, between villas with swimming pools and adobe huts with five or six people crammed into a tiny room, between the elegant life of the *licenciados** and the utter misery of the poor who come on their knees to the porch of the most famous of all basilicas, Guadalupe.

You have only to go a few kilometres out of Mexico City to come upon Indian villages where modern comfort and hygiene are totally unknown. Yet the city itself is something unique in Latin America. Though Rio de Janeiro may be the *cidade maravilhosa*, Lima the ancient city of the kings of Spain, and Buenos Aires by far and away the largest, Mexico City has a soul of its own. Gangs of boys, from Jalisco or Michoacán, will one day leave their village and come to the capital to form another group of *mariachis*. You see them near the Tenampa : gaudily dressed, wearing wide sombreros, strumming guitars and blowing discordantly on their trumpets. It is an ancient tradition dating back, we are told, to the days of the empress Charlotte. But these *mariachi* bands have more to them than just the music which veers between the wildly happy and the wildly sad : it is the joys and sorrows of the people from the very heart of the Mexican countryside that they are pouring out into the night.

Mexico City is one of the leading intellectual, artistic and scientific cities in Latin America. Its Institute of Cardiology, directed by Ignacio Chávez, has won a worldwide reputation, and is one of the world's most important centres of study and research into heart disease.

*

Querétaro, Guadalajara, Guanajuato, Puebla, Morelia : legendary names, rich in history, follow one another along the highlands of the central plateau. Guadalajara and Puebla

* See page 264.

sprang into new life with the coming of the hydro-electric industry. Textile factories, cellulose works and canning plants have replaced the old mining industry. Cuernavaca with its jacarandas and tamarinds is only 85 kilometres south west of Mexico City; once the home of the Empress Charlotte, now a weekend resort for those who live in the capital, it is also the gateway to the south Pacific. From Mexico City you come to Cuernavaca having first gone up to the summit of a col. From Puebla the road winds down to Oaxaca and the isthmus of Tehuantepec. Mount Orizaba (5,594 metres), the highest volcano in Mexico, is a perfect cone dominating the chaotic downward sloping of the *sierras* towards the green and moist depths of Chiapas. Armies of giant cactus stand guard over the pink and mauve edges of the last deserts in front of Oaxaca, Mitla, the town of the dead, and Monte Albán, the capital of a civilization which flourished 400 years before Christ. The Tehuantepec Isthmus widens out to Tapachula where the rainy season brings the most apocalyptic downfalls, but by then one is really in Central America.

The violence and loneliness which characterize the Mexican landscape are reflected in the temperament of its people. No one gives a more profound insight into the soul of this people than their own poet, Octavio Paz. The Mexican, introverted, turned in upon himself, always remote, always smiling, goes forward feeling his way along the dark walls of a labyrinth leading inevitably to death. 'He goes through life,' writes Paz, 'with insolence. Between himself and reality there is an invisible but totally impassable barrier of impossibility and distance. The Mexican is always remote, remote from other people, remote from the world. Even remote from himself.' To attempt to escape from that loneliness which they inherit from their distant Indian past Mexicans fling themselves into celebrations, into noise, into distraction. Of 365 days in the year, the Mexican calendar shows 120 as holidays. Each one of these holidays is planned with the most rigorous ceremonial and care. Even in everyday life the Mexican is forever seeking to define his personality. One word sums this up : *macho*. Being a *macho* means being a man. This explains his frenzy for living, his violent and various loves, and also his indifference to death. 'The Mexican does not seek to escape death. On the contrary, he approaches it, taunts it, braves it. It is one of his favourite amusements and the most faithful of his loves.' On All Saints' Day children munch little sugar coffins under the loving gaze of their mothers. And on the island of Janitzio, near Pátzcuaro, All Souls' Day is a fantastic mixture of paganism and Catholic piety. Cakes, sweets and fruit are all placed as offerings on the crosses of the tombs, lighted by hundreds of candles, and then, at dawn, are brought back to the houses of the living. The frontier between life and death is barely perceptible. It is all one. Great disasters, mourning, even the most unjust and unexpected blows of fate are all welcomed with the same uncomplaining and dignified fatalism. Poverty too. Amid all the mass of insipid and sugary melodramas usually put out by the Mexican film industry, one film has appeared in recent years which makes no concessions of any kind, and casts a pitiless light on the despairing reality of the daily life of the poor and especially of the women, who seem always to be in mourning. Called *Raices** it shows a child, blind in one eye and forever teased by his fellows, who loses his good eye in a firework explosion. And his mother thanks God for saving her son from the curse of the half-crippled and enabling him henceforth to earn a decent living as a blind beggar. *Los Olvidados*† cynical and violent as ever, are still hurling the bodies of their murdered mates onto public rubbish dumps.... *Que viva Mexico!*

*

* Roots.
† The Forgotten Ones: title of a Buñuel film in which such an incident occurs.

Apart from Castro's Cuba, no other Latin American country
has so exalted revolution as Mexico. Revolution is a formidable and state-supported abstraction. It is present in everyday
life, in political speeches, in trade union statements. It inspires
editorials. It is in fact institutionalized and the party in power
is precisely that: the Institutional Revolutionary Party, PRI.

Many foreigners are amused by this outrageous language,
this revolutionary floweriness. Yet at first its claims were
justified. The first shots in the Mexican revolution were fired
on 20 November 1910. Chronologically it preceded the Russian revolution. It too was a social uprising. Bands of *peones*
from the *haciendas* took up arms to demand land. Emiliano
Zapata was a small farmer in the state of Morelos, closer to
the Indians on the sugar estates than to the mestizos. The
leaders of the movement – especially the austere and intellectual Madero – can have had no idea of the forces they were
unleashing when they uttered the call to revolt. But unleash
them they did: the 1910 revolution was no ordinary *pronunciamiento*, but a real uprising of the people against the
large landowners and the representatives of foreign capitalism. No such movement occurred anywhere else in Latin
America until the revolution of Fidel Castro – thus giving
Mexico fifty years' lead. But what is the situation now? The
harshest observers describe the revolutionary lyricism of
Mexico as so much verbiage, and are convinced that every
reference to 'revolution' should be replaced by the term
'counter-revolution'. More moderate critics consider that
Mexico was too early with its revolution, and is too late with
its reforms. The painter Diego Rivera, in his violent and
aggressive frescoes on the walls of the Palacio Nacional in
Mexico City, exalts the revolution, retracing the exploitation
and liberation of the Mexican people. There is a similar
audacity and turbulence in David Alfaro Siqueiros's paintings
on the façades of the university centre – veritable paeans of
praise for permanent demands and legitimate revolt. Diego

Rivera and Siqueiros are undoubtedly, together with Orozco, the most brilliant representatives of what is generally known as the Mexican school of the twentieth century, still almost unknown in Europe. Diego Rivera, born in 1886, studied in Paris at a time when artistic life there was more than usually exciting. He was a personal friend of Modigliani and visited Apollinaire, Picasso and Braque regularly. This Mexican aesthete from Montparnasse was a communist, then a Trotskyist, then an orthodox communist once more, and was eventually to die of cancer in a Moscow clinic. Siqueiros, who commanded a motorized brigade on the republican side in the Spanish civil war, is a communist too. Orozco is dead. Diego Rivera is dead. Siqueiros was imprisoned for the fiftieth time in 1965, for 'attempted social dissolution', and his imprisonment is perhaps symbolic: the men who did most in their own domain of the arts to keep alive the tradition of the great revolution of 1910 were ultimately rejected or disowned by all the new élite – apart from a handful of artists and determined idealists. If one really wanted to schematize the history of Mexico in this century, it could best be presented in the form of a sinusoidal curve: it rises from 1910 to 1920, goes down again until 1934, climbs once again from 1936 to 1942, and then falls gradually from 1944 until the present. A further rise is logically possible, and indeed a great many Mexicans feel it is likely to come soon. But the situation is rather more complex, for that curve only represents what one may call the revolutionary aspirations which Mexico has always claimed, and what was possible in 1911 or 1938 might not be so today in a totally changed international context.

*

Mexico certainly presents an extraordinary historical continuity. The 1810 revolution for independence was the forerunner of the revolution which was to drive out Porfirio Díaz a century later. Zapata, Pancho Villa, and Obregón, the leaders of the anarchistic but courageous forces of the 1910 rising, were peasant sons of peasant fathers. The heroes of the struggle for independence were country priests who were disowned by their superiors. In Venezuela, Peru, Colombia and Chile, the leaders who seized independence for South America from the hands of their Spanish masters were creoles, many of them officers and all aristocrats. In Mexico they were ordinary men. But it was the same shock that caused the downfall of Spanish dominion in Mexico as in South America: the entry of Napoleon's troops into Spain.

On 16 September 1810 Hidalgo, the village priest of Dolores, sounded the first call. He was a man of sixty, convinced by the liberal ideas of the French revolution and deeply concerned over the lives of the Indian *peones*. He was part of the Querétaro group of conspirators. The signal for the revolt was to be given during the course of December, but certain indiscretions had alerted the Spanish authorities, so Hidalgo took matters into his own hands and decided to act quickly, and unleash a movement that was, in the event, to take a direction rather different from that intended by the officers and gentlemen who had organized the Querétaro conspiracy. At the end of October groups of Indians revolted, with cries of 'Long live independence!', and captured Guanajuato, Guadalajara and Valladolid. The rising immediately took on a violent and ruthless quality; massacres, demands for money, the sacking of towns and villages, all multiplied. This guerrilla war, in which it was hard to establish what proportion was sheer banditry, spread rapidly. It was another obscure parish priest, Morelos, a friend and pupil of Hidalgo's, who stirred up the State of Guerrero, and organized the struggle against Spaniards and *gachupines** there. Now it became clearly a matter of settling long-standing racial and social accounts: the mass of the revolutionaries were Indians, and though at first the leading

*Spanish settlers.

spirits were creoles, they themselves ended by fading into the background before this gigantic demonstration of hatred by the people. But because of these hesitations and gradual defections on the part of the leaders, the Spanish repression was able to get organized and moved to the counter-attack. Hidalgo, defeated, was captured and shot at Chihuahua on 31 July 1811. Morelos carried on the torch: he was a mestizo, and though even more exhausted he still demonstrated that he was the better man of the two, both as a war leader, and as an administrator in the liberated areas. Morelos managed to hold the Spaniards at bay for nearly four years, moving from *sierra* to *sierra*, from *pueblo* to *pueblo*, cutting off all the roads round Mexico City, and even at one point looking as though he might capture it. He was in complete command of the tropical Pacific coastal area. On 6 November 1813 representatives of all the provinces that had risen met under his inspiration at Chilpancingo, and proclaimed Mexican independence. Morelos was popularly acclaimed generalissimo. Slavery was abolished, and what was perhaps most significant of all, all racial barriers were suppressed by law. Morelos went on to think in terms of agrarian reform, sharing out the large estates, and giving back to the *ejidos*, the communes, the land taken from them since the conquest. However the Spaniards, under the leadership of the dynamic Calleja, once again launched a counter-offensive. Within a matter of weeks almost all the areas liberated by Morelos had been reconquered, and the guerrillas of José Ignacio Rayón, who were Morelos's allies, forced to disperse. Morelos then took up the desperate burden of protecting the rear-guard of his retreating army. On 5 December 1815 he was ambushed at Techuacán, captured as Hidalgo had been four years earlier, and this erstwhile priest, now a revolutionary general, was shot near Mexico City. His death left the guerrillas totally disorganized; his successors fought over a power that was gradually distintegrating.

The Chilpancingo Congress was dissolved, and only one group leader continued hopelessly haunting the first battlefields of independence – Guerrero. Paradoxically it was just when the disturbances seemed to be calming down, just as the early leaders of the revolution were dead or handing themselves over to the Spanish authorities, that Spain at last accepted Mexican independence. The date of liberation was in fact brought forward, partly because of general restlessness all over the American colonies, and partly because of the weakness of the metropolitan power locked in battle with the armies of Napoleon.

*

But Mexico as it now was had little in common with the Mexico of which Hidalgo and Morelos had dreamed. The property of the Spaniards was left intact; the influence of the Church, despite its many compromises with the political power since the conquest, remained as strong as ever. Iturbide, an ambitious but a-political general, who had finally engineered the break and come to an agreement with Guerrero, published the Iguala plan in February 1821. Within six months the major towns in Mexico, apart from the capital, had accepted it. And on 24 August 1821, the new Spanish viceroy, Juan O'Donojú, gave formal recognition to Mexican independence. A governing junta set up a ruling council with Iturbide as its president, and he had himself proclaimed emperor on 18 May 1822. It was to be another two years, during which the emperor Iturbide abdicated, came back to Mexico and was executed by the republican heirs of the first revolutionaries, before a federal republic on the American model was at last proclaimed. Now, fourteen years after Hidalgo's first call to revolt, Mexico was at last free. Politically the struggle for independence had won the day; but the ideals of the pioneers had been betrayed, forgotten or misconstrued, and the new republic was a conservative one. The mass of Indians who had provided the infantry for the Mexican troops were not part of it. It was largely to improve the lot of the *peones* that Hidalgo and Morelos had fought, yet the social inequalities of 1825 were quite as appalling as those of 1809. Political power was seized by the landowners; the Church and the Army, preserving and indeed increasing their privileges, contributed to the general impoverishment of the country right up to the middle of the nineteenth century. The endless flow of *pronunciamientos* led to anarchy and left the state unable to act in face of the expansionist intentions of the U.S. In 1836 Texas revolted and seceded. The war of 1846–8 with the U.S., famous mainly for the incident of the Alamo, ended badly for Mexico which finally had to surrender Texas, California and New Mexico for good in exchange for the derisory sum of 15 million dollars. According to the Mexican historian Lucas Alemán, this dark time from the fall of the short-lived Iturbide empire to the loss by Mexico of half its territory was dominated by the personality of Santa Anna, a devious, weak and extravagant general. Neither his extravagance nor his political acrobatics are in any doubt. For instance, he had a leg he had lost at Vera Cruz buried with great pomp in the cathedral in Mexico City; and his repeated political balancing acts made it possible for him to come back to Mexico several times through the window after he had been driven out by the door. But Santa Anna's trickery is not the whole story: the incredible greed of Iturbide, the stupidity of the Church and the rivalries among the military were certainly the major factors which contributed to bringing Mexico to the verge of bankruptcy and balkanization. Then came Juárez.

*

It was an Indian, born near Oaxaca, a silent, discreet and determined lawyer, who was to save the threatened independence of Mexico. For Mexicans the name of Juárez is linked with reform – a reform which tried to erode the exorbitant privileges of the Church and destroy the last traces of the colonial past. Such reform is rightly considered by Mexicans as an essential element in their history, and in fact it represents one of the constants in Mexican political life since the beginning of the nineteenth century. Europeans remember Juárez primarily as the implacable and victorious enemy of the French troops of Bazaine, sent to Mexico by Napoleon III in an attempt to save the tottering empire of Maximilian of Austria. These two sides of Juárez's struggle were closely connected. Before his coming to power, the property of the Church represented at least a third of all Mexico's wealth. In 1855 the victory of the Reform Party (at first confused with the Liberal Party) was clearly a grave threat to the clergy. In 1855 the special ecclesiastical courts were abolished by Juárez; the Jesuits were dissolved; the anti-clerical campaign continued with a new law in 1856 which forced the clergy to sell part of their land. The Church, thus threatened, rallied to the fight, calling on conservatives, officers and large landowners, all determined to present a firm front to their common enemy, and ready to use any and every means, even treason. Religious houses were turned into arsenals. First a civil war – the so-called Three Year War – and then foreign intervention combined for a time to make the clergy hope they would succeed in defeating the anti-clericals and liberals. When the War between the States began in the U.S., it looked to Napoleon III like a chance for achieving one of the great ambitions of his reign – that of creating in Mexico a large Catholic and Latin empire which would act as a counter-balance to the Protestant and Anglo-Saxon influence of North America. The landing of Spanish, English and French troops at Vera Cruz in 1861 and 1862 enabled the Mexican conservative and clerical alliance to become entrenched behind this foreign power. The French army besieged Puebla for a year, finally capturing it, and marched upon Mexico City. Juárez withdrew northward to San Luis Potosí at first, and then closer to the U.S. border.

In Mexico City a triumvirate, symbolically presided over by Archbishop Antonio de Labastide, declared Maximilian von Habsburg emperor of Mexico. This curious interlude lasted for three years. Maximilian, filled with good intentions, tried to reconcile conservatives and liberals. But the conservatives and the clergy, whose first concern was always to preserve their own privileges, abandoned their monarch with his liberalizing tendencies, and the liberals remained loyal to the obstinate Juárez. In 1866, with the end of the Civil War, America was in a position to intervene diplomatically (under the guise of the Monroe doctrine) and militarily (by giving arms to Juárez). The tragic end of the episode took place at Querétaro where Maximilian, betrayed, beaten and taken prisoner, was shot on 19 June 1867. Juárez, returning triumphantly to Mexico City in July, did not survive his victory long enough to get his reform laws properly established. Having been himself unable to read up to the age of twelve, he realized the urgency of the fight for literacy, and he decreed that every village and every *hacienda* must have its school, and a national training school was formed to prepare the teachers. But Juárez died in 1872.

*

In the forty years following the revolution only one name stands out : Porfirio Díaz. Díaz's dictatorship in fact lasted for thirty-five years. He seized the presidency after a revolt based on the slogan of 'No re-election'. Once in power, Díaz stuck to it, and was re-elected several times. Only from 1880 to 1884 was he *not* president, and then he remained a minister and a puller of strings behind the scenes, while his friend Manuel González was actually president. Not until the uprising of 1910 was this old man of eighty-eight finally removed from the dictator's seat to which he clung. Photographs of Díaz, taken around 1900, show a man wearing splendid uniform, laden with decorations, wearing a plumed hat, with a lively gaze and a flourishing moustache. He was a liberal who had fought bravely alongside Juárez against French intervention. But as the years passed, he gradually came to see himself as the executor of the will of the people, and thus naturally developed into an absolute ruler. Francisco Madero has said of him: 'He had no political passion; his enemies were merely those who stood in his way, and his friends those who supported his plans.'

Politically, Díaz's regime was a dictatorship determinedly ignoring the social problems smouldering in the country until they burst into the explosion of 1910. But economically this cazique who thought himself something of a scientist undoubtedly assisted Mexico to lay the foundations for a modern economy. From 1894 onwards there was a balanced budget for the first time since independence. In 1876 there were 600 kilometres of railway lines and by 1911 there were 24,700. Foreign trade increased tenfold. Mining and industry advanced fantastically. But there was a darker side to the picture, for this economic development was only possible because of enormous investments of foreign, and especially American, capital. In 1910, U.S. investment alone was over a thousand million dollars – in other words, more than all the capital in Mexico. When the Díaz dictatorship came to its end most of the industrial enterprises, the oil deposits and other mineral wealth belonged to foreigners. Of 15 million Mexicans, 10 million owned no land at all, though 75 per cent of the population were country-dwellers. It was first and foremost these economic and social structures that were to be shattered by the revolution.

*

The political movement launched by Francisco Madero in November 1910 against the further re-election of Porfirio

Díaz was rapidly and easily victorious. Led in the north by the legendary horse-thief, Pancho Villa, guerrilla warfare gradually spread over the country like a trail of gunpowder and Porfirio Díaz had to resign himself to becoming an exile in Paris. In November 1911 Madero was elected President. Forces held in check for too long exploded, and Mexico entered upon another decade of violence, war and bloodshed. General Huerta had Madero killed, and then was himself driven out in his turn. The troops of Carranza, Obregón, Pancho Villa and Emiliano Zapata were all swept into a raging whirlwind in which it was hard to distinguish any remains of the ideals that had inspired the early months of the revolution. Massacres, shootings, demands for money, looting – there was chaos everywhere. As in 1810, the revolution soon became a frantic revolt by Indian and mestizo masses against all landowners, clergy, government agents and foreigners.

The 1917 Constitution seemed to satisfy the deepest longings of both peasants and workers. Article 27 declared that ownership of all lands and minerals reverted to the state. Article 123 stated the principle that there must be a code of work enforcing a minimum wage, an eight hour day and safeguards for farm workers. But these two basic points were in fact never actually put into effect by the Carranza government. Zapata was murdered in an ambush, and a large number of the tradeunion leaders were killed. One last burst of violence brought Carranza's rule to an end; he was murdered in his turn in the country outside Puebla, and Alvaro Obregón, the last of the great popular revolutionary leaders, became president in November 1920.

This date marked the official end of the killing, but rebuilding this devastated country was slow work indeed. In particular the reforms sought by the real leaders of the 1910 movement – a repetition of those demanded in 1810 – never got past the planning level. In 1930 Mexico was still a country

where large landowners called the tune, and the social inequalities were appalling.

*

There is of course a great temptation to explain the swings in
Mexican politics in terms of coming and going between left
and right. But in Mexico the traditional western ideas of
left and right are not an accurate description of the subtle
interplay of forces and the deepest sentiments of the
people. *Tierra y libertad*, Land and Liberty! – that was the
war-cry of Zapata's men. Agrarian reform was the overriding
concern of the most popular, and probably most disinterested,
of the leaders of the 1910 revolution. There could be no doubt
that Zapata's heart was on the left. But as for Carranza,
Calles or Obregón? Yes and no. It is hard to be sure. Some
Mexican historians liken Calles to Stalin – others to Combes
in France. After so many bloody and turbulent years of revolution, Mexico's prime need was certainly for stability and
order. Obregón and Calles, the two presidents who ruled from
1920 to 1929, ensured that order by the most energetic action.
They mercilessly put down all attempts at *pronunciamientos*,
though both were in fact liberal men. But their first priority
was to fight against the power of the Church and restrict the
privileges of the military – neither objective to be gained
without meeting great resistance, and a lot of political
manoeuvring. François Weymuller rightly says in his *Histoire
du Mexique* that 'the presidential dictatorship after 1920 was
supported by the military, and moderated by the principle of
non-re-election and by assassination'.

After Obregón's defeat in 1928, the anti-clerical policy of
his successor, Calles, resulted in bitter conflicts and the revolt
of the *cristeros*. The number of priests was greatly restricted
and they were forbidden to wear clerical dress. After
Obregón's tragic death, in fact, Calles managed to keep a close
control on Mexican political life. To help him he could de-

pend on the workers' and peasants' trade unions, especially the CROM (Regional Confederation of Mexican Workers) founded in 1918. The better to secure his power, he created the National Revolutionary Party, with a party machine which could ensure the election of the presidential candidate chosen by the ruling group. Calles's party later changed its name to the PRI, Institutional Revolutionary Party, but its objectives are still the same. Since his day there has never been an instance of a candidate chosen by the PRI failing to win a presidential election. The principle of non-re-election, so dear to the heart of Madero the idealist, has been twisted into something very different from what he meant by it. Yet it can happen that a new president, groomed for the job and carried to the presidential palace in a chair above the heads of an enthusiastic crowd, does not do what is expected of him. That was what happened in 1934, with Lázaro Cárdenas.

*

Cárdenas was the candidate both of the Revolutionary Party and of the Calles clique. He was elected without much of a fight for the period from December 1934 to December 1940, but immediately made it clear that he wished to do his own governing. The first innovation was his presentation of a sexennial plan – a plan for speeding up the distribution of land to the Indians, for improving methods of aiding the *ejidos*, for the development of agricultural credit. Cárdenas was as good as his word : from 1934 to 1938 his government distributed over 15 million hectares of land to more than 800,000 penniless small farmers. To get some idea of the magnitude of this, it must be noted that in an earlier four-year period, from 1920 to 1924, the Obregón government succeeded in distributing no more than 1·6 million hectares. A president was for the first time really putting Article 27 of the 1917 constitution into effect, confirming that the nation alone owns the whole of the nation's land. Cárdenas, in thus satisfying the Mexican peasants' everlasting thirst for land, was carrying out a kind of tropical 'new deal' which made it possible to lay the foundations for a genuine political democracy. 'The Mexican people,' he said one day, 'must learn that there can be government without terrorization.' Faced with violent opposition at home and the hostility of foreign businessmen, especially from the U.S., who looked back longingly to the happy days of Díaz, Cárdenas did his best to keep in direct touch with the people. Every day there was an hour when the telegraph service could be used without charge by any citizen – and especially anyone poor – who wanted to put his complaints to the far-away *Casa presidencial*. In 1936 Cárdenas got rid of Calles, sending him under guard to the U.S. and the Callist machine which had worked so marvellously for ten years began to break down. Cárdenas, though a left-wing liberal, many of whose colleagues had definite Marxist sympathies and tendencies, put a stop to the fierce wave of anti-clericalism unleashed by his predecessors. He permitted the sale and distribution of religious propaganda leaflets, and forbade the attacks on the Church which had become the norm in state schools. On the international level, Cardenas's Mexico was a model democracy. It took a first stand against Mussolini's fascism and Hitler's nazism, and opened its gates wide to refugees from Spain after Franco's victory. Cárdenas's greatest stroke was in March 1938, when he nationalized oil and expropriated the foreign oil companies. All over the country there was rejoicing; it is said that peasants came from their far-off villages to the capital to bring their mite – perhaps a chicken – to the president's house to contribute to the payment of Mexico's vast debt. There was a strong rumour that the U.S. was not really hostile to the step taken by Cárdenas, and that the nationalization of Mexican oil was a surgical operation carried out under American anaesthesia. It must be admitted that nationalization was not part of Cárdenas's six-year plan as announced when he first became president. He was forced into it, though his decision was due more to a wish to have Mexico's political sovereignty accepted than to any purely economic reason. But in fact the oil companies had for two years been waging a small war of attrition against the Cárdenas government, above all refusing to negotiate any collective bargain with the unions. They also refused to carry out the decisions given by the Mexican supreme court. Roosevelt had been in power in Washington since 1933, and the U.S. ambassador to Mexico was a personal friend of Cárdenas. The Washington government, however, subjected to fierce pressure from the oil lobbies, announced economic sanctions against Mexico, and demanded the payment in full of the debts incurred by its expropriations. After March 1938 the American companies, especially the Sinclair Oil Co., threatened to let Mexico 'drown in its own oil', organizing a boycott on sales. Only after the boycott was broken by the purchase of Mexican oil by Nazi Germany did the American companies agree to negotiate on the matter of compensation. Cárdenas, who wanted Mexico to become a genuinely socialist state, was thus obliged to appeal to a totalitarian fascist state in order to save his country – and this painful incident left profound traces on the Mexican intelligentsia.

In a sense, indeed, Cárdenas was a forerunner of Castro. He was forced into adopting international positions not of his choosing by pressure and lack of understanding from U.S. economic interests. However, Cárdenas was doubly lucky in 1938: first, in that Washington was officially practising a 'good neighbour policy' with Latin America under the Roosevelt administration, and then in that his nationalization speech was barely noticed outside the American continent. From 1958 to 1960 Fidel Castro on the other hand had to deal with a Republican administration dominated by financial lobbies, and his every slightest word echoed round the four corners of the world. In 1940 Cárdenas quietly retired as his

term came to an end. He set off for the Michoacán countryside where he was born and until 1959 he scrupulously ob-
served the rule of non-re-election. Nor did he try to exert any
influence on Mexican political life. He ultimately emerged
from his retreat only to proclaim publicly his sympathy with
the Castro regime. Settled in his rancho, 1,000 kilometres from
Mexico City, Cárdenas looked, listened and judged. His prestige remains considerable.

*

Following Cárdenas the decline was slow and imperceptible.
The machine continued its forward thrust in the early period
of Ávila Camacho's presidency; the battle against illiteracy
waged by Cárdenas went on, due in large part to the efforts of
Torres Bodet, the Minister of Education. But the distribution
of land to the small farmers, and the formation of the *ejidos*
slowed down a lot between 1940 and 1946. It soon became
clear that the Camacho government was trying to get the
support of the new industrial and commercial bourgeoisie, and
no longer concentrating on the effort to raise the standard of
living of the poorer classes. Ávila Camacho was a general, one
of the last of the military 'old guard'. Cynical popular writers
in Mexico City record this sally attributed to Camacho's
brother: 'If you build a road costing 75,000 pesos, and pocket
1,000 pesos, everyone is shocked and scandalized. But if you
build one costing 75 million, and take a rake-off of a million,
no one even notices ...'

Under Camacho the soldier, the Mexican revolution became
more or less inactive. But under the civilian Miguel Alemán
it decayed into a gradual and open corruption. Alemán's
arrival at the presidency in 1946, with his fine bearing and
eloquent speech-making, marked the handing over of power
from the military to the *licenciados* – these being generally
doctors of law, but in any case, men who have done post-
graduate studies. Before he became President, Miguel Alemán

was governor of Vera Cruz state. The Mexican papers published stories of embezzlement and corruption by officials in which the government had been involved. One review was even so bold as to tell the whole story of the tax situation in Vera Cruz, and the very next day had its presses destroyed by an unknown gang, while the editor of another opposition paper was murdered. After that the papers became more circumspect. President Alemán launched upon an ambitious plan of public works and spectacular achievements. The *políticos* around him developed a taste for country estates, especially, it seemed, where there was a government plan for irrigating the area, or building new roads. Alemán made frequent tours round the provinces, and whichever town he was visiting, the press would end the account of the visit with the same sentence: 'The president then withdrew to his nearest ranch.' Those were great days for the Mexican *carpas* – theatres set up under canvas or in some kind of hut – where singers from the capital would tear all the politicians to bits with their jokes and puns, and the President always provided them with fuel for endless satire and attack. But in the end Mexicans became too sick to respond with wit or astonishment any more. None the less, at the end of his term, Alemán presented an economic balance sheet that was objectively very impressive. 'Alemán,' said people, 'is a bit like Adhemar de Barros in São Paulo. He has stolen a lot, as he did, but he has built a lot too. Which is better? A dynamic and not quite honest president, or an honest but ineffective one?' Certainly great numbers of roads were built in Mexico between 1946 and 1951, and it was during Alemán's presidency that the University of Mexico was begun. In a way Alemán did a lot to speed up the pace of industrialization in the country.

The judgement of the Revolutionary Party, however, was different. Alemán was in fact hoping for re-election – which would have once again upset a basic principle of present-day Mexican political life. The caziques of the Institutional Revo-

lutionary Party met in the autumn of 1951 to choose someone to be president from 1952 to 1958. Arguments raged.
But the Alemán clique at once succeeded in getting their man
accepted – a man who looked likely to carry on along the
lines of his predecessor, being one of his closest colleagues.
The papers had little more to say about him, thinking him as
good as elected.

*

The candidate chosen was Ruiz Cortines, formerly governor
of Vera Cruz, like Alemán, and Minister of the Interior.
There were four candidates in the election on 6 July 1952:
Ruiz Cortines, competing under the PRI label; Lombardo
Toledano, head of the Popular Party and an influential union
leader; González Luna, supported by right-wing Catholics
and those of fascist leanings, and General Henríque Guzmán,
who was said to have the sympathy and support of Lázaro
Cárdenas. There was an unusually large poll and the first
results were inconclusive. Toledano, Ruiz Cortines and Henríque Guzmán all declared with equal certainty that they
were going to win. There was great excitement, with rowdy
meetings, troops called in, and hundreds of people arrested.
Ruiz Cortines was declared the victor, and calm was slowly
restored.

Then accusations against Alemán began coming to light.
One of the best-known people in the PRI, General Francisco
Aguilar, publicly castigated Alemán and his friends for
having made large fortunes and deposited hundreds of millions of dollars in Canadian and Swiss banks. Other equally
circumstantial allegations were made against several of
Alemán's ministers – with a publicity that would have been
unthinkable a few years before. They were clear indications
that people wanted a new style of government heralding a
period of austerity. Ruiz Cortines, shy, self-effacing and

modest, had never been part of the spectacular clique of his predecessor : more of an administrator than a politician, he certainly represented no real danger in the opinion of the super-dynamic Alemanist *caballeros* who had for six years been skimming the cream from the country's finances. The efficient and honest former governor of Vera Cruz was both a representative of compromise and a badly-needed new broom. Supported by the communists, Lombardo Toledano's trade unionists and the friends of Cárdenas, Ruiz Cortines set about sweeping out the stables of the Zócalo. But it was clear from his record that he would always be more of an executive and a competent administrator than a leader of men.

He had started work at the age of sixteen as apprentice in a bookshop. When Mexico was submerged in the 1910 revolution he enlisted in the army and served for eight years, but most of that time he spent as a clerk or accountant. After the revolution, he patiently worked his way up the stages of civil administration, and thirteen years later was directing the statistical bureau. In 1936, this punctilious official made the acquaintance of the young and brilliant Miguel Alemán. Ruiz Cortines' political fortunes were thus beginning. He became an adviser in the office of Alemán when he was Minister of the Interior, and then, thanks to Alemán's influence, governor of Vera Cruz. But Cortines did not alter his own way of living as a low-paid official. In Jalapa, the capital of Vera Cruz state, he settled in a small cottage, and went on foot each morning to his office. In Mexico City, where he went as Minister of the Interior in 1948, he rented a flat in a quiet district, and fulfilled this key position with the same discretion and absence of ambition he had shown in every other function.

On 1 December 1952 he took over the Presidency and made a statement which removed the smiles from the faces of the Alemanists : 'We must put an end to government protection of monopolies. I shall take a hard line with all dishonesty in officials.' That same day, when he announced the composition of his cabinet, it was realized that it did not contain a single member of the Alemán clique. A few days later he published a complete inventory of his personal goods, and demanded that the other 250,000 state employees do the same, making it clear that their wealth would be re-examined when they lost their official positions. His Minister of Communications received an invoice for a 100-kilometre road ordered by the previous administration : Ruiz Cortines went to see it and found not a trace of any roadworks. He fined the unscrupulous contractor a sum equal to three times the payment he was demanding. As good as his word, Ruiz Cortines also set to work on the monopolies. One of the most lucrative was Jorge Pascual's petrol business. Pascual was removed, as was another of Alemán's friends, Antonio Díaz Lombardo, director of bus companies and social security services. On the international level Ruiz Cortines tried to loosen the close bonds linking Mexico to her powerful northern neighbour. Porfirio Díaz had said, long ago, 'Poor Mexico – so far from God and so near to the United States !' The Minister of Foreign Affairs appointed by Ruiz Cortines, Padilla Nervo, was a friend of Cárdenas, and Mexico's voice would now be heard in meetings of the OAS (especially in Caracas in February 1954) or the United Nations, demanding more justice and more consideration of the real needs of Latin America.

*

The wave of austerity lasted for about two years and then lost its momentum. Stories of *mordida* began once again to go the rounds, both on the ministerial back-stairs and in the streets – *mordida* being the equivalent of 'perks', in this case a commission taken by officials as their reward for services rendered. It is not a specially Mexican phenomenon. In Venezuela, at that time, foreign firms allowed for the considerable percentages they would have to pay to the senior officers and ministers of Pérez Jiménez when working out their budgets. But in Mexico the corruption seemed more damaging than anywhere else, because the chances spoiled by it were correspondingly greater. In the final years of the Ruiz Cortines government, however, the general atmosphere was still so very austere and honest as to make it inevitable in everyone's eyes for there to be some reaction against it.

The handing over of the Presidency from Ruiz Cortines to López Mateos in 1958 was uneventful; once again, the PRI had so ordered its machine as to make any unpleasant surprises impossible, and once again it was tiny nuances that made the difference. López Mateos was more dependent than Ruiz Cortines on the business middle class. In itself, the fact of a Mexican government's being able to run the country by counting on a rich national class was, and indeed still is, an encouraging phenomenon. Throughout Latin America the establishment and consolidation of a middle class and a bourgeoisie thrown up by industrialization is a very good sign. Only countries like Argentina, Brazil, Uruguay, Chile, and to a lesser extent perhaps Peru, can begin to play an effective international role because their economies are escaping – or are on the point of escaping – from the desperate situation of monoproduction.

But this development also has its negative side : generally – and Mexico is no exception – the industrial and commercial bourgeoisie becomes a tool or ally of foreign interests, which in Mexico means North American economic and financial interests. The stringency of Ruiz Cortines's government, on which great stress was laid in the American press, might have reassured the directors of the big American companies, but in fact it alarmed them. The return to economic liberalism in 1958 assisted the growing influx of American capital into Mexico. However, that liberalism was modified by certain authoritarian state measures, such as the nationalization of the electrical industry and petro-chemicals; and the Mexicanization of the mines was intensified.

López Mateos was born on 26 May 1910 at Atizapán in Mexico State. After studying at the French college of Toluca, where he took his baccalaureate, he went to live in the capital, got a law degree, and set up shop as a barrister. Thus this president – exactly the same age as the revolution itself – was first and foremost what is known as a *licenciado*. His political career followed a more or less traditional pattern, in that his friends and relations played as important a part in it as his own will to succeed. López Mateos was undoubtedly a man whose whole education had been in the hothouse of the PRI. As Private Secretary of the Governor of Mexico State, then adviser to the president of the PRI a few months later, this austere and hard-working young lawyer was on the right road. He held jobs as diverse as that of agent of the Republic in Toluca, and secretary general of the teachers' trade union. For some time he was a junior director of the Fine Arts Department; he was a member of the Mexican delegation at the conference of OAS Foreign Ministers in Washington in 1951. A senator in 1946, secretary general of the PRI in 1952 during the delicate manoeuvrings which preceded the removal of the Alemán clique, López Mateos was called on once more by Ruiz Cortines to direct the committee of the economic development plan. Thus he was definitely a party man, but it was a party identified with the government, the revolution and the State. López Mateos described himself as a progressive.

*

In fact the López Mateos government had a hard time striking a balance. Liberalism in economic affairs had made it possible for foreign capital to get a firmer grip than ever. One of the most outstanding and dynamic members of the López Mateos government was Torres Bodet, the Minister of Education.

Earlier a minister in the Avila Camacho government, once Director General of UNESCO, and a former ambassador to Paris, Jaime Torres Bodet, a poet and man of letters, decided to tackle the illiteracy problem with renewed energy. In 1944 he had produced the slogan: 'Every citizen should be the teacher of another citizen'. In 1962 his ministry's budget represented 20 per cent of the whole – which would have been a high proportion anywhere in the world, not only in Latin America. His eleven-year plan got under way in 1959. 'In 1970,' he said, 'we must have classrooms for seven and a half million children of school age.' Already 20 million textbooks were being handed out free by the government, from which young Mexicans could learn the history of their country in an objective fashion. They taught that the rebels who determined the Texan secession had different customs and traditions from those of the Mexicans, and President Santa Anna was described as 'a despotic dictator' – which is the unadorned historical truth. Thirty factories were given orders to make prefabricated schoolhouses for the country, and in 1962 2,000 schools of this kind were opened, each consisting of one large teaching hall and living quarters for five teachers.

López Mateos sought for a middle path between those who still demanded Cárdenas and his programme, and those who supported the *status quo*. The former were not a large group, being influential mainly in university circles. They called for a vigorous return to agrarian reform, and equally vigorous measures to free the Mexican economy from the grip of North American capital. López Mateos's decision to nationalize electricity therefore looked like a pledge to the left wing, but he tried at the same time to reassure the U.S. His government on several occasions stepped in firmly to stop railwaymen's strikes, and set its face against the rebirth of any genuine trade unions – those in existence being rotten with corruption and lack of organization. From this standpoint it was clear that a democratization of the unions was a *sine qua non* if the nation's revolutionary ideals were to be brought alive again. The more sophisticated of the proletariat, as well as railwaymen, electricians, telephone employees and teachers, were becoming more and more dissatisfied with the paralyzing dictatorship exercised by the middle-class pundits of the official unions. Ruiz Cortines had used force in the last years of his term to repress the movement to democratize and clean up the unions. López Mateos made no change.

*

The bitter struggle between national industrial development and private enterprise was nothing new. Even during the Alemán government it can be said that Mexico was trying to let capitalism exist alongside socialism. Agrarian reform, though slowed down somewhat, never actually came to a standstill. It developed fastest under Cárdenas but since 1940 nearly another 15 million hectares had been given or given back to the *ejidos*. Alemán had attempted to change the basic direction of the agrarian revolution by saying: 'The agricultural revolution, historically considered, is no more than the incorporation of agriculture into the capitalist economy.' But at least he did nothing to stop it.

This land reform even recovered some of its vigour. The terms of the law were respected : according to the decrees for agrarian reform, no individual might own more than 150 hectares of irrigated land, or more than 300 of non-irrigated land; pastureland might be owned up to 5,000 hectares. But it was also – and indeed chiefly – a matter of redistributing the common land. Each family around the *ejido* got an allotment of up to 2 hectares of irrigated and 4 to 5 of non-irrigated land, and one part of the *ejido* was shared by the community as pasturage. Thus this institution which existed long before the Spanish conquest was once again coming into being. In 1945 there were some million small landowners, and about 1,400,000 *ejidatarios*. To realize the revolution this represents one has only to compare these figures with those of 1906, when 97 per cent of all land belonged to a thousand large landowners, and 830 landowners employed the incredible number of 3,120,000 labourers. This reform, speeded up by Cárdenas, and later carried on with greater or less enthusiasm by his successors, did not of course take place without some difficulties and injustices. The share of the irrigated land handed over to the *ejidos* in particular tended to diminish after fifteen years or so, and the granting of credit to farmers caused endless controversy. Agricultural credit was organized by the State, and the delays in administration were perhaps more keenly felt in this sector than any other. The National Bank of Agricultural Credit and the National Bank of Ejidal Credit were to run the operation.* Schools were set up in Chapingo, Narro, Ciudad Juárez and in Sonora state to popularize modern farming methods. Education, land reform, technological advance, irrigation – so many essential elements that no government could afford to neglect, for 24 million Mexicans, more than half the total population, live and work in the country. Yet farm wages are still on average six times lower than those in other sectors of the country's economic activity.

As in 1910 the problem of the land was still, and had to be, in the front line of the government's priorities. Since 1917 forty million hectares had in fact been distributed, but a great many Mexicans, notably Jesús Silva Herzog, still consider that the revolutionary attempt to bring back a truly collective form of farming has failed. Though this is undoubtedly often to be put down to lack of credit and technical aids, it is also, and even more, due to the fact that the large landowners have so often (especially in Sonora and Sinaloa states) been able to reconstruct vast new estates. It would appear, in fact, that 30 percent of the *ejido* lands are not being used to the profit of

* These two have since merged under the name Banco Nacional Agropecuario.

their real owners at all. It was in an attempt to stop this trend that the Díaz Ordaz government in 1967 proclaimed a return to the agrarian collectivism of the first stage of the revolution.

The massive return to land distribution by the López Mateos government was ultimately only a palliative; it affected mainly the semi-desert pasturelands of the north where few people lived, and consequently few people bene-fited. Any serious study of the real results of Mexican land reform is very difficult, given the immense variety of the land, the greater or less importance of irrigation, closeness to roads, and the great variations in yield as between tropical and cooler areas.

As Claude Bataillon points out, 'one cannot either con-demn or approve the "capitalist" deviations of the *ejidal* farming system *en bloc*. It is clear that the moment they get beyond the stage of subsistence farming, the *ejidatarios* need credits: the amounts granted by the Banco Ejidal are inade-quate, and the cumbrousness of the administrative machinery limits their effectiveness still further. One can hardly blame those *ejidatarios* who have good land and enough of it for securing their own prosperity as best they can: thus it is inevitable that the most enterprising growers should race ahead, and try to increase the land they have to cultivate. Yet it is easy to see that it is only a step from flexibility to abuse...'

Thanks to this system Mexico is continually increasing her exports of agricultural produce to the U.S. It is doubtful therefore whether any attempt will be made to re-mould the structures in the richest areas for the sake of greater social justice. Yet the peasant population in the poorer areas is grow-ing fast, especially in the centre of the country where maize is grown. Though the rural exodus is large, it does not get rid of the whole of the manpower surplus. Absolutely speak-ing this rural labour force grew from 3·8 million in 1940 to 6·3 million in 1960. The number of farm workers not owning any land has also increased (under two million in 1940 and over 3 million in 1960). The fact of an ever-growing rural proletariat is undeniable, and to make matters worse these peasants who have no land and no hope of ever having any land are young – 65 per cent of farm workers are under thirty-five. In such conditions, it is evident that the dangers of social tension are increasing and pose a problem which the government will have to face.

*

The conflict between private enterprise and national investment has become one of the essential features of modern Mexico. The fear of revolutionary contagion will often lead to American or other foreign firms making concessions and compromises of one kind or another. A law passed in 1960 ruled that Mexicans must hold the majority of shares in all the country's mining enterprises. Between now and 1985 Mexican silver production, the largest in the world, will also come into Mexican hands. But the line between state control and freedom is as hard to define in Mexico as anywhere else. Some private enterprises which claim to be Mexican and national in fact represent foreign interests. President López Mateos favoured the establishment of a national workers' centre, combining the unions for electricians, textile workers and sugar cane producers (with 375,000 members). This national centre was intended to 'fight against communism while at the same time liberating the working class from political or economic compromises with capitalism'. This idea of a union 'third force' was symbolic of the way the López Mateos government was moving, avoiding any Castroist or communist influence, while also keeping its distance from big business. But Cárdenas's men obviously wanted something more : they wanted the total eviction of the American monopolies. They pointed out that foreign investment had reached a fantastic level – estimated in 1945 at 18 million dollars, in 1958 it had reached 112 million, and by 1961 the total was reckoned to be two thousand million. And of this the U.S.A.'s share had continued to grow : in 1938 it had been 60 per cent, while in 1962 it was over 82 per cent. 'Economically we are a colony of the United States,' declared Cárdenas's friends, who would have preferred closer ties with the neutralist powers of the Third World, and above all with Cuba.

The López Mateos government banned Lázaro Cárdenas from going to Cuba to demonstrate his solidarity with Castro after the American military intervention of April 1961. When he learnt of this decision in Mexico City, the old general took a taxi down to the Plaza del Zócalo and gave an impromptu speech to the excited crowd who gathered round him. Yet it was this same government which authorized a Latin American conference on national sovereignty, with Chinese, French, Italian, Soviet and African delegates taking part. Thus the balancing act going on in the economy was also being carefully applied to foreign policy. And up to now there has been nothing to suggest that the wish to keep a balance is likely to change. The machine of the revolutionary party is still powerful and efficient enough to prevent any attempt to establish a 'pure and strict' republic as certain individualists would like.

There are not many communists in Mexico. The Mexican CP was founded in 1919, but has, since its inception, been racked by a number of internal crises. It cannot put candidates forward for election, because the federal electoral law stipulates that a party must have at least 75,000 members before it can be registered. In 1951 the CP supported Lombardo Toledano, the Popular Party candidate. The orthodox far left was not, it seems, very fierce. The impact of the Cuban revolution and the revision it imposed of old dusty party doctrine had a similar effect in Mexico to that in other neighbouring countries. Communists loyal to the Moscow line were continually threatened by a revolt from their own left wing: the most genuinely revolutionary elements in the intelligentsia and the university here, as elsewhere, rallied to non-Communist Party positions (pro-Chinese, revolutionary Communists, Trotskyists, Castroists, Guevarists). The student upheavals of spring and summer 1968 showed very clearly how far behind was the pro-Soviet Mexican Communist Party. The anti-American reflex in Mexico is still very powerful (long ante-dating the Cuban revolution), and there is a great temptation among liberal intellectuals to justify automatically everything Castro may do. Significantly López Mateos, though he forced Cádenas to be discreet in his pro-Castro demonstrations, set his face against any condemnation of the Castro regime. 'Our basic principle,' he said, 'is self-determination and the sovereignty of peoples. The Cubans are free to choose what political institutions they like, and Washington has no right to interfere . . .' in this López Mateos's sympathies were with the left wing of the PRI inspired by Cárdenas rather than with the right wing restored to life at the end of 1961 by the Alemán clique in collaboration with U.S. business firms.

It became clear with the election of López Mateos and then Gustavo Díaz Ordaz that Mexico was quietly and tenaciously continuing along a well-marked road with no apparent possibility of surprises. Gustavo Díaz Ordaz, another *licenciado*, was Mexico's sixtieth president, and the twelfth since 1910. He took office on 1 December 1964.

He had been chosen on 16 November 1963 by the leaders of the PRI as their candidate and his election on 5 July 1964 by 8,391,205 votes (as against only 1,015,716 for his nearest competitor, José González Torres) was without incident. Though there could be no doubt as to the outcome of the election, Gustavo Díaz Ordaz went through all the proper motions, with a real American-type electoral campaign that took him from the north of the country to the south, setting out the major lines of his programme. He was hardly an unknown man when he was finally acclaimed as president.

Carefully nurtured by the PRI, the new president was born at San Andrés de Chalchicomula in Puebla state. The son of a farmer and a teacher in a training college, he himself studied first at Oaxaca and Guadalajara. After a course of general studies at the Oaxaca institute of arts and sciences, he went on to study law at Puebla, and got his degree at the age of 26 in 1937. But from 1932 on he worked for the department of the interior of the Puebla provincial government. First as recorder, then temporarily in charge of the Tehuacán public ministry, and finally as president of the Puebla state high court. A jurist, a university teacher, an official, a member of the Institutional Revolutionary Party – it would be impossible to find a more ideal *licenciado* than this unassuming president – whose marked Indian features were incidentally also a great reassurance to the masses of peasants.

Though it was not realized by the many foreign dignitaries invited to the inaugural ceremonies on 1 December, there could be no doubt that this new president, strengthened by fifteen years of political and administrative experience, would follow the major lines of López Mateos's policy. Under the latter's presidency Mexico, paradoxical though it may appear, had become banker to the south American continent. From 1954 to 1964, an extraordinary influx of both North American and Latin American capital had contributed to an economic and industrial development which was beginning to make Mexico something of an outsider in the Latin American family, and from one viewpoint decidedly closer to the U.S. than most of the others. Díaz Ordaz, in the first months of 1965, appeared even more resolved than López Mateos to intensify this collaboration with foreign capital. 'There is a vast field of possibilities,' he declared, 'for both public and private investment in Mexico. . . .' All indications were that the Díaz Ordaz government intended to stress economic and financial expansion and leave doctrinaire and political subtleties more in the background. It might further have been thought that the appointment to the Foreign Affairs Ministry of Carillos Flores, well known as pro-American, who had been ambassador to Washington from 1958 to 1964, pointed to a possible hardening of attitude towards Cuba. But Díaz Ordaz made it clear that he was not going to stray far from the López Mateos line. In March 1965 the Mexican government appointed an ambassador to Havana – and in fact relations between the PRI's Mexico and Castro's Cuba had never been broken off. At the beginning of 1965 Mexico was actually the only Latin American country which had not broken with the Cuban revolutionaries who had been isolated by the OAS by urgent command of Washington. There had been a Mexican *chargé d'affaires* in Havana since 1963.

Mexico gave Europe tomatoes, sugar and cocoa. Not, however, the calendar: Mexican logic is not the same as the West's, nor has time the same value in it. But no one could have foreseen the effects that would be produced by the explosive cocktail of Castroism and Cardenism, shaken once too often, in this country which constitutes a natural bridge between the U.S. and South America.

Though in 1968 Mexico still gave the impression of a certain political independence, despite ever stronger pressure from north American capital, there were quite a number of pointers to suggest the presence of internal unrest. The murder of the peasant leader Jaramillo in 1962, though virtually unnoticed in the Mexican national press, had caused anxiety in the most liberal circles. The growing proletarianization of the farming class began in 1963 to lead to incidents which though only relatively important were tending to become ever more frequent. In Guerrero state there was a definite undercurrent of banditry. Those who live in the capital have always described the people of Guerrero – one of the states most active in the 1910 revolution, and most loyal to Zapata – as *Gente muy matonera*, which means, freely translated, 'People quick on the draw'. But in 1966 incidents along the road from Taxco to Acapulco were becoming alarmingly frequent. Peasant unrest was also felt in the trade unions. Traditionally, the CNC (Peasants' National Confederation) had close links with the government and with PRI headquarters – being the rural equivalent of the CTM (Confederation of Mexican Workers). Its members are drawn from among the hundreds of thousands of *ejidatarios* who benefited from the country's agrarian reform, and therefore naturally tend to identify themselves with the regime. In January 1963 this farming union which supported the government was split by the setting up of an Independent Peasant Confederation (CCI) with specially strong roots in Nayarit and Guerrero. By the end of 1963 it had 75,000 members. At last, in May 1967, there were serious confrontations between the peasants and the army in Sonora, a state which is extensively agricultural, and where there has been a considerable amount of reconstitution of the large estates.

In 1964, as President Díaz Ordaz took office, it was evident that the two spheres in which urgent and determined action was most imperative were those of agriculture and the democratization of institutions. Irrigation has always been linked with agrarian reform, and the possible reserves of new land which could be cultivated without a lot of money being spent were continually going down. At that stage they were reckoned to be about five million hectares: according to government estimates, agricultural production could not possibly keep pace with demand, and it was estimated that by 1975 the gap would reach 8 per cent. Given that the agricultural sector receives less than a fifth of the national income the problems were obviously bound to grow worse, especially since the natural population growth was more than enough to outweigh the relative advantages brought by agrarian reform. The fourth general assembly of the PRI had reminded the government of the need to give new impetus to agrarian reform and to extend it to those northern districts where the large estates were coming back into being. But the credits earmarked for rural reorganization were barely increased in 1965 and 1966. The government ordered a limited extension of the social security system in the countryside in December 1965, but this made little difference. While stressing the need for a return to revolutionary sources in 1967, Díaz Ordaz pointed out that there was less and less spare land available for cultivation. He spoke openly in favour of increased mechanization for agriculture, an argument fully justified in terms of profitability, but hard to reconcile with a return to the 'revolutionary sources'.

Díaz Ordaz's behaviour during the crisis that shook the governing party was equally revealing of his right-wing sympathies; he evidently favoured the Alemanist clique with all its north American ties. When Minister of the Interior, in 1959, he had put down a railwaymen's strike with great firmness. Now as President he found himself at odds with Carlos Madrazo, president of the PRI, who was working for a movement to renew and purge the revolutionary leadership. Madrazo had gathered round him a team of dynamic activists to achieve this programme which would obviously have a hard time overcoming long-established habits of conformism and vested interests. During a trip round the country he declared that 'the party was one thing, the government another'. Nothing could have made his difference with the Díaz Ordaz government clearer. The fourth general assembly of the PRI in April 1965 enabled Madrazo to win one significant point, though most of the delegates would have preferred to soften all antagonisms as far as possible. A motion to get candidates for local elections – up to then always presented and imposed by the party machine – chosen beforehand by the rank and file was adopted, but it was soon evident that it would be impossible to implement it. This was made absolutely clear at the end of the summer of 1965 in a local election in Sinaloa state in which the governor, the direct representative of the Díaz Ordaz government, managed to get his own candidates in. Madrazo, having failed in this, and under fire from the union bosses whose corruption he attacked, resigned in November 1965, and Díaz Ordaz made no attempt to keep him.

The purge of the leadership begun by Madrazo was undertaken with an enthusiasm which betrayed the fear felt by ordinary people of the institutionalized machine. After two years in comparative seclusion Madrazo returned to the charge in 1968. His 1965 revolt had left its mark on the party and on those sincere activists who were sure that the Mexican revolution, now an elderly lady of 55, was now just so much old-fashioned verbiage. 'Though government is the responsibility of the majority party,' declared Díaz Ordaz in September 1965, 'minority parties have not merely a right but a duty to criticize it, and to make known any mistakes, omissions, abuses of power or corruption on the part of its functionaries, thus making their proper contribution to the country.' This somewhat new approach did not however really lead to any new action.

The democratization of Mexican institutions, in 1968 as in 1965, was identified with a democratization of the PRI. After Madrazo's setback the party seemed more than ever paralysed by an omnipresent bureaucracy. But the birth of a genuine public opinion, fostered by an enormous increase in education, resulted first and foremost in the departure from the PRI of the most representative and effective elements in the population. There was increasingly forceful criticism of the pressure from business circles connected with foreign interests (of the hundred largest businesses in Mexico 50.27 per cent were foreign- or largely foreign-owned; 13.52 per cent Mexican or largely Mexican; the remainder nationalized). It was clear that the deals taking place in Mexican business circles (the Confederation of Chambers of Industry, Chambers of Commerce, Banking Associations and Insurance Companies) which presented a unified front to the government were threatening the very principle of national independence. All these associations had fiercely attacked all President López Mateos's plans for 'Mexicanizing' the economy, and then persuaded Díaz Ordaz to get all such projects put off indefinitely. Undoubtedly the actions and statements of the López Mateos government had led to a certain recession due to a flight of capital. Díaz Ordaz set out from 1965 to 1968 to stabilize the economy, but by the end of 1968 it was a question whether there remained any possibility of freeing that economy from the ever-tightening grip of foreign capital and interest. The angry shouting of the students in Mexico City on the eve of the Olympic Games certainly showed how little respect there was for 'institutionalized revolution' among the intellectual young, whose desire was to see genuine progress and independence – a desire thwarted by the subsequent bloody battles with the police and by the brutal imprisonment of many of the students.

CHAPTER 6

Central America

For a long time Guatemala (Chapter 7) had no real existence outside geography textbooks. To most educated people it was an imaginary country, vaguely exotic, and inhabited by crocodiles and Indians wearing feathers. As for Nicaragua, (Chapter 10) a Parisian society woman not long ago described it with conviction to the Nicaraguan minister in Paris as 'an island somewhere in the Pacific' ! Central America really only became known to the world at large in 1954. From the narrowing at Tehuantepec in the north, to that of Darien in the south, the isthmus which links the two halves of the western hemisphere by an area of nearly 200,000 square miles, is made up of six independent republics : Guatemala, El Salvador, Honduras, Nicaragua, Costa Rica, Panama, one English colony still dependent on the crown, British Honduras (whose capital is Belize), and one American enclave, the Canal Zone. The accident of geographical proportions has not been helpful to these small but exciting countries : in effect, the smallest of them, El Salvador, is as large as Israel; Nicaragua covers an area somewhat larger than Greece; and both Honduras and Guatemala are slightly larger than Portugal.

They lie close together on a contorted strip of land – the result of past volcanic eruptions – punctured with lakes, the largest of which is Lake Nicaragua, a land that changes its colours at the start of the rainy season rather as jungle snakes change their skins, turning suddenly to a deep green and getting rid in a matter of days of the yellow patches which widen gradually during the Central American summer, from October to May.

Fifty per cent of the people on the isthmus live on the Pacific side, where the climate is far healthier than on the Atlantic – the Caribbean shoreline being low-lying, swampy, humid, broken by endless lagoons and overgrown by tropical forest; it rains there almost all the year round, and the rhythm of dry and wet seasons so marked in the highlands or on the Pacific coast is scarcely felt.

Apart from Managua and Panama City, all the capitals lie on the central plateau, with cool nights. All year long the ports doze in a humid torpor. There remain some colonial towns – like Antigua, still standing ruined and splendid, at the foot of a volcano which might at any moment erupt and bury it once and for all.

*

Most of the people are illiterate and desperately poor. But the isthmus has produced some enormously talented writers and poets, such as Rubén Darío who returned to die in his Nicaraguan homeland after living in exile in Paris, or Miguel Angel Asturias, who has given lyrical expression to the infinite and violent despair of the Indians of his beloved Guatemala. The reactions and temperaments of the people vary from state to state quite as much as they do in Europe. In Guatemala, for instance, the majority of the population is pure Indian. On the other hand, El Salvador, Honduras and Nicaragua have a more mixed population. On the Caribbean coast, blacks, mulattoes and Syrian-Lebanese *turcos* mingle together in the ports, while Costa Rica, with its Galicians, Catalans and Andalusians, its Scandinavians and its Germans, is a most surprising island of whiteness in a sea of colour. Though it is the most southerly of all the republics apart from Panama, its capital, San José, is the most European of all Central American towns. And here the social differences so clearly defined elsewhere fade into insignificance.

Ultimately it is the Indians, pure-blooded or otherwise, more or less closely linked with their past, who make Central America what it is. They are a short people, smiling and peaceable, still sometimes dressed in cloth of rich and harmonious colours, endlessly trotting along the mountain trails with tens of kilos of pottery, fruit or other merchandise on their backs; these Indians who still live in the Middle Ages are the soul of Central America.

In Honduras, Salvador and Guatemala archaeologists have only scratched the surface in their excavations of the treasures and ruins of the first Maya empire. The temples and pyramids of Santa Rosa de Copán in Honduras can bear comparison with those of Chichén Itzá in Yucatán or Palenque in Chiapas state in Mexico. Zaculeu, in Guatemala, is only beginning to be restored, and no one can say for certain how many ruins, temples, tombs, statues, ornaments of gold, jade or volcanic glass lie hidden in the still unexplored forests of Petén.

If they were formed into a Central American federation the five republics of the isthmus (Panama being a special case) would, with a total population which in 1968 was over the 14 million mark, take fifth or sixth place in Latin America. Their mineral wealth would be as great as Mexico's, and if they were to develop their economies in common they could certainly deal more effectively with the highly explosive social problems they face.

Well aware of this, the five Central American states—under the influence of President Kennedy – launched in 1961 the beginnings of a common market which has developed fairly rapidly. In seven years the volume of trade among the member countries had grown sixfold. A great many small industries developed as a result of the inflow of capital and gradual removal of customs barriers. During that same period the volume of foreign investment grew from an average of 30 to 100 million dollars a year. Honduras, alas, has been something of a poor relation in this association, which has been of greatest advantage to Guatemala and El Salvador. Tyres made in Guatemala were being sold all over Central America in 1968, and the same is true of Salvador's fertilizers and the pharmaceutical products of Costa Rica. These promising facts must not make us forget that in 1967 Costa Rica was the only country to have achieved the growth rate which the Alliance for Progress took as a norm. Though by comparison with the ALALC (Latin American Free Exchange Association) its progress might appear hopeful, optimism over the Central American Common Market is tempered by realization of the constant conditions imposed from the wings, so to say, by the U.S. (which, though not itself a member of the Association can make its views felt because of its indirect financing of the enterprise) and the difficulties faced in planning any self-sufficient industry. Despite all their efforts, the countries of Central America, apart from Costa Rica, still suffer from the most appalling social inequalities and economic obstacles.

*

Central America is also an essential line of defence in the American Security Triangle in the Caribbean: air bases in Trinidad, in Puerto Rico and in Panama protect the oilfields of Venezuela and the vast refineries of Curaçao and Aruba, as well as the immensely vulnerable Panama Canal.

A hundred years after the dissolution of the first Central American Federation, the dream of Francisco Morazán, the prophet and hero of unity, is still the hopeless ambition of the most dynamic and disinterested political thinkers of Central America.

Francisco Morazán was born in Honduras and there is a

statue of him in the main square of Tegucigalpa in front of the cathedral. For ten years, from 1828 to 1838, Morazán did his best to bring peace to the various states of the federation, moving from Honduras to Salvador, from Salvador to Guatemala, and then on to Nicaragua. He was ultimately forced to retreat before the hordes of Carrera, a Guatemalan mestizo who was cruel and brave, and a complete fanatic. Morazán fled to the Colombian province of Panama, and then to Peru. On his return to Costa Rica in 1842, his determination to create unity alarmed the other states, who had meanwhile abrogated the Federal Pact in 1838. Morazán was captured at Cartago, and shot in San José on 15 September 1842.

In him, Central America lost the greatest champion of unity it had ever had. Apart from the brief and legendary epic of Sandino in this century, fighting against American military occupation, no leader worthy of the name has since taken up the torch, nor managed to overcome local rivalries, arguments between villages and economic interests which, it must be admitted, are becoming ever more divergent.

In 1935 Juan José Arévalo published a book, *Isthmania*, which became and has remained the Bible for those who believe in unity. And in 1951 there was a move towards economic and social federation, which could have been the prelude to a political reorganization. The San Salvador charter set up an organization of Central American States, ODECA, patterned on the UN and the OAS. A flag was chosen, but the attempt was unsuccessful and its original purposes altered. ODECA had barely come into being when it was condemned to death by an encircling movement aimed at isolating the democratic government of Guatemala.

Those who supported unity appealed to economic arguments: the five countries had developed certain export crops (sugar cane, coffee, tropical fruit) but were without any local industry. Thus they still largely depended on the U.S. for raw materials, manufactured products, and certain essential foodstuffs. The division of Central America into competing states had for years been of the greatest advantage to the American companies, in particular the United Fruit Co. Governments could do nothing to defend themselves against arbitrary price-fixing, and carefully managed competition among the various countries enabled the buyers to call the tune.

Of course there were arguments against this, and in fact the major obstacles arose from within the states themselves. Their economies were more competitive than complementary. The percentage of each country's exports is very revealing: coffee, bananas and cocoa represent nine tenths of Costa Rica's exports, gold and coffee are the main source of wealth for Nicaragua, bananas form 80 per cent of Honduras's trade, while coffee and bananas add up to 90 per cent of Guatemala's. The means of communication within each republic are still directed to transporting the products of the soil to the Atlantic or the Pacific, rather than linking the states to one another. Only the Pan-American highway provides the beginnings of any real link and that is still unfinished; its construction was solely due to the war and America's need for access to the Panama Canal – for which reason it is still sometimes called the 'Hirohito highway'. Only a real union will make it possible to rescue the masses from their desperate poverty, and that cannot happen unless communications are improved, the middle classes strengthened and the old feudalists overthrown.

None of this looks like happening soon. It was undoubtedly from a wish to 'de-balkanize' Central America and establish a relatively prosperous buffer between Mexico and the Panama Canal that the Kennedy administration urged the Central American leaders to form a 'mini Common Market'. President Johnson's trip to San Salvador in 1968, where he met the heads of state of the four other member countries of the

MCCA, showed clearly that the U.S.A.'s prime concern was to preserve order in the area, and that there was no intention on Johnson's part of looking too closely at the methods used to this end by some of the 'policemen' then in power.

CHAPTER 7

Guatemala

STATISTICS

Area: 42,042 square miles
Estimated population in 1967: 4,717,000
Population density: 112 people per square mile
Annual rate of population increase 1960–65: 2·9 per cent
Annual increase in average per capita income from 1960 to 1966:
  2·7 per cent.

PRINCIPAL PRODUCTS

Coffee, bananas, maize, cotton, cocoa, tobacco, resin gum, chicle
  (juice of the sapodilla, used in the manufacture of chewing-
  gum).
Salt, silver.

John E. Peurifoy arrived in Guatemala shortly before Christ-
mas 1953. This new and lively ambassador from the U.S.
came as a successor to Schoenfeld, a prudent and self-effacing
man. The change was revealing. Peurifoy, an excellent golfer,
with many cups to his credit, already had a firm reputation
as a dashing diplomat. He was in Greece in 1947 during the
communist rising and the dismal days of the civil war, and
his role there had been anything but negligible. Dynamic
and effective, avoiding nuances and subtleties in getting
straight to the point, Peurifoy was a man for confidential
missions and difficult situations. His appointment to a small

Central American republic might at first sight have seemed
odd, and even suggested a demotion. But no well-informed
person could think that: it was in fact the first act in the
U.S. plan for intervention in Guatemala.

Up to 1952, the U.S. government had shown no special
interest in what was, after all, just one among many Caribbean banana republics. The one unique feature of which
Guatemala was proud was the *quetzal* – a brightly feathered
bird found only in the deep and largely unexplored forests
of the Petén, between the Mexican border and British Honduras, and which according to legend dies if it is ever shut up
in a cage.

In the country's coat of arms a magnificent *quetzal* grasps
in its claws the parchment of 15 September 1821 declaring
Guatemala's independence. The bird symbolizes unyielding
freedom and the grasping of independence and it has also
given its name to the country's coinage.

For four centuries there was a 'kingdom of Guatemala', and
from Antigua, its ancient and splendid capital, the Spaniards
controlled the lands lying to the south which were to become
the united provinces of Central America. When the Federal
Pact was broken, Guatemala was left to a solitary fate. Like
so many other Latin American nations it had during the
nineteenth and early years of the twentieth century an
obscure and tragic history, with a merely formal rivalry between liberals and conservatives, the period of Carrera's
absolute power, the struggle against the Church and the
Jesuits, and barely disguised pressure from its powerful
Mexican neighbour.

*

Geographers and tourists alike depict Guatemala in the richest
and rarest colours, and this, the second most heavily populated state in Central America, fully lives up to its reputation.
The major airport, La Aurora, most nearly resembles a Swiss

chalet standing amid pine trees shaken by the breeze. The capital is laid out like a chessboard, with avenues running north and south, streets east and west. The houses tend to be low, not usually more than two storeys, because of the ever-present, ever-feared possibility of earthquakes. Sixth Avenue crosses the entire length of Guatemala City, lined with smart shops, modern cinemas, and American-type drugstores. At one end a huge square contains the Palacio Nacional and the Cathedral. All demonstrations inevitably end in this square, where a bandstand rises up unexpectedly among the rose-beds. The echo of cheers and gunshots seems to linger under the arcades of the patios of the Palacio Nacional, for these are the two sounds which have always marked the tumultuous rhythm of Guatemala's political life. And on each occasion the fate of its $4\frac{1}{2}$ million people has been decided within the confines of this illuminated square.

According to CEPAL statistics 67 per cent of the population of Guatemala is pure Indian – the largest proportion in the whole of Latin America. The Guatemalan Indians live mainly in the mountainous area in the west of the country, and are descended from those Mayas whose melancholy and brilliant civilization extended over the whole Yucatán peninsula before it vanished, no one quite knows why : no logically satisfying answer has yet been found to explain the crumbling of that remarkably sophisticated civilization.

The old Maya empire, whose apogee was some time between 400 and 600 A.D., contained a series of cities of which little is now left – Copán, Tikal, Piedras Negras, Uaxactún, Palenque and Quirigua – in a line strung out from the east of Mexican Yucatán to the wooded peaks of what is now Honduras. The Mayas used the decimal system and had immensely advanced architecture and astronomy. They also made ceramics, knew how to weave, and did incredible gold- and silver-work. Every city was autonomous, as in the Greece of Sparta and Athens, but because communications were difficult, and even more because of their permanent rivalries, they hardly did any trade with one another.

The Palenque bas-reliefs, the gigantic and enigmatic statues of Copán, the Bonampak frescoes and the Quirigua steles, all date back to that golden age when the Mayan civilization was producing masterpieces worthy of a highly developed society. Yet by the end of the ninth century all these towns were abandoned.

The new empire became established in the north only to crumble slowly and inexorably away. The arrival of the Toltecs, aggressive conquerors from central Mexico, gave both a new lease of life and a different direction to this neo-Maya and then warlike civilization. After two centuries of relative peace around the cities of Chichén Itzá and Mayapán, a cycle of civil wars added further disasters to the ravages effected by epidemics and cyclones. By the time the conquistadors arrived at the foot of the steps up to the *Castillo*, and the warriors' temple at Chichén Itzá, Maya civilization was only a pale shadow of what it had been. Today, in the mountains of Guatemala, short dark men, smiling and peace-loving, still live in the same closed economy of ancient times.

*

Guatemala undoubtedly owes the fact of being one of the most beautiful countries in the world to her Indians, who daydream at the foot of volcanoes whose melancholy inactivity is only apparent. There are no fewer than twenty-eight – from Tacana, near the Mexican border, to Chingo – including the 4,120 metre high Tajamulco, and the twins, Agua and Fuego. These two between them destroyed the first two capitals of Guatemala. The first city, founded in 1527, was torn to bits by a torrent of stones rushing down from the summit of Agua; the second, rebuilt in 1543, more beautiful than ever, and immensely proud of its palaces, its thick-walled monasteries, and its sixty churches, was in its turn wiped from the map on 29 July 1773 by another outburst of rage from the angry giants. There remains a cool and dreamy city : Antigua, rebuilt around the vast ruins overgrown with wild flowers and age-old brambles. Antigua is the first stopping place for tourists who seek to find in Guatemala a perfect copy of what southern Mexico was, fifty years ago.

From Antigua, one of the most romantic journeys in the world takes you up to Chichicastenango by way of the idyllic shores of Lake Atitlán and the precipitous Panajachel road. The Indians' own world never changes. It extends no further than the 50 kilometres lying between them and Copán, Chichicastenango, Huehuetenango or Quetzaltenango. They live on maize, black beans, and a little dried fish. They have walked from time immemorial along paths of red earth, bending forward under their huge bundles of pottery, which they carry with the aid of a headband. They know nothing of mules or carts, but themselves do the work of both. When they have sold their burden in the market they replace it with huge stones, so as to preserve the same balance and way of walking. They come trotting and panting home along the mountain tracks. When they have troubles, they go to see the witch-doctor, or they pray to Our Lady in a church, or to one of those Maya idols concealed by a hilltop or in the forest.

At Chichicastenango one day a Spanish priest, under standing, or perhaps devious, allowed the Indians to come and pray in their own way in his white church : with breeches caught in at the knee, and brightly coloured ponchos down to their hips, making them look like pirates, they came up the slippery steps to the church door, shaking pots of incense – the church itself being empty, and lit by hundreds of candles standing on the floor of the nave amid a scented carpet of pine needles. On the rectangle of beaten earth in front of the church the men talked seriously among the baskets and awnings of the market until early afternoon. The women as usual wore full blue or black skirts and scarlet blouses. The purchase of a pair of chickens, a bundle of irises, or a handful of maize occupied the morning. Meanwhile a slow procession sang its way up the steep, worn steps to the church : phantom-like shadows gesturing through the smoke of mingled incense, pine cones and charcoal. The sound of praying rose above the bargaining of the market. To please the gods – both those of their Maya ancestors and the one brought by the Spaniards – the Indians strewed the nave in front of each altar with rose petals, white for the living, golden for the dead, and green leaves for eternal life.

As the sun began to go down over the top of Chichicaste-nango the crowd grew excited. The early drunkards, dizzy as much from fatigue as from the crude spirits they were drinking, shouted and staggered about as though struck by some tropical frenzy. The coppery faces became more than ever closed to outsiders. In a corner of the square *marimba* players (this being a kind of trapeze-shaped harpsichord made of two planks of pine, with battens of hard wood nailed across) struck their instruments, never smiling, their gaze far away, beating out that heavy despair that seems so old and so distant.

This area around Lake Atitlán is so mountainous and cut off and the Indians are so closely bound to their communities that modern civilization has made very little progress. The land belongs to the people as a whole.

*

Guatemala's other aspect is coastal : along the shore of the Pacific, with its mass of lagoons, as well as along the Caribbean coast, the air is more humid and the people more exuberant. From Puerto Barrios, where whole families live in disused railway carriages, to Livingstone at the mouth of the Río

Dulce, blacks, mestizos and *zambos** predominate. The misty lakes among the volcanoes and the pine trees of the high plateaux are replaced by the dark green carpet of the tropical forest, and the banana plantations of the United Fruit Co.

Guatemala and the *frutera* – that is, the United Fruit Co. – emerged from the obscurity of history together in 1954, obviously not by coincidence. The *frutera* had suddenly become defendant number 1 in Latin America's lawsuit against the U.S., starting in Guatemala. In effect, the private interests of the company were so directly under attack from the Arbenz government that the most naïve of diplomats could no longer claim to be neutral in the dispute between the David of Guatemala and the Goliath of the U.S. But it took five years, and the return of their diplomats to Washington, to get the Americans to admit frankly that Dulles had had a plan for intervention in Central America in June 1954. Yet at the start of the Guatemala operation the North American press spoke in complacent terms of the financial aid given by the United Fruit Co. to the anti-Arbenz rebel forces working from Honduras and Nicaragua. In New York the villains are always Jews, Italians or Irish. The United Fruit Co. had the relative advantage of having among its first founders a few genuine adventurers and one Bessarabian Jew. Besides, there is no doubt at all that the pressure of the banana lobby supported by the United Fruit Co. played a considerable part in Washington's decision to get rid, by fair means or foul, of the Arbenz government. It was rendered easier by the fact that John Foster Dulles himself, as a member of the law firm of Sullivan and Cromwell in New York, had taken part in the drawing up of the *frutera*'s new contracts with the Guatemalan government in 1930 and 1936. A lot of historians today, however, consider that the part played by the *frutera* was neither unique nor even perhaps decisive. In any case, it

* Indian and Negro half-breeds.

was lucky for the United Fruit Co. that it was helped out of a difficult spot by the fears of the Pentagon and the State Department of communist infiltration in Central America.

The United Fruit Co. was and still is, though to a lesser extent, a state within a state in a number of the Caribbean countries where it operates. From this point of view the tropical fruit business is a major factor in political life in Central America.

The United Fruit Co. took just over fifty years to become the largest company in the world's entire banana industry. It swallowed, or eliminated, its three chief rivals, in particular the Cuyamel and the Atlantic Fruit Companies, whose spheres of exploitation were respectively Cuba and Jamaica. The operations, contracts, legal battles and wars of this total vertical trust provided inspiration for numerous economists, and led to the most impassioned polemics. As early as 1921 a leading authority declared that the influence of the United Fruit Co. alone was weightier than that of all other American companies put together.

Two men guided its early steps: Preston and Minor Keith. The former founded the Boston Fruit Co. which was the first draft, so to say, of the later firm. The latter began cultivating banana plantations in Costa Rica in 1872. He was the real pioneer in a systematic conquest of the Caribbean lowlands, so fertile in tropical fruit, and with his three brothers he embarked on the laying of a railway line, the first in Central America, from Puerto Limón to San José. From 1899 when it was founded, to 1920, the United Fruit Co. extended its activities to most of the countries of the isthmus. By 1950 it owned a fleet of 50 ships, symbolizing power and luxury, the famous White Fleet. It controlled port development, railway lines and roads in all the states with which it had signed contracts – contracts which were for the most part greatly to its advantage. It owned telephone lines, such cable companies as Tropical Radio, and most of the shares in twenty or so firms or companies whose operations were directly or indirectly connected with the tropical fruit trade.

In Guatemala itself, by the end of the Second World War, the United Fruit Co., the International Railways of Central America (IRCA), and the Compañía Agrícola Guatemalteca (CAG) were all in a single trust. In 1945 the profits after tax of the United Fruit Co. reached the tidy sum of 18,900,000 dollars; in 1948 they were 52,700,000, and in 1950, 66,150,000.

By that time the United Fruit Co. had clearly won its spurs among the giants of American Big Business. In its list of directors we see O. Cameron Forbes, Floyd B. Odlum, George Davidson, and Jefferson Coolidge, who among them basically represented the Boston, Morgan and Rockefeller groups.

*

One of the most profitable contracts for the United Fruit Co. in Guatemala was given by President Jorge Ubico, elected in 1931. Ubico, whose candidature had been quite openly supported by the U.S., had promised to respect civil liberties and not to stand for a second term. But like so many of the dictators thrown into the arena by Washington, he savagely repressed all signs of unrest in the opposition, especially in 1936, and finally remained in power for fourteen years. Even before the Spanish war was over he had recognized the Franco regime. But he was a strong character and he ruled Guatemala by decrees that were unhesitatingly obeyed. The Indians affectionately nicknamed him 'Don Jorge' because he used often to go and visit them in their wretched *ranchos*, and had no hesitation in partaking of their *frijoles*** and *tortillas*.† In one decree he had declared them freed of their hereditary obligations of serfdom. But by a further decree he transformed thousands of them into forced labourers, whose efforts provided Guatemala with a large network of perfectly-kept roads. Don Jorge

* Beans. † Pancakes.

admired all things foreign. On the road to the airport he had a miniature Eiffel Tower built, having seen a copy at the Chicago World Fair. The agreement he made in 1926 with the United Fruit Co. gave them the best land in the country in return for a promise (which they never kept) to build a port on the Pacific. When he left the country for an enforced exile, he said, ironically and phophetically, 'watch out for communists and clericalists'. That was on 24 June 1944. Don Jorge yielded up his power to a military triumvirate, who were in turn overthrown on 20 October by a popular uprising. For the first time in Guatemala's history a rising was led and brought to victory by liberal officers. The first president of the new democracy of Guatemala was Juan José Arévalo, triumphantly elected with five times more votes than all his opponents put together : he took office on 15 March 1945. A man of humble origins, a brilliant and magnanimous teacher, who had sought refuge from the Ubico dictatorship in Argentina, he was also an honest politician, perhaps even too much of an idealist. When his term ended on 15 March 1951, he left office without any fuss; over the six years he had had to deal with twenty-eight attempted coups d'état. He left behind him a Code for Workers and a plan for agrarian reform which his successor, Colonel Arbenz Guzmán, was to start putting into effect. Arbenz was elected by an absolute majority – over half the total votes. He was the son of a Swiss-born pharmacist from Quetzaltenango, a town whose narrow steep streets are reminiscent of Toledo.

Arbenz Guzmán was one of that group of young nationalist and progressive officers who had overthrown both the Ubico dictatorship and the military one that followed it. He was a member of the revolutionary junta from October 1944 to March 1945, then Minister of Defence in the first Arévalo government, and now, at the age of thirty-seven, he had become the youngest head of state in the western hemisphere. His objectives were two : first, to achieve an agrarian reform that would destroy the feudal system forever (in 1945 twenty-two families owned half of all the cultivable land, and 300,132 small farmers half the rest); and second, to create a united and powerful trade union movement.

*

No one has ever settled the question of whether or not Jacobo Arbenz Guzmán was a communist. In May–June 1954, Washington, the Pentagon, the United Fruit Co. and a large part of the American press declared that he was, with suspicious unanimity and fervour. It may be significant that whereas Professor Arévalo sough refuge first in Caracas and then in Santiago de Chile to think over the results of a resounding failure, Arbenz went to Switzerland, and then to Cuba and Mexico. But that is hardly proof. It seems most likely that Arbenz was an ambitious young officer with no definite political education, filled with goodwill but maladroit, and immensely influenced by his wife and by such communist or communist-sympathizing union leaders as Pellecer, Fortuny and Victor Manuel Gutiérrez. His wife, the beautiful María Cristina, née Villanova, was a Salvadorian. Her father was a member of the 'Fourteen families club' which had run the country since the conquest, and was in 1931 adviser to President Martínez, dictator and theosophist, who ordered the massacre of almost 20,000 Indians. The incident would seem to have left María Christina with a horrific memory, a hatred for 'pious people' and a fondness for Marxist reading.

Whatever may have been the personal or political reasons that led young Colonel Arbenz to emerge from his formerly obscure way of life, it immediately became clear that his government had every intention of acting.

Agrarian reform was decreed on 17 June 1952. Its general principles were moderate, but the first American warnings of communist danger in Guatemala coincided with the first expropriation of unused land owned by the United Fruit Co.

The general nature of this agrarian reform was such as to bring into being a new class of small landowners: estates of less than 90 hectares, whether cultivated or not, were not touched by the decree. All that was handed over to the new *campesinos* (land workers) – with compensation paid to the former *terratenientes* (landowners) or the United Fruit Co. – was land lying fallow and land not being used at all by its owners or their agents. The department of Escuintla, between the Pacific coast and the chain of volcanoes, is the area with the richest land : 80 per cent of the sugar, 20 per cent of the coffee, 95 per cent of the cotton and 40 per cent of the livestock of the whole country come from there, and it was there too that agrarian reform was first applied. But clearly it was not enough just to distribute or let out land : this mass of newly-propertied peasants would have to be educated. The hardest battle was that against the atavism of the Indians, who were content to produce only what they needed to keep themselves alive. Yet the government still did nothing to stimulate the creation of cooperatives and collective farms.

In 1954 there was only one centre for mechanization (and only one technician) which lent its forty tractors to peasants who wanted them.

All other social reforms decreed and partially carried out by the democratic government of Guatemala were equally lacking in revolutionary dynamism. The inspirers and advisers for the projected reform were Mexicans, and the first thought of the brains trusts summoned by Presidents Arévalo and Arbenz turned to the example of their northern neighbour, whose human problems were so like their own.

Social security barely got beyond its first tottering steps, getting no further than providing help for accidents at work and maternity. As for public works, the building of a national port at Santo Tomás (30 kilometres from Puerto Barrios), virtually controlled by the United Fruit Co., had been entrusted to an American firm which set to work enthusiastically so as to pocket the considerable first payment promised by the government; a so-called Atlantic highway, intended to link Santo Tomás with the capital and provide effective competition to the United Fruit Co.'s railway from Puerto Barrios to Guatemala City, was begun, but the American bulldozers often stood idle.

Arbenz Guzmán's Guatemala was – as is to some extent Castro's Cuba – a victim of its own verbal exaggerations and revolutionary romanticism. Guatemala's *revolución de octubre** was praised by its organizers with the fervour of recent converts. Idealist officers, socialist intellectuals and Marxist trade unionists in Guatemala all believed that ten years of reformism justified their waving their still modest banner on high. They also believed that they could say aloud what many Latin Americans only dared to think.

On 1 May 1954 thousands of peasants marched before the Palacio Nacional bearing banners protesting against the 'imperialist war in Korea' and the 'filthy war in Indo-China', and declaring the solidarity of the workers and peasants of Guatemala with all the oppressed people in the world.

*

Who was responsible for all this? The communists of course. And how many communists are there? 'Five hundred, with perhaps twenty of them actual party members,' said the Foreign Affairs Minister, Guillermo Toriello. 'Over 3,000,' retorted the growing ranks of the opposition. The communists, under the title of the Workers Party (PGT), had won 14,000 votes in the 1951 elections in Guatemala province.

But the controversy was not really a matter of percentages. The communists were certainly a tiny minority. Only four deputies in Congress claimed the PGT label, while the two other parties which supported the Arbenz government, the PAR (Revolutionary Action Party) and the PRG (Guatemalan

*October revolution.

Revolutionary Party) counted forty-one deputies between them. But neither the PAR nor the PRG had a properly thought-out ideology; they had only an ideal and leaders. The Guatemalan Communist Party, on the other hand, was very well organized: with cells at the base and an extensive committee at the summit, with such sympathetic organizations as the 'Movement of Guatemalan Women' and the 'Democratic Students' Association', with cultural bodies like the *Saker Ti* group (*saker* meaning dawn), and the house of culture in which Raúl Leiva the poet was the moving spirit. Its leaders were intelligent and dynamic men, real personalities: Pellecer, a deputy from Escuintla, Gutiérrez, secretary general of the CUTG (Confederation of Guatemalan trade unions), and Fortuny.

Victor Manuel Gutiérrez, Leonardo Castillo Flores (a member of the PAR and leader of the farm workers' trade union), Gabriel Camey (the mayor of Escuintla) and José Manuel Fortuny had, in late 1953, visited the far side of the iron curtain. It looked as though the PGT had had encouragement from Moscow, and for the very first time in Latin America the Soviets glimpsed a possibility of harassing the United States. It was an unexpected piece of luck – and just next door to the Panama Canal. For the first time, too, the Monroe doctrine, 'America for the Americans', was to start cracking. But we can see now that the Soviets had no intention of going very far to help any Latin American government merely because it had the support of a handful of communists. When American intervention became a real threat, Fortuny voluntarily resigned as secretary general of the PGT, and the word went round that the 'national bourgeois' government of Colonel Arbenz must not be embarrassed. Too late, however: the powerful American counter-offensive was already under way.

In June 1954 Guatemala was not a communist country, nor was it on the point of becoming one. There was complete

Guatemala 305

freedom of the press and opposition groups were far more vocal than the communists, with daily papers regularly publishing denunciatory warnings to President Arbenz. They had a circulation of anything up to 50,000, and they had the monopoly of commercial advertising, while the government papers struggled along painfully with circulations of 10,000.

The only interesting question was whether Guatemala could become the first American country under communist control? America's clamp-down was so rapid that we shall never know the true answer. But the U.S. intervention, camouflaged though it was, and following on so many other examples of the 'big stick' policy in the Caribbean, aroused a quite unusual wave of disapproval all over the continent. The Guatemala affair was, and still is, instructive from another important standpoint. During the final months of the Arbenz government, under continually greater pressure from the U.S., the communists equally became continually more influential. The American policy of force thus achieved in a few months what nine years of patient organizing and hard work by the PGT leaders had failed to achieve: what happened in Guatemala in 1954 was merely a prologue to what happened in Cuba from 1959 to 1962. The gradual slide to the left of a nationalist revolution in which the communists were no more than chance supporters (as in Guatemala) or eleventh-hour recruits (as in Cuba) was largely the result of a failure of understanding in Washington. In both cases there was bad miscalculation: the Cuban revolution is firmly entrenched despite all the diplomatic and military assaults it has undergone; and though since 1954 order has continued to reign in Guatemala, it is highly precarious. The recent rumblings we have heard are a clear sign that only a short extension of time has been won.

*

The day after his first private interview with Arbenz Guzmán, Peurifoy sent an urgent confidential report to the State Department. Its conclusions were categorical: Peurifoy was convinced that there was no time to lose. John Foster Dulles was given the job of working out a plan of action on the diplomatic level. His brother Allen Dulles, head of the counter-espionage service of the CIA, got together a group of specialists to plan a military operation. These supposedly secret preparations were naturally soon known to the Latin American embassies and consequently to the Arbenz government, who negotiated the purchase of arms and military equipment first, and unsuccessfully, in western Europe, and then successfully in Eastern Europe. The arrival of the cargo ship *Alfhem* in Puerto Barrios, laden with military supplies for Guatemala, brought the crisis to a head. Dulles at once accused the Arbenz government of having the strongest army in Central America (which was not true), and of having spent a sum quite out of proportion with the country's budget on the purchase of arms (which *was*). The Nicaraguan government summoned home its representative from Guatemala and the Honduras embassador also left. The U.S. gave arms to Nicaragua and Honduras, where Guatemalan exiles led by Colonel Castillo Armas hastened their preparations.

The first of Castillo Armas's troops crossed the border on the afternoon of Thursday 17 June 1954, using three major bases from which to enter, Macuelizo, Copán and Nuevo Ocotepeque respectively. It was the feast of Corpus Christi. Normally it would take ten or twelve hours by horse or mule to get from any of these places to the border; rain-soaked trails led across peaks, down into gorges where palm and banana trees vanished, were cut short by rivers in flood. At Aguas Calientes, above the river, just past the frontier-post, rebel scouts fell upon one lieutenant, and two soldiers, who were at once killed. This was the only incident of the day.

In Guatemala City people were not yet aware that war had begun. It only became official news the next day, Friday, when the ports of San José and Puerto Barrios received their first aerial bombardment, while rebel leaders simultaneously made an attempt to occupy them. The rebels were repulsed from Puerto Barrios back towards Santo Tomás and Morales, along the Motagua river and into the various lagoons stretching out at the foot of the 'Mountain of the Monkeys'. The difficulty, indeed impossibility, of communication by telephone resulted in the spread of the wildest rumours, and proclamations of victory from both sides. No one really knew what was happening along the frontier during the first three days – even in the rebels' headquarters from its base in a low-lying house with firmly barred windows in Tegucigalpa.

The government's one determination was at all cost to keep the rebels within thirty kilometres of the frontier where the Chiquimula plain began, and thus to keep the threat contained; their one hope was to involve world opinion and the United Nations in their problem. On the first day Castillo Armas had fewer than a thousand men in the occupied border areas, but all peasants of an age to bear arms were mobilized or 'voluntarily' enrolled, and added to units mainly composed of Guatemalan exiles from Salvador, Honduras, and Nicaragua, but with a considerable strengthening from Dominicans, Hondurans, Nicaraguans and Costa Ricans. Weapons, on the other hand, were plentiful – various in the extreme, but good: German and Russian rifles, sub-machine guns, American grenades and revolvers, Swedish, Italian and American mortars and automatic rifles. And, more important, the rebels had some aircraft: a few DC3s and Thunderbirds painted steel-grey, taking off from sites in Honduras or Nicaragua, and usually piloted by Americans. In the end, the only major air operations of the insurgents were the bombardment of Zacapa and the railway near El Progreso, where a single lucky hit broke up an entire military convoy.

*

These planes suddenly appearing from the clouds sowed terror among the civilian population, and even, oddly enough, among the regular troops. Hundreds of women and children left their villages to seek refuge in the mountains. Castillo Armas's planes had the same effect on the peaceful Indians of Guatemala as the horses of Cortés and Alvarado had had on their Maya ancestors in the sixteenth century. These small and slow fighters met with no opposition from any government planes: the few that would have been available to support the ground forces stood idle on the airstrip at La Aurora, near the capital, for lack of qualified pilots, fuel and bombs.

Yet Guatemala is ideal terrain for guerrilla warfare. A few dozen determined and well armed men could have withstood a force as heterogeneous and poorly mechanized as that of Castillo Armas for several days. It would only have needed massive distribution of arms to the peasants, who were the government's natural support, and the establishment of people's militias to halt the increasing chaos. But no such order came. The army were against it and the groups of supporters hurriedly mustered by some of the trade unions had not even the time to be given guns.

There was no counter-attack on the rebels by the regular troops, and they advanced slowly but surely from village to village. While the Arbenz government dithered, Colonel Miguel Mendoza, one of the hard-liners in Castillo Armas's staff, was establishing new units in a matter of hours from among the primitive and timid *peones*. The kernel of rebel 'shock troops' advanced, but they left no gaps behind them. The attack on Chiquimula was the only real battle in a conflict whose result was a foregone conclusion. All day on 24 June, Castillo Armas's men fought with sub-machine guns, automatic rifles and grenades. By evening they had reached the barriers. The regulars (of whom there remained 200 inside the building) massed their machine guns in the windows of the first floor, and the battle lasted for two hours. Finally Chiquimula was occupied, and the encirclement of Zacapa began, but by now the 'snowball' operation was succeeded by the *tortilla* operation : before cooking *tortillas*, the women knead the corn dough in their hands, beating it like washerwomen, so that the *tortilla* can be described as 'a pancake you turn over and over'; it was during this second phase that most of the political leaders suddenly gave way under pressure from the infantry.

The fate of the Arbenz regime was in fact decided in less than twenty-four hours, during the night of Saturday 26–Sunday 27 June. The general staff painted an extremely dark picture of the military situation. Toriello, Minister of Foreign Affairs, had a lively argument with Charnaud MacDonald, the Minister of the Interior, and offered his resignation – but it was refused.

The increasing rivalries among the leadership, coupled with the lack of any determination, showed the true weakness of a government which had lost the support of most of the armed forces. Peurifoy, a *deus ex machina*, made a brief appearance, and at that very moment a group of officers demanded that Arbenz dissociate himself from his communist friends. This he refused to do. It was the last decision he was to make. A few hours later, having announced his resignation on the radio, Arbenz in his turn crossed Sixth Avenue from the Palacio Nacional to the Mexican Embassy. The compelling and supposedly forceful president had become a deflated and embittered political refugee. Arbenz was not yielding because of the threat of Castillo Armas, whose forces were by then only 200 kilometres from the capital, but because he was unable to follow the direction of his own failing logic. At heart he was still a soldier, and only a mediocre politician, and now that he was abandoned by the officers of the general staff, he felt utterly deserted. It never occurred to him to make any serious attempt to seek the full support of the peasant masses.

The unexpected and rapid fall of the president left Castillo Armas somewhat taken aback: his plans were completely overthrown: his forces had begun to encircle Zacapa – they could be seen arriving at La Cumbre, a ridge of hills equidistant from Chiquimula and Zacapa, in trucks, jeeps and small red buses with the windows gone. A battery of twenty mortars, just liberated, was in position near the last village before the metal bridge, and as the rain teemed down, people were scrambling for the best positions from which to fight a war that was over.

*

Once again there was a short interregnum, a junta under the chairmanship of the Minister of War, further activity by Peurifoy, and a peace conference in San Salvador. To Castillo Armas's demand for unconditional surrender, Colonel Monzón replied on behalf of the junta that the honour of the Guatemalan army must have the first priority. It took almost a whole night of talking to realize that no agreement could be reached, but once again Peurifoy saved the situation. Colonel Osorio, president of Salvador, his ambassador to Guatemala, Commandant Funes, and the apostolic nuncio, Mgr Genaro Verolino, succeeded among them in bringing about another meeting between Monzón and Castillo Armas, and Peurifoy hastened from Guatemala City to give America's blessing to the finel settlement. Castillo Armas's entry into the capital was a memorable occasion: the people went mad with enthusiasm; rockets, bursting into white clouds of smoke, went over the heads of the human sea swirling around the palace, pushing forward, thrusting against the guards who defended themselves with their rifle butts, but eventually retreated before the shouting of advancing women. At the corner of Sixth Avenue girls were running about in the sunshine, and on all sides there were blue and white flags, rosettes and placards borne at arms' length. There was intense and childish excitement among this overjoyed mass of people and they advanced towards the green stone steps of the presidential palace. Pale and thin, his hands gripping the microphone, Colonel Castillo Armas, in civilian clothes, appeared on the balcony, and in a quiet monotone made his first speech. He promised to defend the country, the rights of workers and citizens, and the Church: *primero Dios!** He might just as well have recited the multiplication table – the acclaim he got would have been just as loud and universal: he had won the hearts of the people. At the end he went back into the main hall, and wiped away his tears as delighted officers crowded round to embrace him.

Three years later, on 23 July 1957, Castillo Armas was assassinated – less than twenty yards from that same balcony of his triumph. His Tarpeian rock was in fact very close to the Capitol. No one has discovered the exact details of the affair: there are indications that there was some dispute between Castillo Armas and other officers over the establishment of night clubs in the city. Castillo Armas, who had not been a dashing or colourful president, was shot dead. His murderer, a bodyguard, was killed on the spot. But who had inspired the deed? In the weeks that followed there were a number of changes and semi-dismissals among the top ranks of the military and diplomats of this small republic, but though that may have settled some accounts, it made no real difference. The only practical result of the assassination was that the president stopped living in the presidential palace – the walls of which still bear traces of the gunshots that killed him. Ydígoras Fuentes, a general and the former leader of a group opposing the Arbenz government, exiled in Salvador, became president of Guatemala in 1958, but he lived in the *Casa crema*, a curious building, vaguely Persian in style, near the Polytechnic.

*First of all, God!

The history of Guatemala since 1954 can be easily summed up. The sudden fall of the Arbenz regime did not result in a total about-face in relation to the past ten years of experimenting in the social field. Those who succeeded Arévalo and Arbenz called themselves, and would still call themselves, democrats. Indeed the Catholic conservatives and large land-owners were to discover to their annoyance that Castillo Armas had liberal tendencies – in the sense implied by 'liberal' in the days of Ubico. Thus Castillo Armas vetoed any return to the preferential status the Church had enjoyed in Guatemala prior to 1871. Certainly the 1952 agrarian reform law was set aside: the obligatory renting out of land owned by individuals was stopped, and the United Fruit Co. got back some 200,000 acres of its expropriated land – though the company had the grace (or wisdom) to hand back half of it at once to the new government. But there was a new reform programme set on foot, involving the distribution of land on a basis of ownership rather than tenancy to almost 5,000 poor families. The national farms, which consisted of land taken from Germans during the war, were in large part given to the people working on them. All these steps were a clear indication that there was no possibility of destroying from one day to the next the hopes the 1944 revolution had aroused among the Indian and mestizo masses. Despite everything, however, the Castillo Armas regime soon lost what little popularity it had, and the big central trade unions of North America (the CIO and the AF of L), which had not raised a finger to defend Arbenz, positively opposed his successor. In 1954 Castillo Armas' ambiguous victory over Arbenz had created a new star in the international sky, but not for long.

His tragic death in 1957 only got a few lines' notice in the American press. This poor little colonel who, three years earlier, had been able to trick the archangels of anti-communism, his revolver in his belt and his medal of the Blessed Virgin on his chest, had disappointed his supporters without

managing to win over his enemies. After his murder there
was a period of confusion. Elections were arranged to find a
successor in an uneasy atmosphere of pressure and uncer-
tainty. The first ballot had to be declared void because it had
been too obviously rigged. At a second attempt, Ydígoras
Fuentes won the day: a conservative, an engineer, an impassioned archaeologist, he was one of Washington's men,
representing the right wing of the opposition to those who
brought Arévalo to power in 1945. The U.S. would have preferred a man more concerned over social reform, and more
determinedly anti-Castro, but Rómulo Betancourts are not so
thick on the ground among the Central American volcanoes.
After some weeks of remaining aloof the State Department
decided to establish the most cordial relations they could
with Ydígoras Fuentes, who remained in office until 31 March
1963, drawing his main support from the army, and apparently remaining cool towards the conservative group. Washington found a number of causes for satisfaction: troops
intended for a landing operation in Cuba were authorized
to do their training in the remote jungles of Guatemala – a
step which caused profound uneasiness in an army in which
the Arbenz Guzmán type of liberal officer still existed in considerable numbers. The military rising of 13 November 1960
was a direct result of this unease. The rising failed, but it
gave birth to a movement of armed resistance which had still
not been quelled by 1971, despite vigorous activity by both
the government and the forces of conservatism.

The United Fruit Co. got back yet more of the land con-
fiscated from it by the Arbenz government – however, by
now it was too late for their needs, and in Guatemala, as in
Honduras, the Company set about gradually abandoning its
increasingly less profitable plantations.

Electric Bond and Share agreed to give a substantial rise in
wages to its Guatemalan employees, thus making them the
best-off of the urban proletariat. But the general picture

remained so uncertain that U.S. State Department experts were inclined to judge Ydígoras Fuentes unfavourably : 'He has shown more of a democratic spirit than might have been expected,' they said, 'but the incompetence and weakness of his administration are a danger ...'

*

The Americans tried to help the president of Guatemala, hampered as he was by his own parliament's hostility towards any attempt at tax reform. The conservatives and landowners were far more interested in gambling on the American stock market than taking it on themselves to finance vital industrial development at home. This shortsighted and selfish attitude on their part is quite enough to explain the immense prestige of Castroism fourteen years after the inglorious fall of Arbenz. Students and intellectuals were as left-wing in 1964 as they had been in 1945 or 1953, and though it looked highly unlikely that Colonel Arbenz would return to the forefront of the political scene after the intense humiliations of the chaotic days of June–July 1954, Arévalo's popularity seemed unimpaired. Though living in exile, he gave cause for some concern to the regime, for he was precisely the kind of president Washington wanted to see in office. Arévalo had already declared his intention of standing in the presidential election of 1963; in a letter to his supporters he proposed that all the political or trade union movements which had made common cause in 1945 should again form a United Front.

Arévalo very skilfully planned his campaign as though the history of Guatemala had ended in 1951 – the end of his own first presidential term. He behaved as though the Arbenz regime had never happened. The first trial of strength for the Arévalo forces took place at the beginning of 1962, with the congressional elections. Guillermo Palmieri, a supporter of Arévalo, made a speech on the radio asking that all Arevalists leave their voting papers blank : 15,000 electors responded –

which, if expressed in national terms, meant a third of the electorate. However, there were a number of indications that the democratic Front, which for ten years had supported the Arévalo and Arbenz Guzmán regimes had still not fully recovered from the traumas of July 1954. While Arévalo, the moderate liberal, presented himself as a possible future Guatemalan Betancourt, a highly organized and dynamic reformist opposition developed. It was led by Mario Méndez Montenegro, and it looked early on as though the first battle for the presidency would take place in 1963 between these two men who had always been personal enemies. Ydígoras Fuentes was by way of remaining neutral, declaring that 'Anyone in Guatemala can stand for office. But it must not be forgotten that some elements are strongly anti-communist ... !'

Everyone in Sixth Avenue realized that he was alluding to the ex-president Castillo Armas's Movement for National Liberation. The country's landowning aristocracy was quick to label 'communist' any politician so foolish as to mention words like 'reform' and 'progress'. President Ydígoras Fuentes himself was not immune to the criticisms of the wealthy – he was altogether too liberal and far too keen on opening schools in the countryside. 'If the Indians learn to read,' they said, 'they will become receptive to Castroist propaganda. It is a great mistake therefore to build schools.' After eight years of relative inactivity, the forces now for the first time confronting one another before the world's television cameras gradually burst into action.

In point of fact that 1963 election never took place. Giving as their excuse the campaign being waged by Arévalo, with the quasi-official support of Washington, the military overthrew the Ydígoras Fuentes government on 31 March 1963. The revolutionary junta which took over was led by his own Minister of War, Colonel Enrique Peralta Azurdia. The activity of all political parties was suspended 'to save the nation from the permanent threat of communist subversion'. It was a facile and rather overworked excuse, but the Guatemalan officers considered it such as to provide reassurance to the U.S. Even in Washington, however, no one was taken in by it. In fact this is a particularly illuminating example of the problems faced by the State Department in working out a policy for Latin America. Juan José Arévalo was precisely the type of candidate wanted by the Kennedy government, but the lobbies of the big fruit companies and the strategists of the CIA thought otherwise. Thus the fall of Ydígoras Fuentes was really a personal defeat for Kennedy and his Alliance for Progress. It was quite peculiarly absurd to accuse the true blue conservative, Ydígoras Fuentes, of communist sympathies; and as for Juan José Arévalo, his traditional democratism and loudly proclaimed anti-Castroism would certainly have satisfied anyone less allergic to political analysis than the Guatemalan officers. All one can sense behind their action is the permanent fear of the rich few, their hostility to the slightest measure of reform, and their determination to delay the arrival of elementary social justice as long as possible.

One may even have reservations as to the genuineness of the *pronunciamiento* of 31 March; it is possible that Ydígoras Fuentes was himself a party to it. Certainly he had scarcely arrived in a neighbouring republic before he began urging all the American governments to recognize the military regime which had supplanted him! And his statement that 'Arévalo represented a serious threat to Guatemala' would seem to confirm the real reason for the putsch.

Four months after these events there were confrontations between soldiers and guerrilla groups in the district of Izabal in the north east. Similar incidents broke out throughout 1964 and during the early months of 1965. In April 1964 the Colonel commanding the mobile military police was killed by guerrillas in Puerto Barrios. Eleven years after the fall of Arbenz the country of the *quetzal* bird could already be put on the list of those in which revolutionary guerrilla warfare was a fact which no amount of military proclamations and decrees could unsay.

Luis Turcios Lima, a young officer, had been still under twenty when he took part in the military rising of 13 November 1960, under the command first of Alejandro de León and then Yon Sosa. At fifteen he had entered the military academy, having previously been to school in Catholic colleges. In 1959, as a sub-lieutenant, he continued his military studies at the Ranger School of Fort Benning in Georgia. Back in Guatemala he was for some time in command of a jungle post in Petén. The November mutineers were inspired by the same feelings which had inspired the young officers who destroyed the Ubico dictatorship in 1944 – but their fate was very different.

Having captured Puerto Barrios in a surprise attack, they were soon in turn overwhelmed by the forces which remained loyal to the government. It looked as though that was the end of a minor attempted putsch of a kind common enough in Guatemalan history. But in fact, it was the start of one of the best organized revolutionary movements in the whole of Latin America since 1959, and the beginning of a long period of collaboration between Guatemalan communists and young revolutionaries – whether idealistic intellectuals like César Montes, or liberal soldiers like Turcios Lima and Yon Sosa. In February and March 1961 serious trouble broke out in the capital. There was a general strike, and demands that the government resign from people of all shades of opinion.

The repression the government used was on the same scale as this quite exceptional unrest all over the city. In March and April 1962 fresh trouble broke out which the authorities managed, though with difficulty, to repress. It was then that several of the PGT (Guatemalan Workers' Party, a communist party) leaders, together with the officers involved in the 1960 rising, among them Yon Sosa and Turcios Lima, decided that the only way to escape the repression and get their movement properly organized was to create a guerrilla *foco* in the hills.

By December 1962 MR 13 (the 13 November Revolutionary Movement) had a *guerillera* base camp, though the various revolutionary movements gathered together in the FAR (Revolutionary Armed Forces) had not fully ironed out all their differences. As in the rest of Latin America the orthodox communists, especially the older party activists, had reservations over the principle of the armed struggle as 'the fundamental way to revolution'. The last secret CP congress in 1960 had elected a central committee of which most of the members tended to prefer the tactics of 'power won by peaceful means'. On the other hand it seems that a certain number of active Trotskyists managed to influence the leadership of MR 13 (centred around Yon Sosa) to some extent at this period, though the dispute among orthodox communists, Trotskyists and Castroists was in fact to come dramatically into the open some time later.

The whole revolutionary movement also suffered from a great many reversals between 1962 and 1964, resulting mainly from a considerable degree of unpreparedness. In Guatemala the party did not have, and still has not really got, any hearing among agricultural workers, apart from those areas where the agrarian reform of the Arbenz government had begun to operate. Orthodox communists still insisted that the leading role in the revolution must be played by the industrial workers. Consequently two opposing tendencies stood out within the PGT, and in February 1966 (following the Tricontinental Conference in Havana) the theory of the armed struggle finally received the approval of a remoulded Central Committee.

It was at the end of that Havana conference that Castro made his violent attack on what he described as 'Trotskyist infiltrations' in the Guatemalan FARs. With nothing but

praise for Turcios Lima, the leader of the Guatemalan delegation at the conference, he roundly condemned Yon Sosa, the
MR 13 leader still in Guatemala. As a result relations between
the orthodox communists and Castroist revolutionaries began
to get worse in a situation of dispute between the MR 13,
now outside the Latin American revolutionary family gathering in Cuba, and Turcios Lima's FARs which were still prepared to remain in harmony with the communists. In point
of fact the breach between the Trotskyists or supposed
Trotskyists of Yon Sosa's group and the revolutionaries
identifying themselves with the Cuban experience dated back
to March 1965, but even the most careful scrutiny of the
statements put out by both parties did not make it easy to
distinguish any profound ideological divergency between
them. Indeed, one might well reckon that there was a certain
hair-splitting involved, given that the revolutionary forces
had to deal with an army and police trained in anti-guerrilla
tactics by North American instructors. There can be no doubt
that the many setbacks in the guerrilla war, especially in 1966
and 1967, were due to the comings and goings between town
and country of the guerrilla leaders for discussion. The importance given to 'the town' may have helped the communist
leaders, but in the long run it could not but alienate the
guerrilla military commanders. To the PGT's warnings
against the 'dangers of left-wing deviationism, and radicalism,
the tendency to move too fast, the danger of over-valuing the
military at the expense of other forms of struggle', the revolutionary leaders finally responded by attacking 'the PGT
clique which kept providing ideas while the FAR were providing dead bodies'.

The 1966 presidential election was to crystallize these
divergencies. The communists called on their supporters to
vote for Méndez Montenegro, described as a 'well-known
democrat', because it was important 'to sharpen the contra-
dictions within the ruling classes and weaken the political

and social basis of the dictatorship'. The guerrilla leaders and Turcios Lima opposed this stance taken on behalf of the armed rebel forces and not merely the official communist party. 'For us revolutionaries' declared Turcios Lima, 'to take any part in these elections, or call on the people to take part – whether to vote for Méndez Montenegro's revolutionary party or any other opposition party – would be equivalent to giving our support, the support of our principles, our revolutionary approval and the support of the masses who believe in us to people whom we know to be utterly unscrupulous, and the accomplices of reaction and imperialism.'

As angry voices were raised more fiercely between Communists and Castroists, Yon Sosa (whose guerrillas had reformed near Lake Izabal) and Turcios Lima (whose forces were chiefly to be found in the Zacapa area) tried to achieve a reconciliation, Sosa making it known that he had got rid of all 'Trotskyist influences'.

Turcios Lima accidentally killed himself near Guatemala City early in October 1966; his place as leader of the FAR was taken by César Montes, a man of 25, formerly a university activist, and one of the founders of the guerrilla group called the Edgar Ibarra Front. He had been an active communist since 1958, but was now far closer to the ideas of Turcios Lima than those of the Guatemalan CP bureau. His taking command coincided with one of the army's regular attacks on the guerrilla *focos*. On 1 July 1966, shortly after taking office, President Méndez Montenegro had in fact proposed a general amnesty in exchange for a cease-fire. This the guerrillas rejected, so he gave the army the order to attack without mercy in the Zacapa area. In May 1967 the Méndez Montenegro government considered that the guerrillas had been effectively wiped out. And indeed there had been very heavy losses among them at the point when Fidel Castro's speech of 13 March 1967 made the breach between the Havana leaders and the political bureau of the Venezuelan Communist Party official (the Venezuela party's theories being very similar to those held by the Guatemalan party). It was not however until 10 January 1968 that the breach between the military commanders of the FAR and the leadership of the Guatemalan Communist Party became official. On 21 January César Montes confirmed it. As in Venezuela a year earlier, the revolutionaries in favour of the armed struggle adopted the theses of Guevara, despite his spectacular failure in Bolivia, but their numbers had decreased and their enemies were more powerful than ever.

What happened was that the guerrilla terror met with the response of a white counter-terror. 'Militia', organized directly by army officers and North American instructors, had been effecting more and more summary executions since the end of 1966. Sequestrations, kidnappings, mutilations, executions: this sad catalogue of violence had produced several hundred deaths in under two years. Various well-known communist party leaders, among them Victor Manuel Gutiérrez, appeared on the list of the missing. In January 1968 two American officers, one the head of the U.S. military mission in Guatemala, were murdered in the capital. In August that same year the U.S. Ambassador himself was killed as he came out of the Ministry of Foreign Affairs. Méndez Montenegro, whose 'pacification' scheme seemed to have failed completely, was virtually a prisoner of his own army, and his sole concern was by then simply to survive. But it looked as though the chain of bloody violence would never come to an end.

CHAPTER 8

Honduras

STATISTICS

Area: 43,277 square miles
Estimated population in 1968: 2,500,000
Population density: Nearly 58 per square mile
Annual rate of population increase: 3·3 per cent
Annual increase in average per capita *income from 1960 to 1966:*
  2·7 per cent.

PRINCIPAL PRODUCTS
Bananas, coffee, black beans, timber.

The Caribbean shoreline is fringed with a thick dark green carpet on the land and little white waves coming in from the sea. The carpet is dense and unbroken, save only by the long snaky movement of a river the colour of reddish mud. It even covers the first foothills, where the capital Tegucigalpa is lodged. It belongs to the American United Fruit Co.: they have 1,750,000 hectares of land, and 11 million hands of bananas to be exported every year to the U.S.

Honduras is the second largest country in Central America in terms of land area. But with 2,500,000 inhabitants in 1968, it is less populated than two of its closest neighbours – Guatemala and El Salvador. U.N. statistics of living standards and annual *per capita* income place it fourth only, after Panama, Nicaragua and El Salvador, and equal to Guatemala.

The disproportion is easy to explain : four fifths of Honduras is covered in mountains of anything up to 2,500 metres high. The lowlands are literally submerged in tropical vegetation, while the north shore is swampy and difficult to live in. The population centres are scattered on the high plateaux of the south west, among the valleys and coastal plains of the north, and are often cut off from one another by bad weather, or lack of communications. Even the capital has no direct access to the sea. The silver mines which made it rich and famous for two centuries are now virtually abandoned. Tegucigalpa, at a height of 1,000 metres, is dominated by an imitation Greek temple, a monument to peace and men of good will, which was built by Tiburcio Carias the dictator; but it has neither a road nor a railway station. Humorists declare that its people have never seen trains or engines except at the cinema. It has frequently been insisted that the United Fruit Co. build a railway from Tegucigalpa to the sea, in return for all the privileges it has received. Indeed a promise to do so has several times been embodied in contracts agreed between the company and the Honduras government, but on one pretext or another it has never been kept. The *ferrocarril* still only goes from Puerto Cortés to the lovely shores of Lake Yojoa, some 70 miles north west of the capital.

*

Its neighbours say of Honduras, 'It is a land of herds and bananas. The herds belong to Carias. The bananas belong to the United Fruit Company.' Unhappily, Honduras is an almost perfect copy of the picture painted by an American journalist at the beginning of the century of a 'banana republic'. It is first, by a long head, on the long list of countries all over the world exporting tropical fruit. For Honduras, during the last few years, bananas have represented 70 per cent of all exports. Back in 1932 banana plantations already spread over almost 200,000 hectares – over a third of the cultivated land of the country. The record for exports was reached in 1929, with 29 million hands valued at 23 million dollars. Then the mysterious *sigotoka*, the banana disease, and a particularly violent hurricane combined to destroy thousands of plants. The company consequently gave up huge areas where it had become impossible, or too costly, to fight the advance of the disease effectively, and removed their activities to areas not yet used where it would be possible to prevent the disease from spreading. Thousands of workers found themselves jobless from one day to the next and were faced with either remaining unemployed or leaving their homes.

This almost completely single-crop economy, controlled by foreigners, is clearly a handicap to any rational development of the country's economy. Yet the potential wealth is enormous: sugar cane, tobacco, cotton, rubber, valuable woods, and mines of amianthus, platinum, iron, gold and copper. These things are barely being touched though they could transform the entire nature of the country. Since 1959 industry has made some modest efforts, but it still only represents 10 per cent of the national income. Factories have been built for food processing and weaving, as well as some flour mills, but on a totally inadequate scale.

The problems Honduras has to overcome if it is to resolve the absolutely vital problem of transport undoubtedly make all the efforts the government is now making towards modern economic planning quite illusory for the present. The great highway from Mexico to the Panama Canal, which follows a tortuous route down the isthmus, deliberately bypasses the vast eastern areas – their wealth not realized when it was built – known today as Honduras. The conquistadors' road naturally ran alongside the volcanoes of Salvador and the Gulf of Fonseca, and the Pan-American highway more or less follows the same path. Still, today, huge areas of Honduras are reached only by poor and difficult roads which, especially during the rainy season, are almost impassable by wheeled vehicles. The Hondurans have long been searching round for various solutions, but none have been sufficient for this mighty problem – a peculiarly infuriating situation for a country with two sea-coasts, one of which is extremely long. To some extent the aeroplane has produced one satisfactory solution, during the past ten years or so; the increase in air transport, at least to the major centres, put a sudden end to the age of the mule and cart. Twin-engined planes can move quickly from one airstrip to another, despite the continual cloud and rain, all over the republic. San Pedro Sula, the second largest town, and since 1960 the 'boom-town' of Honduras, is only half an hour from the capital, and the magnificent Maya ruins of Santa Rosa de Copán less than forty-five minutes' flight. The Mayas, coming down from Guatemala, built in this still little-known border area temples, palaces, steles – an entire town covering some twenty square kilometres, which has been slowly and inexorably overrun by jungle. Though archaeologists generally consider the Copán ruins to be as beautiful and worthy of study as those of Piedras Negras in Guatemala, or Palenque in Mexico, the inscriptions on their pillars have still not yet been completely deciphered. Copán was an abandoned town even by the time the first Spaniards reached it, and the grimacing or terror-stricken carved faces visible on its moss-covered stones have not yielded up all their secrets yet.

*

The strike among the workers on the Atlantic coast banana plantations broke out suddenly on 4 May 1954. It was absolutely unanimous and yet there had been no previous indication that it would occur. From one day to the next 40,000 workers refused to go back to work until the company acceded to their demands. In the plantations the workers' universal tool is the machete, a kind of short curved blade : thus they are known as 'machete-men'. Their list of grievances was detailed : they wanted a 100 per cent increase in wages, decent housing for as many workers as possible – not just for the favoured few – and medical care not just in theory but in fact. To these demands they held despite threats and pressure. The leaders of the strike were the skilled workers : mechanics, railwaymen and office workers. It was the first time a dispute on this scale had ever broken out, not just in Honduras, but in any of the United Fruit Co.'s areas of exploitation. It was clear from the start that the strikers had no trade-union experience, and hardly any political training. Their strike, though unique in the history of Central American workers, remained virtually unknown outside Honduras itself. At the time all eyes were on Guatemala where the Arbenz Guzmán government was in its death throes; the big American newspapers sent their best reporters and war correspondents, men who had been through Korea and Indo-China, to cover what was expected to be the lively battle between the rebels of Castillo Armas and the Guatemalan regular forces. They knew absolutely nothing about this workers' movement which was ultimately to have consequences almost as great for the history of Central America as all the comings and goings of Castillo Armas's mercenaries between Esquipulas and Chiquimula. However, affairs in Guatemala made it possible for the Honduras government and the United Fruit Co. men to accuse the strike leaders of collusion with the unionists and the leaders of the Guatemalan workers' party, i.e. the communists. Still, a month and a half after the strike had begun, the United Fruit Co. had already lost 20 million dollars, and by the end of August the company decided it would be wisest to yield. The workers received a substantial increase in wages, and a number of extra privileges, all of which combined to create a kind of revolution in the company's methods of work. That this was so only came to be grasped later : this first blow in fact marked the beginning of the decline of the United Fruit Co. in Central America.

*

By a curious twist of fate the company suffered its first serious setback in a country whose political life it had up to then controlled to an extent achieved nowhere else.

Honduras had for a long time what amounted to two governments : the real one, and the secret one; the one working from the Palacio Nacional and the one whose orders came forth from the offices of the United Fruit Co. a few hundred yards away. Hondurans always knew full well that the latter was the one that mattered most. The first company to become established on their shores was not in fact United Fruit, but the Cuyamel Fruit Co., whose name derived from the area where it worked. Cuyamel was run by a Boston businessman, Zemuray, a Bessarabian by birth. The story of the struggle for power between Cuyamel and United Fruit in Honduras was really for at least fifteen years a mirror-image of the political conflicts of the area. For instance, in 1924 Cuyamel supported Miguel Paz Barahona as candidate for the presidency of the republic, and he was elected. Tiburcio Carias, whose electoral campaign had been financed by United Fruit, was defeated. In theory the 'reds', i.e. the liberals, were ready to do business with Cuyamel, while the 'blues' or conservatives would have preferred the profits to go to United Fruit. But all that these election results really proved was that Cuyamel at that time had more funds than United Fruit. Zemuray, who was not only an astute businessman but also a man who would take great risks, had encouraged and helped to finance the military expedition of Manuel Bonilla, an ambitious Honduran general. Bonilla, who landed at Puerto Cortés on the Atlantic coast with his handful of mercenaries, seized power with an ease which astounded the Hondurans themselves, and at once granted enormous concessions to Zemuray, who had placed such confidence in him. A lot later, Zemuray finally sold his rights to United Fruit for 30 million dollars, becoming at the same time one of their largest shareholders. United Fruit was now alone in the field, and naturally continued to call the tune in all the elections – now without opposition from anyone else. To the people, however, these apparent struggles for power, these alliances and share-bargainings between rival financial groups, all meant little. They knew that, whatever its name, whatever north American company was established in their midst was bound to make Honduras effectively a colony of the U.S. and that the disappearance of Cuyamel from the scene meant the coming to power of Carias.

*

Tiburcio Carias was a forceful mestizo of humble origins. He had to make relatively little effort to remain in power, for the cards were so stacked in his favour, and the whole game took place in the triangle of which Tegucigalpa was the tip, and the Caribbean coast the narrow base. Tall and heavy, his huge bushy eyebrows forming a line across his good-natured and shrewd face, Carias was a man of action rather than words. To United Fruit, whose main concern was to see peace reigning in the country, he was the ideal *caudillo*. Though he was in power from 1933 to 1944, his fame barely spread beyond the bounds of his own small country. Yet in some ways there was little to choose between him and some of the most cruel and famous of the Caribbean dictators – Gómez, Trujillo, Somoza. He did manage to create one innovation however: that of bombarding rebels from the air. To put down one peasant revolt, he used aircraft of the TACA (Central American Air Transport Company). This effective and highly successful method received some publicity at the time, and was later copied by a number of South American dictators, especially Laureano Gómez in Colombia, where the groups of permanent revolutionaries paid for their activities with some thousands of dead during the course of five years. In 1936 Carias altered the constitution, making his power absolute. The only people whose advice he was forced to heed were the United Fruit Co.'s representatives in Tegucigalpa. However, in 1944 the great wave of liberalism which swept over all of Central America was felt even here. The people began to grumble against the oppression of this long dictatorship. There were demonstrations in the capital, and in San Pedro Sula where the army had to be called in. 'Down with Carias' was a cry first heard under the arcades of the central square, in front of the cathedral of Tegucigalpa, and even under the very windows of the United Fruit Co. and the American Embassy. The company's Number One concern had not changed : peace at any price – so Carias had to be abandoned for the moment. There were elections and the winner was José Manuel Gálvez, not, apparently, a very great change from his predecessor. Gálvez was in fact a Honduran lawyer who had spent several years dealing with the *frutera* and its disputes; it seemed out of the question that his government would dare to undermine in any way the privileges won by the United Fruit Co. under Carias. Yet something new was evidently happening. Carias had been a perfect caretaker, who knew his place and was devoid of any political imagination. Gálvez, leader of the nationalist party, soon made it clear that he was a man of dynamism and intelligence who was absolutely determined to lead his country out of the stagnation and obscurity in which it had lain for so long. He brought together a group of skilled and courageous men; he launched a plan for modernization, finding funds for the building of roads and barrages. In 1954, at the end of his term, something like public opinion had come into being, and there was a growing desire for genuine independence. In June 1954 the Hondurans were profoundly shaken by the invasion of Guatemala, and for a week there were violent student demonstrations in the streets of Tegucigalpa, protesting against 'government complicity'. For in practice Gálvez was unable to do anything to prevent, or even to warn against, the preparations for the attack on Guatemala, though the rebel headquarters was openly set up in Tegucigalpa itself. That the omnipotence of the Boston giant was beginning to waver was at least as much due to the whims of nature as to the efforts of men : between 1955 and 1961 a series of unusually disastrous hurricanes destroyed thousands of hectares of plantations. The series of such catastrophes which befell the fruit company after its open intervention in the Guatemala affair combined – though belatedly – to produce certain effects. Two major decisions were made by the Department of Justice in Washington : 1. The United Fruit Co. was obliged to dispose of all its shares in the International Railways of Central America by 1966; 2. By 1970 it had to have handed over part of its plantations to an independent company which could produce at least 9 million hands of bananas a year.

*

On the other hand competition from other banana-producing countries, especially Ecuador (which had almost caught up with Honduras), made itself felt, with the natural result of overproduction and a fall in prices. In the past ten years the profits of the United Fruit Co. went down from 90 million dollars to just over 3 million; during that same period the value of the shares also fell drastically. The directors of the executive council had a special meeting in their Boston offices and decided to do the logical thing : a letter went out to all shareholders early in 1962 from Sunderland, the president, making it clear that United Fruit was gradually going to cut down its activities, especially in the sphere of production. In has already given up the larger part of its plantations in Ecuador, Colombia and the Dominican Republic. But whatever decisions the company may make, it seems unlikely that the mass of hatred it has acquired during sixty years of exploitation can be so easily disposed of. In fairness it must be noted that the company drained swampland for cultivation, built schools, hospitals, railways and roads (though the latter of course for its own exclusive use). It paid its workers on average two or three times more than local farm workers got. But these items on the credit side can never, in Honduran eyes, make up for its merciless grip on their political life. The general feeling is that United Fruit exploited *their* national soil solely for the benefit of *its* shareholders. The tragedy here is that the total and immediate departure of the United Fruit Co. would quite certainly leave the country at first in greater poverty than ever. For nothing – or almost nothing – has been done in preparation for the transition that must be made.

The presidential elections in 1954, to find a successor to José Manuel Gálvez, were so muddled that no one had a clear majority. The Carias clique used every pressure they could to get the tired, intransigent old dictator back. But Carias, with Gregorio Reyes as his vice-presidential running-mate, still believed that the label 'nationalist' was enough to secure victory. So convinced was he that his party's electoral machine was in advance of all the others, that he was quite astounded to discover that the people were weary of all the old empty, vote-catching promises. The two other candidates, General William Calderón, formerly a minister under Carias, and the *licenciado* Villeda Morales, were no better off, though the latter with some justice protested against the irregularities that militated against him. Villeda Morales, popularly nicknamed the *Pajarito* (little bird), was a good lawyer and a brilliant leader of the liberals, but he had in fact to wait another three years before being able to move into the presidential palace for a six-year term. From 1954 to 1957 there was a colourless interlude with Vice-President Lozano Díaz established as acting president, on the ground that the electors could not make up their minds about what they really wanted. After three years of a power threatened by a great many popular protests, there was another election, culminating in the victory – admitted by all, both civilians and army – of the *Pajarito*. A liberal and convinced democrat, Villeda Morales tried to carry out a plan of economic development that was both reasonable and moderate. A plan for agrarian reform was set on foot by a specially convened council of eight, with the assistance of foreign advisers. The new president, unlike his predecessors, was not without humour. His electoral programme was 'Always one step forward ...' His wife told how one evening, on returning to the palace, she found the nurse singing a lullaby in which that phrase was the chief refrain. When asked why, the nurse replied, 'You have put a whole people to sleep with your slogan. Surely if I sing the same line I can put one child to sleep with it?'

Villeda Morales certainly did not put the people of Honduras to sleep, but so huge were the obstacles to be overcome that six years of his liberal regime was only long enough to make a start. The hated United Fruit Co., though certainly less powerful and ambitious, was still there, and still to be reckoned with. To deal with the Castroist propaganda which was appearing here as in other Latin American countries, *el Pajarito* decided it wiser not to make any frontal attack on it, but allow it freedom of expression. The 1963 general elections would show whether such a liberal attitude would prove more rewarding than a more repressive one.

But they never took place. On 3 October 1963 the armed forces of Honduras, led by Colonel López Arellano, overthrew the Villeda Morales government. The presidential palace was shelled and street fighting took place between the rebel army and the *Pajarito*'s remaining supporters. Over a hundred people were killed. Villeda Morales was accused 'of blindness in face of the danger of communist infiltration', and Washington at once broke off diplomatic relations with Honduras. Obviously the military revolt here had the same causes and the same consequences as the putsch of 15 September 1963 in the Dominican Republic. In both cases, within a month, the Kennedy government received spectacular setbacks with the possibility of disastrous consequences. The fall of two presidents with reformist and pro-American tendencies – Bosch and Villeda Morales – proved that forces opposing the Kennedy plan were stronger on the ground than the official representatives of Washington. Villeda Morales was no more a communist than was Bosch, and he had made numerous declarations of his hostility to Castro's Cuban regime. He sought temporary refuge abroad but made a spectacular return on the eve of the general elections to take place on 16 February 1965.

Thousands of enthusiastic people were waiting for him at the airport, and provided a triumphal cortège to the centre of the capital. It looked as though the army might have been foolish to allow the liberal leader so outstanding a demonstration of his popularity. But the result of the election proved that, on the contrary, they had taken full precautions. The conservative party, supporting Colonel López Arellano for president, won enough votes to claim an absolute majority in the new Chamber. So, indirectly, the October 1963 coup had now been legalized.

On 31 March 1968 there were municipal elections – the first since the promulgation of a new constitution by the López Arellano government. Voting under duress and cheating, especially in country districts, were so patent that the liberal party demanded that the results be scrapped, and the party leadership asked their own 25 deputies to resign in protest. Only two obeyed this order which cost them a salary of a thousand dollars a month. And the man responsible for rigging the elections, Ricardo Zúñiga, a member of López Arellano's national party, made no secret of his intention to stand for president in the 1971 elections.

CHAPTER 9

El Salvador

STATISTICS

Area: 8,256 square miles
Estimated population in 1967: 3,100,000
Population density: Nearly 384 per square mile
Annual rate of population increase: 3·1 per cent
Annual increase in average per capita income from 1960 to 1966:
 2·8 per cent

PRINCIPAL PRODUCTS
Coffee, cotton, bananas.

There are fourteen of them. Their names are emblazoned outside the air-conditioned office blocks, the banks, the trading firms and the insurance companies of San Salvador. They play golf. They give parties by their swimming pools. They join exclusive clubs. They own vast coffee *fincas** in Libertad and cotton fields around Sonsonate. These fourteen heads of families have a close grip on the whole political and economic life of El Salvador. You find them, their sons-in-law, their nephews or their cousins, running every business, and most of all the coffee industry, which is Salvador's greatest wealth. They control cotton, cocoa, sugar, palm oil, phosphates and livestock; they control cement-works, transport, the sales of Coca-Cola, mineral drinks, beer and American cars. Without

*Farms.

themselves taking any direct part, they have created or destroyed almost all the governments that have held office since independence. A study of El Salvador's Business Yearbook tells you everything you could possibly want to know about all the political intrigues of a country barely larger than Wales.

The Duenos, the Regalados, the Hills, the Mes Ayaus, the De Solas, the Sol Milets, the Guirolas, the Alvarez, the Meléndez, the Menéndez Castros, the Deinnigers, the Quinónez, the García Prietos, and the Vilanovas: this white oligarchy runs the lives of three million mestizos. Within the group itself there are complex precedences relating to how long a given family has had its money, and the number or quality of its highly-placed connections. The Duenos gather 40,000 quintals (a quintal=50 kg) a year of a coffee rightly considered one of the finest on the New York market. The Mes Ayaus have a beer monopoly, and Don Benjamín Sol Milet is the major shareholder of the Agricultural and Commercial Bank. The Meléndez provide their fellow-citizens with electricity, and the Quinónez are the largest importers of machinery, tractors and refrigerators. Some of these patrician families of Central America came from Estremadura with the first of the Spanish conquistadors. Others, on the other hand, are of Jewish ancestry, English or Dutch perhaps. But they have one trait which sets them apart from all the other Latin American oligarchies: the 'fourteen families' of El Salvador invest all their capital and income in the national economy. They are protected by the *ley de fomento de industrias de transformación** of 1952, which allows them to pay no import duty on heavy machinery and tools. They have faith in the destiny of their country, though there have been signs recently that their omnipotence is starting to be questioned and perhaps even positively attacked.

*

*Law promoting processing industries.

The road from San Salvador towards the Guatemala border – a branch of the famous and still unfinished Pan-American highway – looks like a winding, sunken black line in a landscape of various shades of violent green. The plateau is no more than 800 metres high, and with an atmosphere as moist as a greenhouse, the earth is incredibly fertile. Coffee trees follow banana trees, giant eucalyptus protect brilliant bougainvilleas; not far from the road there are plantations stretching for dozens of kilometres. Then suddenly you come to wretched villages consisting of straw huts filled with a human mass, barefoot, ill-clothed, eyes burning feverishly. Salvador comes second only to Haiti as the most heavily populated republic in America. The majority of the people live in the western provinces where the production per hectare is twice that of Guatemala or Costa Rica. It is also the world's richest coffee-growing land; in fact, tiny Salvador is the world's third largest coffee exporter.

The first coffee plant appeared in Salvador as long ago as 1838. From its beginnings in Santa Ana province, the cultivation of this green gold spread rapidly to the areas of Sonsonate, Ahuachapán, San Salvador and San Vicente. By 1880 it was the country's major export. And the great majority of coffee producers nowadays have every kind of modern equipment for the most varied and complex operations: removing the fleshy part of the fruit, fermentation, husking, washing, drying, and classifying the beans. The rhythm of life in these overpopulated country areas is thus almost precisely what it was over a century ago. The harvest, which generally continues from November to May, attracts all the *peones* who live by seasonal work, who live just as they always have. Later on the cultivation of cotton came to represent an additional important source of foreign currency for Salvador: Salvadorian cotton, similar in quality to Egyptian and therefore much in demand. During the Suez crisis,

France in particular bought several million dollars' worth.

*

The secret of the record productivity of these coffee plantations is simple: the Salvadorian *peones* are tremendously
hard-working. They go barefoot and ragged, live in straw
huts, eat each day no more than two or three *tortillas*
(maize cakes), a handful of *frijoles* (black beans), and also
fortunately a number of wild herbs rich in vitamins – twenty-
five different varieties have been identified. When they are
in work, their wages are incredibly low, and they rush to
spend them on the local brand of rough and nauseating
liquor. You often meet them on the road, zigzagging back
home, each trying to find his home with the help of a less
drunk or harder-headed mate. The *colonos* (farm workers)
generally remain on the *fincas* where they work all the year
round. They live in conditions that can only be called appalling. Following a recent inquiry, a UN technical mission to
Salvador published the following figures: 60 per cent of
Salvadorians live on less than 480 dollars a year; in the
country, less than 5 per cent of all dwellings have even the
most rudimentary sanitary facilities; meat, fowl and fish are
almost unknown foods among the *peones* who work on the
land; and in the country, the percentage of illiterates is 75,
which is similar to that in the neighbouring republics.

The coffee-growing plateau is fringed by a chain of volcanic mountains along the Pacific coast. The chain of craters,
some slumbering, some active, comes to an abrupt halt beyond Conchagua with two volcanic islands. Near San Salvador, the capital, Lake Ilopango was fairly recently subject to mysterious and alarming turbulence: the waters rose
or fell, for what reason could not be precisely determined. In
1873, for instance, for no apparent cause, the level of
Ilopango suddenly rose by a metre, then remained steady.
Seven years later, there were new upheavals, accompanied

by eruptions of gas and sulphur vapours, which terrified everyone in the capital, who could only believe that a new volcano was appearing. After the turbulence, some tiny volcanic islands appeared in the middle of the lake. On Sundays when the Salvadorians come to bathe on the beaches around it they still look anxiously towards these rocks of black lava. Another phenomenon indicating the undisciplined violence of nature in this most highly populated area of central America is the volcano Izalco, a perfect cone rising to 1,890 metres. Sailors passing the coast of Salvador nicknamed it the 'beacon of Central America' because of the roseate light coming from its crater; and Haroun Tazieff, the authority on volcanoes, honoured it with a long visit during a world tour of volcanoes. At the foot of Izalco lies the swimming pool of Atecozol, the favourite Sunday gathering place for San Salvador's young people. In a hollow surrounded by a clump of huge trees, there is a great rumbling every quarter of an hour or so which drowns the noise of talking and music, while a jet of flame and smoke rises into the sky. At night the effect is tremendous.

*

In point of fact, the whole of El Salvador is a volcano which might at any moment erupt without warning. On 22 January 1932 bands of *peones*, armed with their formidable machetes, marched out of the village of Izalco, beside the volcano, and captured the towns of Sonsonate, Sonzacate and Nahuizalco, killing all the landowners who were at home, and pillaging their estates. It was the sudden and violent explosion of a long-standing blind rage. For three days the poor wretches enjoyed their triumph, getting drunk with the terrified wives and daughters of the landowners they had killed, and applauding the excited speeches of their newly found leaders. On the morning of the fourth day trucks full of soldiers left San Salvador for Izalco, and machetes stood little chance against machine guns. The Indians fought courageously but hopelessly. When the American ship *Rochester*, which had hurried to the spot, cast anchor outside Acajutla, General Calderón could assure the captain that he needed no help and that over 5,000 'Bolsheviks' had already been disposed of.

By the end of the military operation around Izalco over 15,000 had been killed; the operation was commanded by Maximiliano Martínez, who is still known as 'Brujo', the sorcerer, in Salvadorian history. He was a sorcerer but he was a general too, and he had more Indian blood in his veins than Creole. He took power following a *pronunciamiento* on 3 December 1931. Historians now say shamefacedly that President Martínez's democratic feelings were heavily outweighed by his constant concern over public order. This he proved by the strong-arm tactics he used to crush the *peones*' political organizations, a move which somewhat reassured the landowners who were not so delighted by some of the other features of his government. Maximiliano Martínez was in fact much attracted to theosophy and was given to magic formulae, incantations and mystical signs. He managed somehow to subjugate the poor and illiterate peasantry. He recommended a new system of planting maize and the peasants followed it; one day he had bottles filled with red, blue and green water set up on the roof of his residence, and managed to persuade people that these old apothecary's jars contained sovereign cures for rheumatism and heart illnesses. It would seem that magic is the only possible explanation for the fact that Martínez managed to stay in power for thirteen years, despite the doubts – and at times open and bitter criticism – of the 'fourteen families'. Ultimately, however, in April and May 1944, revolution broke out.

The sorcerer's fall did not make any major change in Salvador's political life. The 'fourteen families' went on making the laws, as they always had, and the military leaders now taking turns to be president were careful to do nothing which might really compromise the interests of the coffee oligarchy. After 1944 the presidents were General Andrés Menéndez, Colonel Osmín Aguirre, General Salvador Casteneda, Colonel Oscar Osorio, Colonel José María Lemus – all regular soldiers, linked either by financial or blood relationships with the Salvadorian notables who still ran the country for longer or shorter periods, and in general remained pretty faithful to the Constitution.

Paradoxically that constitution is undoubtedly one of the most liberal of any in Central America. Thus Article 5 contains positive encouragement to revolt against regimes that are too cynically authoritarian. 'Some alternation in the holders of the presidency is indispensable if the established form of government is to be preserved. If this rule be violated, then revolution is obligatory.' One less liberal stipulation of the constitution has, since 1950, forbidden those people considered to be 'extremists' to have their names presented for election.

*

Just what is an extremist? The interpretation placed on the word by the heads of the 'fourteen families' and the military partially explains the way Salvador's politics have developed of recent years. In 1960 President José María Lemus was overthrown. There was nothing new about this – a number of his predecessors had suffered similarly. But this time the conquering putsch was made up of young progressive officers closely involved with the leaders of a left-wing movement which, though small, was quite dynamic and ambitious: the PRAN. PRAN, which declared itself determinedly revolutionary in intent, was authorized to present itself as a political party after the fall of Lemus. Was it an extremist group? The 'fourteen families' and the army considered the point: for three months they considered it while the PRAN leaders made their sympathy for the Castro regime clear beyond any doubt. This was their undoing. The young liberal officers who had organized the anti-Lemus putsch were disowned by the army Chief of Staff. The junta which had taken Lemus's place was dissolved and a civil and military ruling council took over on 15 January 1961: its members were Colonel Portillo, Lieutenant-Colonel Rivera and Professor Avelar.

There was a moment when it looked as though Salvadorian conservatism had taken over control more firmly than ever. But it was not long before it became clear that things were not quite as simple as that. Certainly a number of PRAN leaders were exiled, together with certain officers who had been involved with them. But the civil and military ruling Council soon began taking steps quite unheard of in a country like Salvador, where no government had ever given a thought to any kind of social reform. The Council decreed that henceforth both factory and farm workers must be paid for their Sundays off; rents were to be reduced by 30 per cent – a move which benefited nearly 800,000 people. The Council declared the Central Bank nationalized and set up an exchange control. This last measure seemed quite specially revolutionary in a country where the wealthy classes had always been able to send their capital abroad freely, and were accountable to no one for what they did with it. There was immediate reaction from the coffee oligarchy. During 1961 alone 30 million dollars left the country to be put safely in American or Swiss banks: this flight of capital, a totally new phenomenon, is a perfect illustration of the unexpected way in which the policy of the Council developed after 1961. The underlying reason became clear when the Council announced that its plan for economic reorganization was linked with Salvador's acceptance of the programme proposed by the Alliance for Progress.

*

The 'fourteen families' were on the defensive, but they could still count on the support of the Church – even though there were priests who had – somewhat timidly – begun to speak out against the appalling contrast between the total misery of the majority and the luxury of a tiny minority. They could also depend on a still influential section of the army.

But a new element was introduced which looked like being far more damaging to the oligarchy. The Kennedy administration realized that it might be far more profitable to help to bring to power in Central America teams of liberals and moderates, rather than to support anachronistic military dictatorships or oligarchic rule. The first illustration of this new policy occurred in Santo Domingo between June 1961 and September 1963. Salvador was of course a far more complex case: from one point of view the coffee oligarchy was more progressive than a lot of the antiquated dictatorships in the Caribbean. Yet the risk of a social explosion was far greater there too. To prevent the latter, the State Department experts decided to take the most liberal elements in the army and the intelligentsia into their confidence. The 'fourteen' could still count on the support of influential friends in the U.S. itself – for, curiously enough, Salvador is the only country in Central America whose economy is not wholly dependent on north American interests or business undertakings; it was through the intermediary of the 'fourteen' that the big American firms had up to now exercised their influence in Salvador. This Salvadorian coffee and business lobby was in a position to counter the campaign of the American government. Their principal argument was a simple one: the government which had followed the junta that overthrew Lemus was illegal. Therefore general elections must be arranged. With Washington's support, the Council undertook a race against time. The measures taken were intended to speed up the industrialization of the country, to stimulate production, make a considerable improvement in the lives of farm workers, and set up for the first time a system of old age pensions and sickness and unemployment benefits. These steps, considered by the coffee oligarchy as sheer 'vote-catching', were not even received with any special enthusiasm by the ordinary people, who had all too often been deceived and soothed into inactivity – people in any case with little political education. So, already under attack from the wealthy few, the Council also lost the support of the masses. Ultimately Salvador's real chance in this difficult battle to achieve effective modernization of its institutions lay in its university. The students of Salvador revealed outstanding dynamism and felt themselves to be the true spokesmen for public opinion. They took part in every demonstration. They were the children of a new social group, the lower middle class, and would gather in the town centres with cries of '*Cuba, sí, Yankee, no.*' It was more in the nature of a protest than a statement of any political programme; but the main thing about it was that they had absolutely no faith in the notion that *pronunciamientos* formulated in the drawing-rooms of the landowners, and put into effect more or less successfully by the military, could ever get Salvador any further along the road of progress. They realized that they might well leave university as lawyers without briefs, journalists without newspapers, doctors without patients, because of the still feudal structures of their country. They continued obstinately repeating a fact which must in the end be accepted as such : there could be no hope for Salvador as long as 2½ million out of the country's 3 million inhabitants remained second-class citizens.

The elections of April 1962 brought Colonel Rivera to the presidency, and he took office on 1 July 1962. His term ended in 1967, and he was succeeded by another officer, Colonel Fidel Sánchez Hernández, for the period 1968–72. This election was not as straightforward as Rivera's had been. The right wing of the government party known as the party of 'national conciliation' favoured a different candidate. But the new president had one trump card : a former Minister of the Interior, he had also been president of the junta for Inter-American Defence. In such a position an ambitious and skilful officer could make good friends, and there was nothing in 1968 to indicate that Sánchez Hernández lacked either ambition or skill. The future did not, however, look too favourable, given this transfer of power from one officer dedicated to the interests of the oligarchy to another. The elections of 1972 may well prove more lively. The small Christian Democratic party in 1968 still only had 15 seats out of the 52 in the National Assembly, but it was continuing to grow stronger. The man in whom Christian Democrat hopes lay was José Napoleón Duarte. He was re-elected as Mayor of San Salvador in March 1968, and hopes to stand for the presidency in 1972 with a programme similar to that of Dr Frei in Chile. Until then it is clear that no revolution can be expected in Salvador, free or otherwise.

CHAPTER 10

Nicaragua

STATISTICS

Area: 57,145 square miles
Estimated population in 1966: 1,685,000
Population density: 29 per square mile
Annual rate of population increase: 3·4 per cent
Annual increase in average per capita income from 1960 to 1966:
4·7 per cent.

PRINCIPAL PRODUCTS

Coffee, cocoa, sugar, meat.
Gold, silver, copper.

Nicaragua is essentially an agricultural country whose potential wealth is enormous but inadequately exploited, and indeed in some spheres totally untapped. Sixty-seven per cent of the active population is employed in farming. A CEPAL report states that a third of the cultivated land belongs to 362 landed proprietors, while 26,000 small peasant holdings make up less than 6 per cent. Over half the cultivable land remains unreclaimed, and hundreds of thousands of people who live by raising crops or herds are virtually unable ever to purchase industrial equipment. About 20 per cent of all farm labourers are paid in kind rather than money. Effectively the economy of Nicaragua largely depends on the United States; part of its mineral and timber wealth is in the hands of U.S. or Canadian companies, who make large profits out of highly favourable contracts. In 1956–7, for instance, the companies working the gold deposits paid 500,000 córdobas * in taxes, though the value of the gold they mined during that year amounted to some 8 million dollars. In 1961 the timber companies paid the Treasury less than 3 per cent of the value of the year's exports of wood, while the NIPCO company alone exported 80 million dollars. Virtually all (90 per cent) that is exported from Nicaragua goes to the U.S., which re-sells it in industrial products, machinery and fuel; 75 per cent of its imports come from the U.S. This almost total dependence of the national economy is hampering any rational development of the country. Crises in American industry can have unsuspected but drastic effects in the countryside of Nicaragua.

*

Needless to say the living conditions of the majority of Nicaraguans differ little from those of the Hondurans. Here, statistics cannot really convey much, and those we have are in any case not very recent, so must be treated with a certain caution. It may be said that the general picture in Nicaragua is closer to that of Honduras than to that of Costa Rica. In other words, the great mass of agricultural workers live in specially precarious conditions; a continually increasing middle class is becoming aware of its own power; and a minority of highly privileged people, usually of Spanish origin, have large incomes. But Nicaragua's great tragedy, like that of its neighbours, is illiteracy, with the poverty it always brings. Only 5 per cent of the boys and 0·5 per cent of the girls of school age go to secondary school. Though the housing of the poor is generally of the most rudimentary kind, rent still takes up a quarter of the average wage. Less than 2 per cent of the population have access to water that is

* The córdoba was 7 to the dollar in 1970, or 19 to the £ sterling.

safe to drink. The average life-expectancy is fifty, and over 50 per cent of children die before they are five.

No other Central American country has been as carefully watched by the U.S. as Nicaragua. This is not simply because the country's gold mines are in the hands of American firms: the most important reason is that access to the Panama Canal is controlled by Nicaragua, since it lies just where the isthmus narrows to its 'wasp-waist' and starts to bend. With Lake Nicaragua and the San Juan river it would be easy to supplement or even replace the Panama Canal with a new canal between the two oceans. The Castroist upheavals growing ever more violent in Panama naturally led the U.S. to get their old plans for a possible Nicaraguan project out of the files. So for Washington there can be no question at present of damaging its friendship with the Somoza clique which has been in power since 1936. Scholarships were regularly given to Nicaraguan officers by the U.S. to attend courses in the school of guerrilla warfare in the Panama Canal zone. It is noteworthy that in 1961 seventy-four Nicaraguan officers were sent there, as compared with only twenty-five Ecuadorians and twenty-eight Venezuelans. This difference in itself gives one some idea of Nicaragua's special position in the plans of the Pentagon men.

*

This solicitude has continued under varying guises for over a century. Back in 1838, in fact, Nicaragua became the arena in which American and British interests battled. The union of the Central American states, longed for and defended by Francisco Morazán, had just broken up; and the road across the isthmus in Nicaragua looked on the map like the shortest and most sensible choice for the crossing from the Atlantic to the Pacific. In 1849 the Clayton–Bulwer treaty gave the U.S. exclusive rights to build an inter-oceanic canal across Nicaraguan land. A syndicate led by Vanderbilt was formed in

1850. But then Walker came on the scene. Walker was a man of several professions : a journalist, a lawyer, a doctor, but undoubtedly his greatest skill lay in being an adventurer. The Caribbean coast of Nicaragua had received several visitations from the local pirates during the seventeenth century, and the country's third largest town is still called after one of them, Bluefields. That coast had hardly changed since an Indian chief was crowned 'king of the Mosquitos' by the governor of Jamaica. Today, in Bluefields, where the cottages look like English ones, you hear far more English spoken than Castillian. And the first inhabitants of the city always looked on Managua as a foreign town. But there is no doubt that the exploits of Dutch and English pirates along the Costa de Mosquitos were as nothing to those of Walker, an American citizen of Scots birth. He was a severe, cold and arrogant person; at one time he had considered becoming a priest, then studied medicine, set up as a lawyer in New Orleans, and helped to produce a newspaper in which he spoke in vigorous defence of slavery at the very time when the rest of the world was hoping to have seen it finally abolished. Having heard about Vanderbilt and his steamboat company plying the San Juan river, Walker embarked in May 1855 on an ancient boat which dropped its passengers along the Nicaraguan coast. Four months later Walker was practically master of the country; he held the town of Granada and commanded an armed troop of 600 men, made up of two battalions whom he called simply 'the American phalanx'. On the basis of this he declared himself president of Nicaragua, and got himself officially recognized as such by the American government. His first action as head of the government was of course to re-establish slavery which had been abolished at independence. His second was to confiscate everything owned by Vanderbilt. Obstinate, impatient, avaricious and utterly without pity, Walker set about invading Costa Rica. In the end, his audacity was so outrageous as to bring the combined troops of Salvador, Costa

Rica and even Guatemala (which sent a small troop towards
Granada by forced marches) out against his phalanx. Vanderbilt provided the Costa Ricans with money and arms; British
warships appeared along the Costa de Mosquitos to intervene
against Walker if needed. A year later the head of the 'American phalanx', defeated by sheer weight of numbers, took refuge on board an American warship which was most oppor-
tunely in the port of San Juan del Sur, and returned in
triumph to New Orleans where he was acclaimed with enthusiasm by his fellow-citizens. There this indefatigable pirate
found it easy to get more capital, as well as the promise of
further official support, and once more set off for Central
America, on board the *Fashion*. But miracles do not happen
twice. Santos Guardiola, an extremely forceful man, had been
made governor of Honduras since Walker's previous departure. Walker, whose excesses so disturbed the U.S. that he
lost support from that quarter, was betrayed by some of his
own officers and sought by Guardiola's forces. He committed
one single error, but it was his last: he gave himself up to
the English, who handed him over to the Honduran authorities. On 12 September 1860 he was shot near Tegucigalpa.

*

After this picaresque episode Nicaragua underwent a series
of confused political battles which did not greatly concern the
rest of the world. What is usually said is that two cliques,
'conservatives' and 'liberals', fought for power. The liberal
headquarters was in the town of Leon, while the conservatives' capital was Granada. Leon, where the great poet Rubén
Darío is buried, lies amid the wealth of tropical plants at the
foot of the Morabios hills. The old Leon, founded by Hernández de Córdoba, lay further along the lake shore, in the
shadow of the formidable volcano, Momotombo (written of by
Victor Hugo). Granada, its rival, still lives its old hidden life

behind the elegant, locked façades of the residences of the big conservative families. Managua, the present capital, became so as a result of the rivalry between the two towns, and the dispute between the families on the east and west sides of the lake; the Chamorros against the Castellóns.

From 1863 to 1893 the conservatives were in power, and decreed the separation of Church and State. Then the liberals came in their turn, with Santos Zelaya as president, hotly opposed by those who had preceded him in office. This harmless playing-about lasted almost till the beginning of the twentieth century. Then it became obvious to all Nicaraguans with any common sense that battles over places at 'court' between the great liberal and conservative families were of no importance, and that Nicaragua was threatened by something far more dangerous. It was becoming quite clear, in short, that the Americans had every intention of stepping into the affairs of the sleepy little republic. The Washington government offered President Santos Zelaya a loan of fifteen million dollars, in exchange for which the U.S. wanted not only a monopoly for building an inter-oceanic canal, but also total control of the country's finances and customs payments. Santos Zelaya had the temerity – or innocence – to refuse. His answer had barely reached Washington when a revolutionary movement broke out against his government. This timely revolt was led by a certain Díaz, of whom all that was known was that he had worked as an accountant in a firm in Pittsburgh. Certainly it was astonishing how easy he found it to get the arms, money and equipment he needed for his war from the U.S.

Even so, the rebel troops were on the point of being beaten by loyalists who remained faithful to the Santos Zelaya government – when suddenly units of American marines landed at Bluefields on the Caribbean coast. The excuse given by their commander was the rather poor one of protecting 'the lives and property of American citizens'; what the marines actually did was to go at once to the aid of the rebel troops in their distress. The end was not long in coming. Santos Zelaya was overthrown and a new government was speedily formed and recognized by Washington, with the rebel leader Adolfo Díaz as vice-president. It would probably have been a little too obvious – or difficult – to step straight into Santos Zelaya's place; but it was not long before further disturbances made it possible for Díaz to declare himself president and launch a dramatic appeal for help to the U.S., asking for American troops to restore order. Which they did – quickly and very easily.

*

The marines had only just left their Nicaraguan quarters in 1925 when the dispute between conservatives and liberals broke out again with increased violence. Díaz hastened to appeal to America for help, and the marines returned to start another occupation, which this time lasted until 1933. However this second act of their play was less serene than the first. The American troops had to face guerrillas organized by the great Indian, César Sandino. An infallible marksman, an unwavering patriot, he was determined to see the marines simply as invaders; he led a handful of peasant fighters and faithful followers out into the desolate *sierras* of the country. The ambushes and raids organized by his men were never sufficiently deadly or decisive to get rid of forces as hardened and well-trained as the U.S. marines. But such incessant pinpricks offended the vanity of their officers and were received with enthusiasm by the Nicaraguans. Sandino's 'long march' is still famous all over Central America, and Sandino himself remains something of a national hero. Even his death added to his halo as a martyr to liberty. He was not killed in battle, but murdered in 1934 in a surprise attack organized by the man whose name has dominated Nicaraguan political life for thirty years : Somoza.

Sandino died just when his struggle seemed to be winning the day. In fact the arrival of Roosevelt and the Democrats in Washington in 1933 had the immediate consequence of dropping the 'big stick' policy hitherto followed by the United States. Roosevelt, anxious to demonstrate his conciliatoriness and good will, ordered all American troops off Nicaraguan soil. Sandino's forces, who had been fighting for six years with the fervent support of liberals all over Latin America, felt themselves justified in entering Managua. And Sandino, the modern Zapata, demanded justice for the *peones* and agrarian reform – which amounted to a declaration of war against liberals and conservatives both.

Since the American occupation there had been no police or army in Nicaragua, but only a National Guard, established, trained and equipped by the U.S. None the less, this body represented a considerable force, an instrument in capturing the power which the departure of the marines had left vacant. In 1933, when the fate of Nicaragua hung in the balance, 'Tacho' Somoza was head of the National Guard. Somoza was a jovial character who had studied in Philadelphia, and could thus speak English (with an accent which seems to have charmed the wives of the American superior officers when in occupation).

Back in Managua he sold cars for a time. Then the beneficence of the American military high command won him a Rockefeller scholarship. From then on he rose rapidly to fame and fortune. As the faithful collaborator of the occupying power he had not, properly speaking, any political views of his own. His family came from Leon, and he therefore adopted the liberal label, but this did not involve on his part any promise or commitment. There can be no doubt that he was ready at once to get rid of Sandino – whose demands for social justice enraged the great families on both sides. Sandino was invited to a banquet by the head of the National Guard and murdered in cold blood. After that Tacho got on with his own concerns: in 1936, he organized a putsch, and doffed the tunic of the National Guard in favour of the robe of President of the Republic. He was to keep it for twenty years.

*

The story of Tacho Somoza has much in common with that of Trujillo, who was dictator of the Dominican Republic for thirty-one years. Their political fortunes began in the same way, based on the grace and favour of America. Tacho, like Trujillo, was assassinated with incredible ease, after having escaped dozens of earlier attempts. Trujillo, when he died, was the owner of Santo Domingo; Tacho bought up all German property cheap and set systematically about enriching himself at the expense of his fellow-citizens. His nepotism was at least as enthusiastic as that of his neighbour: his elder son, Tachito, was appointed director of the Military Academy and Chief of Staff of the Armed Forces; his second son, Luis, was president of the Chamber of Deputies; and even today the republic's banknotes bear the profile of his daughter Liliane. Like Trujillo, Somoza naturally chose the convenient banner of anti-communism to justify his greed for power and wealth. He was even more a friend to the Americans than Trujillo, being on several occasions General Eisenhower's guest. He had an equestrian statue of himself placed in front of the Managua stadium, which was illuminated each night. He looked like the paternal and kind 'boss' of everyone in the country. At least a third of the estates in Nicaragua belonged to him, and there is a story that once, passing an estate that took his fancy, he had his car stopped and sent a secretary to find out what it would cost to buy. She returned in some embarrassment: 'You already own this property, General.'

Trujillo always remained a canny countryman who could recognize the value of any animal at a glance. Tacho was the first exporter of cattle from Nicaragua. He owned pasteurizing plants, several gold mines and some cement works. It would be tedious to list all the things acquired by Somoza during his twenty years of absolute power : he became the owner of at least fifty ranches and almost as many coffee plantations. He would not allow freedom of the press, for, he said, 'it is vital not to disturb the order reigning in the country'. He sent his children to the best American schools, and his eldest son to West Point. Again like Trujillo, Tacho Somoza did not remain president uninterruptedly, but ruled through intermediaries when the need arose. His son-in-law, Guillermo Sevilla Sacasa, was given the job of defending his regime to the U.S. government, and the UN General Assembly in New York – which he did, be it said, brilliantly, being far the cleverest member of the family.

The end for Tacho came wholly unexpectedly during a reception given in Leon by the Liberal Party on 21 September 1956. The noise of the gunshots was drowned by the playing of the orchestra. The terrorist was lynched by the bodyguard directly. Tacho himself, though he had five bullet wounds, was not dead. President Eisenhower at once sent a private plane with his own surgeon aboard to try to save the dictator whose friendship for the United States had never wavered. Rushed to the hospital in the Panama Canal Zone, Tacho was to die five days later without regaining consciousness. He was succeeded as president by his son Luis.

It might have been expected that the disappearance of Tacho would have led to the collapse of a regime attacked fiercely by an opposition most of whose leaders had been forced to seek exile in Costa Rica. But it did not. Action by the U.S. ambassador helped to stage-manage a transition during which the change-over of power went smoothly and without major incident. Forty-two deputies and sixteen senators approved the investiture of Luis Somoza. The heir to the throne began to loosen somewhat the reins held so tightly by his father, and to act in a generally more open fashion. On several occasions he referred to the possibility of liberal reforms, and seemed to want to relax the dictatorial regime. But every time he was argued out of it by family considerations. In theory neither Luis Somoza nor any member of his family could stand as candidate in the 1963 presidential elections.

In point of fact it was René Schick, a 54-year-old protégé of the Somozas, who had formerly been both an ambassador and a minister, who was elected in 1963. Yet again a victory for the liberal party. The conservatives, victims of their own inner dissensions, were forced to accept defeat, and hope for better days of power in the future. Energetic, modest, coming from an emigrant family who had settled in Nicaragua in 1905, Schick began his term of office by stressing the problems of reforming education and the agrarian system.

Though the survival – even through intermediaries – of the Somozas was never in any doubt in Managua or any of the neighbouring capitals, the Nicaragua governed by Réne Schick presented a far less aggressively dictatorial image than that of Tacho. Real reforms were undertaken: joining the Central American Common Market, combined with the hope of seeing a new interoceanic canal built to replace the old-fashioned Panama Canal, seemed to offer hopeful signs for future development to everyone in the country.

However, this reassuring but hesitant period did not last long. René Schick died of a heart attack on 3 August 1966, and was replaced by the first vice-president, Lorenzo Guerrero; elections then took place in February 1967. The problem was whether the Somozas would be prepared to rule from behind the scenes as when Schick was in office, or whether Anastasio Tachito Somoza, the commander of the National Guard, would demand the presidency in person. Some of his closest friends tried to persuade him that he could wait for a few years; knowing how impulsive he was, and how far less subtle than his younger brother Luis, they feared the upheavals his coming to power would bring. Nor were they wrong; he became president, and at once set about ruling with an iron hand.

Even what – for want of a better word – one must call the electoral campaign was filled with disturbances. In October 1966 the conservative opposition organized a great protest meeting in the capital against the candidature of Tachito. Allied with the Social Christians and the Independent Liberals, the conservatives formed a national opposition Union – from which communists, however, were excluded. A further stormy protest meeting took place in Managua on 22 January 1967, attended by sixty thousand people. A short popular uprising lasted for two days, and the leaders of the movement, having locked themselves into the Grand Hotel with some American tourists as hostages, capitulated before the troops of Tachito's National Guard, who seized the opportunity to arrest a large number of political leaders, and restore censorship of the press.

Under the banner of the need to 'fight firmly against communism', the new Somoza did not find it difficult to gain the presidency. The result of the January rising was to weaken the opposition of both conservatives and liberals to the power of the Somozas; and they in turn found it convenient to make a point of seeing little to choose among 'liberals', 'conservatives' and 'communists'. The communists (Nicaraguan Socialist Party), for their part, carried out a serious self-criticism. Like so many other Latin American communist parties, they had tried to apply European patterns to Nicaragua, and insisted on the leading role of the urban working class 'in the conquest of power'. They had to admit in 1967 that the 'Nicaraguan working class was numerically one of the smallest anywhere in Latin America' (in fact there were only 40,000 urban workers out of a total working population of 600,000). They consequently determined to devote more energy to building up 'cells' in country areas, but they declared once again that 'the armed struggle in its many forms must be a continuation of a mass movement – otherwise it is bound to fail'. There was nothing particularly original about such a stance, but it contained an implied condemnation of some of the fervent revolutionary guerrilla *focos* established in the Nicaraguan hills by the younger members of sections of both liberal and conservative middle classes.

CHAPTER 11

Costa Rica

STATISTICS

Area: 19,652 square miles
Estimated population in 1966: 1,514,000
Population density: 77 per square mile
Annual rate of population increase: 4·1 per cent
Annual increase in average per capita income from 1960 to 1966
   1·2 per cent.

PRINCIPAL PRODUCTS

Bananas, coffee, cocoa, sugar cane, rice, cotton, tobacco.

Twice a day, at noon and at five p.m., happy noises from
recreation grounds can be heard in the peaceful streets of
San José de Costa Rica. Nowhere in Central America or the
Caribbean are there to be seen so many students wearing
college badges or school uniforms, so many socks and striped
shirts, as in this unusual capital. The thirst for learning seems
all-consuming in Costa Rica. Its 10 per cent illiteracy rate is
the lowest anywhere in Latin America apart from Argentina.

   This almost total literacy is not the only unusual feature
of Costa Rica. It is a white man's country, an island of European blood in a part of the world that is dark brown on the
high ground, coffee-coloured on the low. In Costa Rica there
are only 1·8 per cent of negroes and mulattoes, living mainly
on the coast. The remainder of the population are as white as

in Galicia, Catalonia, Andalucía or Scandinavia – from where the great-grandparents of the modern *Ticos* originally came. The nickname is not a pejorative one : it is the Costa Ricans themselves, with their love of all things simple and friendly, who describe themselves as *Ticos*. And the neighbours with whom they have undoubtedly had the largest number of brushes over the past ten years are commonly known in San José as the *Nicas*. There is nothing aggressive about this capital city, which with its 300,000 people (in 1968) reminds one more of a European provincial town than a city in the tropics. The cottages in the suburbs are unpretentious, the epitome of lower-middle-class comfort; cake shops and tea-shops, of which there are few indeed in the other Central American capitals, are a common sight here. Indeed the *Ticos* reckon that their one failing is greed. Apart from that, their rule of life is as simple as that of the early pioneers. They do not like making their horses and donkeys work to death, as is done in so many Spanish-speaking American countries; there is even a law that no animal may be worked in harness for more than 48 hours a week, the use of any form of goad is barely tolerated, and the newspapers in Costa Rica are at least as full of letters from animal-lovers as those in England or Switzerland.

It seems clear that the Church, whose political and social role is considerable, has succeeded in influencing people's style of life here profoundly, unlike the Spanish clergy in Guatemala who are so often forced to tolerate semi-pagan practices among their Indian flocks if they are not to lose contact with them altogether. Kindness, gentleness, good manners, and a concern for security and well-being are undoubtedly the most notable traits of the *Ticos*, who like to compare themselves with the Swiss.

*

They tend to forget how lucky they are in having a climate

which remains around 20°C all the year round; and how lucky too in the exceptional atmosphere of freedom that pervades the streets of San José, which arises out of a long democratic tradition, and the way in which their society first came into being. The discovery, settlement and colonization of Costa Rica took place under somewhat unusual conditions. First, the Indian groups in this part of Central America were few, and their degree of civilization was nowhere near that of the Mayas, the Toltecs, or even the Aztecs – to mention a few of their nearest neighbours. These Indians of Costa Rica lived mainly on the Nicoya peninsula and along the Pacific coast. They presented no special problems to the first conquerors who were led by three *hidalgos*. Of that early Indian population there remain today fewer than thirty families which – and here again Costa Rica is unusual – are strictly protected by the government. The threat facing the conquistadors came more from the Atlantic coast where bands of pirates later landed, and it was by way of that fever-ridden and unfriendly Costa de Mosquitos that tribes came who were considerably more aggressive than those of the Pacific. Almost unique in the annals of Spanish colonialism, the descendants of the first conquistadors became soldiers and peasants : the first picture we have of Costa Rican society is one of a community of small farmers, working their own land, herding their own flocks and defending their property themselves. The great wave of immigration at the beginning of the nineteenth century imposed a very firm structure on this patriarchal society of people whose needs, like their tastes, remained modest.

The splendid roads now linking San José with Cartago, Alajuela and Puntarenas take you past model farms with white wooden fences, and cars alternating with trains of large-wheeled country carts decorated with patterns of many colours.

*

There has been no army in Costa Rica since 1948; it is forbidden by the constitution. In a continent where *pronunciamientos* are endemic, and people tend to be subject to the whims of ill-tempered colonels, Cost Rica has happily escaped the shower of *coups d'état* with which recent Central American history has been filled. A list of the presidents who scrupulously respected people's freedom and constitutional guarantees would be infinitely longer than one of those who were authoritarian, or corrupt, or whose prime concern was to stay in power. The opposition movement which drove out General Tinoco in August 1919 can barely be described as a revolution; and the only civil war even half worthy of the name dates back to 1948, and is still spoken of with deep feeling in San José. In September 1944 Teodoro Picado had taken over the government. He was a man who gave open-air audiences in the park in San José, and held his court of justice under a tree; he was elected by a tactical alliance between conservatives and communists. The opposing side declared firmly that their candidate, a certain Cortés, standing for the Democratic Party, had really got 85 per cent of the votes. So far a situation not peculiar to Costa Rica. For four years the democrats strained at the leash, convinced that only rigging the election and outside pressure could possibly explain Picado's victory. In the 1948 general election the liberals re-formed under the new title of 'National Union Party', and put forward Otilio Ulate as their candidate. Though the Picado government left no stone unturned to get themselves voted back in, Ulate won. Picado resorted to a step which the Ticos could only see as an alarming sign of barbarism: he annulled the elections.

A small dark-haired man, nervous, impassioned, immensely dramatic and totally unknown, then appeared as the devil in the forefront. He launched a proclamation which resounded oddly in this peaceful countryside where life followed a pattern that can only be called evangelical: 'To arms!' This was José Figueres making his noisy and aggressive entry into the Costa Rican political scene. It must be said that he has never really left it, and that his personality still dominates those of all the other political figures in San José even from a long distance. Figueres, as one can tell at a glance, is Spanish in origin; but it is not irrelevant to know that his parents, solidly Catalan, only came to Costa Rica in 1906. This quicksilver politician brought with him the new note of an emigrant seeking progress, and mistrustful of the old aristocratic families. His father was a doctor with no great ambition, but he won an honourable and successful position for himself in Costa Rica and was determined to give young José the best possible education. At the age of sixteen, he sent him to the U.S., first to New York and then to Boston, where he enrolled at the Massachusetts Institute of Technology.

On his return Figueres took charge of a coffee plantation and began meeting with groups of young Costa Ricans attracted to socialism. When the disturbances arising out of the 1948 election developed, he was still no more than the secretary general of a student movement, but his call to insurrection evoked a favourable response among young people and intellectuals, who were at that time following with fascination the still early days of Arévalo's experiment in Guatemala.

*

The 'civil war' lasted for two months. And it was to Arévalo that Figueres and his friends turned for military help – being themselves without arms or organization, and, especially in the early days of the rebellion, improvising from one minute to the next. However, the support they got from Guatemala was more moral than practical. Arévalo felt the strongest sympathy for this Figueres who came from the same liberal and reformist stable as himself. But in any case the Ticos moved with great speed. Figueres took over three TACA aircraft, which he turned into temporary bombers; his pilots dropped their bombs by hand as they swooped low over their targets. The impetuous Figueres then got together in record time an enthusiastic team of fighters whom he named 'The Caribbean Legion', in memory of the Spanish war which had so aroused the feelings of all liberal Spaniards settled in Costa Rica. In this Legion, though it purported to be broadly international, there were at first only Costa Ricans, Nicaraguans, Dominicans who had escaped from Trujillo's prisons, and a few idealistic Mexicans. It was still forceful enough to wreak havoc among the regular government troops outside Puerto Limón. It was the attack on Puerto Limón which settled the outcome of the civil war. The Archbishop of San José, Mgr Sanabria, whose sympathies seem to have been wholly with Figueres and his men, intervened, thus hastening the collapse of the government forces, and Figueres made a triumphal entry into the capital; a junta was immediately set up, with Figueres as its provisional head.

Everyone recognized the fact that the junta really was a provisional one, and would hand over its powers to the properly elected candidate, Otilio Ulate, as soon as possible – which it did, thus indicating how genuinely democratic Figueres's intentions were. But in its few months of action, the junta carried out some astounding measures. First of all, the army was disbanded – a thing which had never happened anywhere in Central America before. Symbolically the Bella Vista barracks, that breeding-ground for Chiefs of Staff, and home of possible *pronunciamientos*, was turned into a Fine Arts Museum. To make it quite clear that he was neither a left-wing extremist – as the conservatives said – nor a right-wing extremist – as the communists said – Figueres struck a blow on either side. He nationalized the banks; he also banned the Communist Party. He then asked Fr Benjamín Núñez to become a member of the provisional government; Núñez is one of the most colourful figures in the small gallery of Costa Rican 'characters'. He founded a Christian Democrat trade union whose title, *Rerum Novarum**, shows what its programme was, and made it one of the leading political forces in the country.

As planned, in November 1949 Figueres handed on the torch to Otilio Ulate, and this Costa Rican Cincinnatus went back to his coffee growing. For four years one hardly heard mention of him. He then stood forward in the 1952 presidential election as the National Liberation Party candidate. Once again the opposition was a coalition between conservatives and communists. The head of the Costa Rican CP was a first-rate lawyer, Manuel Mora, and his supporters were drawn more from among the intellectuals in the capital than from the mass of small landowners who were naturally attracted by Figueres's promises to improve their standard of living. Mora's major complaint against Figueres was his theoretical pro-Americanism, but such an argument had little weight for most people, and Figueres easily won the election.

*

In the newly elected congress the National Liberation Party held 31 out of the 46 seats. When Figueres became president on 8 November 1953 he acquired the nickname 'Don Pepe', and the open hostility of 'Tacho' Somoza, the dictator of Nicaragua. Somoza had made no secret of where his sympathies lay, nor of the help he had given the anti-Figueres forces during the civil war. In 1952 a bitter struggle began between the two rival presidents – a struggle which produced innumerable fears in Washington, and led to a number of special meetings of the OAS. Somoza sent expeditions into Costa Rican territory, and Costa Rica replied in kind. Up to 1956 the Somoza–Figueres duel represented to Latin Americans a paradigm example of the battle between democracy

* Title of a social encyclical by Pope Leo XIII.

and dictatorship in Central America. Figueres, firmly hostile both to communism and to right-wing military dictatorship, counted and still counts on receiving understanding and help from liberal circles – especially the trade unions – in the United States, to assist in the gradual democratization of a continent which has for so long been at the mercy of its many *caudillos*. During his presidency San José became the place of refuge for democratic leaders forced into exile by the military: he welcomed Rómulo Betancourt with open arms, when he decided to leave Venezuela after Pérez Jiménez's *coup d'état*. Figueres got the United Fruit Co. to pay the state almost 45 per cent of its profits; the company's schools and hospitals were placed under direct government control, and its monopoly of railways, electricity plants, cocoa and hemp production was taken away. For Costa Rica this naturally meant considerable material benefit, as well as a somewhat remarkable diplomatic triumph. Don Pepe's supporters considered it as proof positive that his brand of moderate reformism could ultimately achieve as much as, if not more than, violent revolution. However, it must be noted that the modifications made in the United Fruit contract were put through just after the Guatemalan affair at a point when the company was under pressure from all sides – even in Washington where the American government was threatening it with a prosecution under the anti-trust laws – and ready to make any concession for a quiet life.

*

In 1957, his term of office ended, Don Pepe handed over the keys of his desk without a murmur. As he had done in 1949, he went back to being an ordinary political leader, and to looking after his own business. But it was clear that his party would win the next election, despite the combined opposition of communists, Castroists and conservatives. In 1962 the expected happened: the candidate of Figueres's National Liberation Party, Orlich, got in by a comfortable margin, and the supporters of Don Pepe naturally went on playing a part on the Latin American scene quite out of proportion to their apparently modest means. From San José the periodical *Combate* warmly defended Don Pepe's theories, and among the list of its patrons the review numbered the names of Eduardo Santos, former president of Colombia and Rómulo Betancourt, of Venezuela. *Combate* defended with conviction the thesis of Inter-American cooperation, and the twofold struggle against totalitarianism on both right and left. However, the appearance of Castroism in the Caribbean and in Latin America had profoundly changed the whole political scene. The tactics of Figueres and his friends who led this democratic 'third force' in Latin America had one major weakness – that of counting too much on the goodwill and understanding of the United States.

'We are,' said Figueres, 'Americans first and foremost. Nothing will ever change that. Violent extremism is a waste of time. We must collaborate with the United States, condemning their mistakes and weaknesses when we have to, of course, but also trying to understand their point of view.'

One of Figueres's key ideas was this: we are in the western camp, and must do nothing to assist Russia in the east–west conflict. This determination, together with his anti-communist principles is sufficient to explain most of Figueres's feelings about Castroism. He had already got certain reservations over the way the Arbenz regime was going in Guatemala early in 1954, and it was with similar reservations that he watched Castro's ever more rapid movement towards the extreme left. Freedom of expression remained as great as ever in San José. But it was possible that even in Costa Rica the determinedly pro-American reformism of Don Pepe did not now fully satisfy the naturally revolutionary excitements of the new thinking.

From 1962 to 1965 Orlich's presidency was undisturbed by

any incidents grave enough to attract the notice of the rest of the world. Costa Rica, a country where incidents of any kind seldom occur, has proved that is possibly one of the happiest parts of a continent in perpetual turbulence. The temporary silencing of the Somozas in Nicaragua obviously helped, during this period, to reassure the *Ticos* as to the way Central American politics were going, and the fact that President Kennedy chose their capital, San José, as the venue for the meeting of all the Central American heads of state naturally flattered them. Significantly enough, what gave them most cause for alarm was the volcano, Irazú, above Cartago. It began erupting in 1963 in a spectacular and more violent manner than ever before, and reached a dramatic climax in June 1964 when a stream of lava poured down from the crater and threatened to engulf several villages. A sticky and suffocating dust fell on San José itself, and a UNESCO mission, led by the French volcanologist Haroun Tazieff came to study the phenomenon.

Between 1962 and 1966 the trade unions re-formed around the two major ones – the 'Catholic' one, known as the 'Costa Rican Workers' Confederation' and the 'socialist' CGTC, comprising certain Castroist elements – especially among the United Fruit Company's banana workers.

In the elections of January 1966 Trejos Fernández, the Vice-Rector of the University of Costa Rica, and a believer in economic neo-liberalism, won by a short head, defeating the Figueres candidate, Daniel Oduber. The National Liberation Party kept its majority in Parliament. Thus, twenty years after the almost comic-opera episode of the Caribbean Legion, Don Pepe was still playing a quite special part in the country's political life. But to the United States Trejos Fernández, a liberal, a modest and prudent academic, was at least as useful as Figueres, the friend of anti-communist American liberals.

CHAPTER 12

Panama

STATISTICS

Area: 29,208 square miles
Estimated population in 1967: 1,329,000
Population density: 45 per square mile
Annual rate of population increase: 3·0 per cent
Annual increase in average per capita *income from 1960 to 1966*
    5·4 per cent.

PRINCIPAL PRODUCTS

Bananas, cocoa, sugar, coffee, rice.

There is nothing but a railing between the two worlds. On
one side republican Panama, where life is like a permanent
reproduction of *Porgy and Bess*; or like a piece of New Orleans,
vivid, with singing, shouting and dancing twenty-four hours
a day despite the languid damp heat of the tropics. The
wooden balconies of the old houses and even the pavements
are used to supplement the inadequate living space. In
Panama people live as much in the street as in their homes;
apart from anything else, it is a trifle cooler outside. Swarms
of black, yellow and brown children take advantage of any
sudden downpour to rush out for an open-air shower. Chinese
and Middle-Eastern traders mingle with Haitians, European
immigrants and sailors from all over the world on leave here.
In the stalls at the corners of the lanes and alleys (all utterly
filthy), and sometimes on the pavement itself, you see for sale

all the well-known brands of whisky, the most modern German-made cameras, and pocket transistors made in Japan – all at prices which compare favourably with those in the most comfortably-off free cities in the world. On the other side is the canal, where you suddenly find yourself in an oasis of calmness and trim lawns, aseptic, and at all times under the protection of marines in carefully pressed uniforms; here you are in the CZ, the Canal Zone, ceded in perpetuity to the U.S. government by a treaty made in 1903.

Obviously, without the Canal Zone Panama would not exist, at least in its present form. The zone extends from either side of the canal for 8 kilometres, and contains the various artificial lakes that supply it. The area of the Zone is 362 square miles, and there almost 60,000 civilians and 6,000 troops live under American law, with the American comfort you find in one of those neat, tidy and uninteresting little towns in the southern United States. Their lawns are impeccable, and their little houses have white wooden fences; there are private swimming pools to add a splash of jade-green or turquoise to the tropical exuberance of the local vegetation. Clubs, golf-courses, refrigerators, electronic gadgets, and air conditioners are apparently enough to defy the rigours of a climate which has always been considered one of the most unhealthy in the world. Of 40,000 motor vehicles registered in the republic of Panama, 15,000 drive along the well-maintained roads of the Canal Zone. North Americans who work for the canal company still have salaries three or four times larger than Panamanians doing exactly the same jobs, despite the fact that an assurance of equal pay for equal work has been theoretically inscribed into the most recent agreement signed between Washington and the Panama government. The cooperative stores in the Canal Zone sell their goods – from Coca Cola to electric mowing machines – at far lower prices than the local dealers can.

*

Senator Smathers, a democrat from Florida, cried angrily one day that 'The Zone is an island of luxury in an ocean of poverty.' It is quite true; one has only to compare the standard of living of the few thousand American citizens there with that of the vast majority of the 1,287,000 Panamanians. Despite the proximity of the canal and the enormous profits its 64 kilometres of waterway have brought the American Treasury since 1914, the republic of Panama escapes none of the plagues that affect the other Latin American states: illiteracy, infant mortality, unemployment, malnutrition. Yet as compared with the lot of their immediate neighbours, the Panamanians are in fact somewhat better off. The annual internal product was 520 dollars *per capita* in 1965. Obviously this relative prosperity is to some extent artificial, and affects only part of the population (60 per cent of whom live by agricultural work). But it is true that the republic of Panama is the richest of the six little republics which succeed one another from Tapachula down to the jungle of Darien along that strip of land which is so often convulsed and re-shaped by volcanic eruptions.

Panama has definitely profited from the canal. There are good roads across the isthmus, following the same direction as the famous 'Nombre de Dios' trail of Pedro Arias de Avila which they now supplant, though for three centuries of colonialism it was the only trade route for the wealth of the Spanish American Pacific coast to get across to the metropolis. The Americans' determined battle against tropical diseases has continued to extend; their unmerciful war on mosquitoes, malaria and yellow fever has made Panama the healthiest town in the tropics, though its name is still linked with the deaths of the 40,000 workers who died of fevers during the construction of the canal.

The question of internationalizing the canal is only brought up ocasionally by the Panamanians in an attempt to achieve a better understanding with Washington – it was thus that the treaty of 1903 was revised in 1936, in 1955 and again in 1959. Panama lives off the canal, and would like to live better. Indeed this wish is actually translated into a name that sounds like the name of an illness: *canalera*. The mission sent in 1951 by the International Bank to consider reconstruction and development analysed precisely the causes and consequences of *canalera*. The majority of the people feel a sense of resignation, being not unjustifiably convinced that the country's economy depends wholly and solely on the canal. The wave of Panamanian nationalism which is growing ever stronger is thus in practice as much due to considerations of a psychological nature as to merely material demands. In November 1959 the populace broke the windows of the American information office in Panama City, and tore down the flag from the American embassy. The State Department responded to this disturbing indication of unrest by sending Under-Secretary of State Livingstone Merchant to make an on-the-spot inquiry. The conclusions he brought back after a detailed study were so convincing as to persuade the Eisenhower administration that some kind of gesture was called for. Against the advice of the Pentagon and the House of Representatives the American government decreed that in future the flag of the Panamanian Republic should fly alongside the Stars and Stripes at the entry to the Canal Zone.

*

At first the rent for the Canal Zone brought 250,000 dollars a year into the young republic; in 1936 this was increased to 430,000 dollars and in 1955 to 1,900,000. On each occasion the negotiations were lengthy, cavilling and angry. It took almost three years of talks to achieve the first revision of the 1903 agreement in 1936. The talks which resulted in the 1955 treaty were led for Panama by President Remón. 'We are well aware,' he said, 'that Panama is not Suez. We want the United States to stay. Our greatest source of wealth is our geographical position, but we naturally wish to gain as much from it as we can.'

A new element then entered the negotiations between the two governments: it is far from certain any more that the Panama Canal can go on being exploited indefinitely as it exists at present. There are certain definite indications that this gigantic undertaking of the last century may well become out of date in the near future.

The idea of linking the Atlantic and Pacific by cutting a canal across the Central American isthmus was certainly not a new one. As long ago as 1529 Álvaro de Saavedra Cerón suggested cutting through at one of the four points – Tehuantepec, Nicaragua, Panama or Darien. In 1534 Charles V had a study made of the ground between the Río Chagres and the Pacific. Other plans, the most interesting of which was produced by Humboldt, suggesting nine possible lines to be followed, were put up to gather dust on the shelves along with the earliest suggestions of Charles V's advisers. In the mid-nineteenth century the gold rush brought Panama out of its stagnant state, and the first railway line was built across the isthmus in 1849. Panama then became part of the new republic of Gran Colombia which comprised in addition Venezuela, Ecuador and Colombia. There was still to be one resounding failure and a last-minute about-turn by the American Congress before Panama at last really became one of the essential strategic cross-roads of the world.

The failure was French: Ferdinand de Lesseps, who had conquered Suez, agreed after much thought to undertake the construction of the canal. He was by then 74 and though he remained full of vitality, his son who was more aware of all the problems, tried to dissuade him. 'When a general has won his first battle, he wants to win another,' replied de Lesseps, over-confidently. He established the 'Universal Company for the Interoceanic Canal' and set about finding investors. The first response brought in no more than a tenth of the total needed; then a second attempt, including a journey through America by de Lesseps himself, and a publicity campaign quite unprecedented at that date, brought in twice the amount the company needed to start operations. But serious mistakes in the preparations, the unexpected withdrawal of some firms, and above all, the badly under-estimated difficulties involved in the work, hampered this immense operation from the very first. 'It is impossible,' said André Siegfried, 'to give even an approximate number of the victims. We only know that there have been at times up to 40 deaths a day, and that white staff have continually to be replaced.'

Cutting the Suez Canal required the excavation of 75 million cubic metres of earth: de Lesseps's first calculations arrived at the same figure for Panama. But in fact, when the Americans had actually completed the canal, they had re-moved the incredible quantity of 259 million cubic metres. When at last, after endless hesitations, de Lesseps admitted that his first project could not be successful, it was too late. Despite the tardy and limited support of the French govern-ment, de Lesseps's second battle ended in a rout. The scandal of it all was slow in dying down, and it was not until fifty years later that the objective voice of André Siegfried gave a measured assessment of just where the responsibilities for the failure lay.

*

It was in a critical and unenthusiastic spirit that the Ameri-cans had watched the undertaking begun by the French. Its failure enabled them to reintroduce plans and discussions which had been going on more or less continuously through-out the latter half of the nineteenth century. In 1849 at the time of the gold rush the American banker, Vanderbilt, had a travel service operating across Nicaragua which was ex-tremely successful; and up to the last minute Americans seemed to favour the idea of building the canal there. It did in fact seem the ideal place: Lake Nicaragua is almost 170 kilometres long, and only 35 metres above sea level; the Pacific coast is only 25 kilometres away, and a very deep river, the San Juan, flows gradually downwards towards the Caribbean. Vanderbilt's passengers went up the San Juan, and across the lake in paddle-boats. The first serious study of the plan for a canal across Nicaragua was made at the end of the century by an American commission under the chairmanship of Vice-Admiral Walker.

After de Lesseps's failure in Panama it seemed absolutely certain that the Americans' choice would fall on Nicaragua. In January 1902 the House of Representatives unanimously voted for this, but in May of that same year, there was a disastrous eruption of Mount Pele in Martinique. The anxious Americans looked at their relief maps of Central America and discovered that Lake Nicaragua was surrounded by volcanic peaks; furthermore, the Nicaraguans had the unfortunate inspiration of designing a postage stamp which depicted the Momotombo volcano spurting out flames. All the American senators received copies of the stamp, and the results were instantaneous. The Spooner law voted by both houses of Congress gave the green light to the men who wanted to carry on where de Lesseps had left off.

The French company demanded 109 million dollars to cede its rights. The American government offered only 40 million – which was accepted because ultimately there could be no alternative. The American government still could not get the work started until it had succeeded in getting the treaty made with Great Britain in 1850 revised and, more important, in persuading the conceding power, the Colombian government, to agree.

England was too deeply involved in the Boer War to dispute the matter for long. The Colombians, on the other hand, were violently enraged by this threat to their sovereignty. On 12 August 1903 the Senate in Bogotá unanimously rejected the theoretical agreement made with Washington six months earlier, allowing for the handing over to the United States of a strip of land 9½ kilometres wide in the Panama isthmus. While Colombia havered – actually considering how to achieve the most advantageous conditions – Washington determined to use strong-arm methods. On 3 November 1903 a suspiciously opportune revolt against the Colombian government broke out in Panama; it was led by General Huertas, commander of the local garrison, and a supporter of secession. The American warship *Nashville*, which had arrived in the port of Colón the previous day, prevented Colombian troop reinforcements from landing. Three days later the new State of Panama was recognized by the United States. Two men played the major roles in all this : Bunau-Varilla, whose job it was to liquidate the French company, and who negotiated the agreement between Washington and Panama, and Theodore Roosevelt. 'I took the canal zone,' said President Roosevelt some months later, 'and left Congress to argue. While they went on talking, the canal was being built ...'

The canal came into operation on 15 August 1914 and at once proved its value. In fifty years the Canal Company, whose sole shareholder is the American Department of Defence, has already got back twice the amount of capital originally invested. But this nice little arrangement which brings an average of 40 million dollars a year into the American Treasury may perhaps be coming to an end.

*

During the Second World War the obvious vulnerability of the Panama Canal began to turn opinion back towards the idea of reconsidering the Nicaraguan project. The problem of using and defending the Canal Zone in case of atomic war has now made it a more acute question than ever. Pentagon experts therefore estimate that the political problem of the canal is on the way to solving itself: first because it is rapidly approaching the limit of its capacity; they expect that the canal will be quite out of date before 1980 and that a new inter-oceanic waterway must be begun at once, since it will take ten years to build. The Americans are trying to work out a plan for a canal that will overcome the dangers inherent in the sluice-gate system of Panama in case of atomic war. The extremely unhealthy and uninhabited wild area of Darien has been chosen as being the best in principle. Underground atomic tests have been made in the U.S. to develop a technique for the rapid clearing of the ground in this region. If the project goes forward and it becomes clear that the period of consideration is over, relations between the Panama and Washington governments will totally alter. It seems likely that what is happening in Honduras with the gradual reduction of the activities of the United Fruit Co. will be re-enacted in the Canal Zone. The Hondurans have long and justifiably protested against the outrageous rights exercised by United Fruit in their country; they are now realizing that it is not easy to manage without the company from one day to the next. Similarly in Panama it is more a matter of cherishing this goose that lays the golden eggs than trying to drive it away. Otherwise the nationalist demands of the Panamanians may well turn into the disappointed cries of an audience standing in an empty theatre in front of a stage from which the angry actors have walked away.

From 9–12 January 1964 there were violent riots in Panama in which twenty-four people were killed and almost 400 injured. The president, Roberto Chiari, broke off diplomatic relations with the United States, and a commission of enquiry was sent out by the OAS.

Once again the source of the trouble was a flag. This had

also been the chief cause of the rioting of November 1959. On 13 June 1962 Presidents Kennedy and Chiari had put out a joint communiqué stating that 'their representatives would make sure that the Panamanian flag would fly in the Canal Zone'. But the governor of the Zone decided in December 1963 that it was 'correct according to law and custom' that the American flag should still stand in classrooms and lecture halls there. This decision satisfied neither the Panamanians nor the Americans, since the latter wanted to see their flag outside such buildings, while the Panamanians demanded that theirs be displayed together with the Stars and Stripes in every instance, as the agreement stated.

On 7 January 1964 several hundred American students hoisted their flag outside the Balboa school. On 8 January Panamanian students in the capital protested, demanded an explanation, and insisted the next day on putting up their own flag as well. The American authorities refused, and this, combined with the hostile attitude of the American students, made rioting virtually inevitable. For three days there were violent and bloody clashes between thousands of enraged Panamanians and the troops of General O'Meara, called in to reinforce the Canal Zone police units who could not cope with demonstrations on such a scale. The rioters presented no serious threat to residential areas in the Zone, but the intervention of crack troops with automatic weapons on the American side in fact exacerbated the situation. In Panama City, Balboa and Colón, heavy damage was done to administrative buildings, and a few blocks of flats were set on fire by Molotov cocktails. When the final record of the troubles was made, it became clear that a possibly unbridgeable gulf had been created between the American residents and the local population. The one certain victim of those tragic days was the myth of a fraternal and trusting collaboration between the republic of Panama, created arbitrarily by the U.S. sixty years earlier, and the government in Washington.

A year later, in March 1965, it was evident that the position of the republic of Panama in this unhappy dispute was becoming less and less strong. In December 1964 President Johnson had suddenly announced that the United States was planning to open a second canal to replace the present, now inadequate, one. At the same time he had suggested fresh negotiations between Washington and Panama. Clearly he was trying to kill two birds with one stone. By getting the various governments (Nicaragua, Costa Rica, Panama and Colombia) who would stand to gain or lose by the new project into competition with one another, the U.S. was trying to reduce the claims of each of them, while at the same time making the situation as difficult as possible for Roberto Chiari's government.

An American mission led by Thomas Mann, the then Secretary of State for Inter-American Affairs, and Stephen Ailes, Secretary of State for the Army, made a tour of the capitals of the countries concerned in January 1965. The standing of the leaders of this mission showed clearly enough how concerned and how determined Washington's mood was. The different possible lines for the canal were carefully studied, but the most optimistic hypothesis could not envisage a canal being built before 1970, and it seemed likely that atomic energy would be used, which would raise complex diplomatic problems in relation to the international nuclear test ban treaty. However, none of this was totally insurmountable. On the other hand, the sensitivities of the republic of Panama, still smarting from the January 1964 riots, as well as those of whichever country would ultimately be called on to sign an agreement with Washington, looked like being a far greater obstacle.

Six candidates stood in the presidential election of 1964. Marco Aurelio Robles was elected with the theoretical support of eight political groups, but at least six of them were barely groups at all. In effect he was the candidate of the important families of Panama. As a member of the 'liberal' faction of the oligarchy, Robles drew his essential support from what is called in Panama 'the interior', that is, the farming areas. The end of his presidential term was troubled. During the 1968 election he hoped to get his candidate, the liberal Samudio, in; but the great families were tired of Robles and his ways, and the working class, naturally sceptical and carping, preferred Arnulfo Arias. He was a man of 66 who had already been president twice before (in 1939 and 1949), but was each time overthrown before the end of his term; he had been accused by his enemies of being a Nazi sympathizer during the war; but on a platform of aggressive nationalism Arias was once again elected in 1968, thanks mainly to the voters of the capital. The desperate attempts of the Robles party to 'turn the tide' by a 'massive vote from the countryside' were not enough to squeeze out the several thousand votes they needed; they did, however, give Arnulfo Arias a not wholly unreasonable pretext for accusing them of political malpractice. President Robles attempted, with the hesitant support of the National Guard commanded by General Bolívar Vallarino, to cast doubt on the validity of Arias's victory, and there were bloody clashes between the supporters of the two men. The republic then returned to relative calm, and Arias was in a position to resume the presidential chair which he had twice been precipitately forced to vacate.

Could there be any chance of his achieving any major alterations in the agreement the Robles government had made with the United States over the canal? It seemed unlikely in the extreme. The riots of January 1964 had hardly helped to create a favourable atmosphere for negotiations between the two parties. The president, as was natural after such major disturbances, made a great display of firmness. He denounced the 1903 treaty, broke with Washington, and laid an appeal before the Security Council.

In April 1964, diplomatic relations between the two countries were restored. In September 1965 there were talks which resulted in an outline for an agreement in principle which partially satisfied the Panamanian demands : the 1903 treaty was abrogated, and Panama's sovereignty over the Canal and the Canal Zone was recognized, and plans made for them to be gradually integrated into the rest of the country. On the other hand, the United States were to keep their military bases, whose importance had enormously increased in recent years since they had become the lynch-pin for the whole politico-military infra-structure established by the U.S. in Latin America. From this, which can only be described as a 'Southern Command', the airlines used by the U.S. military planes departed, making regularly scheduled calls on all the capitals in South America and the Caribbean. At any moment commandos 'for civil and social action', and units trained in anti-guerrilla warfare were ready to fly to trouble-spots anywhere in the sub-continent or respond to any 'calls for help' from governments – which none the less made a point of declaring their full independence.

The 1965 agreement also allowed for a second canal, which would replace or supplement the present one, to be built on Panamanian territory. Finally the rules for the use of the present canal had to be laid down afresh by a new statute. This second stage of the negotiations took place in conditions relatively favourable to the Robles government. The compensation paid to the State of Panama according to the 1968 agreement – made on the eve of the general election which brought Arnulfo Arias to victory – was to be considerably increased (between 25 and 30 million dollars a year instead of the 1,900,000 dollars paid up until 1967). What had really happened in fact was an arrangement very similar in nature to those made in the past. The U.S. did not apparently abandon the weapon of its threat to build a new canal outside Panamanian territory. The most likely place would be in

Colombia where the immense Atrato project was warmly supported by the Hudson Institute, which had produced the no less ambitious and 'technocratic' plan of harnessing the Amazon basin so as to create the equivalent of the 'great lakes' in South America.

List of Abbreviations

AF of L	American Federation of Labour
ALALC	Latin American Free Trade Association (Associación Latinoamericana de Libre Cambio)
Arena	National Renewal Alliance (Brazil) (Aliança Renovadora Nacional)
APRA	Popular Revolutionary Alliance (Peru) (Alianza Popular Revolucionaria Americana)
BID	Inter-American Development Bank (Banco Interamericano de Desarrollo)
CEPAL	Economic Commission for Latin America (Comisión Económica para la America Latina)
CCI	Independent Peasant Confederation (Mexico) (Confederación Campesina Independiente)
CGT	General Workers' Federation (Argentina) (Confederación General del Trabajo)
CGTC	General Confederation of Costa Rican Workers (Confederación General de Trabajadores Costaricenses)
CGTG	Confederation of Guatemalan Trade Unions (Confederación General de Trabajadores de Guatemala)
CGU	General University Confederation (Argentina) (Confederación General Universitaria)
CIA	Central Intelligence Agency

CIO	Committee of Industrial Organizations
CNC	Peasants' National Confederation (Mexico) (Confederación Nacional Campesina)
CNT	National Workers' Confederation (Paraguay) (Confederación Nacional de Trabajadores)
CONADE	National Development Council (Argentina) (Consejo Nacional de Desarrollo)
CONASE	National Security Council (Argentina) (Consejo Nacional de Seguridad)
CROM	Regional Confederation of Mexican Workers (Confederación Regional de Obreros Mejicanos)
CTM	Confederation of Mexican Workers (Confederación de Trabajadores Mejicanos)
ENDE	State National Enterprises (Argentina) (Empresas Nacionales del Estado)
FAR	Revolutionary Armed Forces (Guatemala) (Fuerzas Armadas Revolucionarias)
FORA	Argentine Regional Workers' Federation (Federación Obrera Regional Argentina)
FUA	Federation of Argentine Universities (Federación de Universidades Argentinas)
GATT	General Agreement of Tariffs and Trade
GOU	United Officials' Group (Argentina)
IAPI	Argentine Institute for Promoting Exchange (Instituto Argentino para la Promoción del Intercambio)
IMF	International Monetary Fund
IRCA	International Railways of Central America
MCCA	Central American Common Market (Mercado Común Centroamericano)
MDB	Brazilian Democratic Movement (Movimiento Democratico Brasileiro)

MLN	National Liberation Movement (Argentina) (Movimiento de Liberación Nacional)
MRP	Revolutionary Peronist Movement (Argentina) (Movimiento Revolucionario Peronista)
OAS	Organization of American States
ODECA	Organization of Central American States (Organización de Estados Centroamericanos)
PAR	Revolutionary Action Party (Guatemala) (Partido de Acción Revolucionaria)
PGT	Guatemalan Workers' Party (Partido General de Trabajadores)
PRAN	Revolutionary National Action Party (El Salvador) (Partido Revolucionario Acción Nacional)
PRG	Guatemalan Revolutionary Party (Partido Revolucionario de Guatemala)
PRI	Institutional Revolutionary Party (Mexico) (Partido Revolucionario Institucional)
SUDENE	North East Development Corporation (Brazil) (Superintendência do Desenvolvimento do Nordeste)
UDN	National Democratic Union (Brazil) (União Democratica Nacional)
UES	Union of Secondary Students (Argentina) (Unión de Estudiantes Secundarios)
UGT	General Workers' Union (Argentina) (Unión General de Trabajadores)
UNCTAD	United Nations Conference on Trade and Development
YPF	State Oil Deposits (Argentina) (Yacimientos Petrolíferos Fiscales)

Index

The Pelican Latin American Library

The Twenty Latin Americas Volume 2

Marcel Niedergang

The second volume deals with Chile, Bolivia, Peru, Ecuador, Colombia, Venezuela, Dominica, Haiti, Cuba and the states of the Caribbean.

Capitalism and Underdevelopment in Latin America*

Andre Gunder Frank

'It is capitalism, both world and national which produced underdevelopment in the past and which still generates underdevelopment in the present.' This study includes historical essays on Chile and Brazil, a discussion of the 'Indian Problem' in its relation to capitalist policy and an analysis of foreign investment in Latin America.

For The Liberation of Brazil

Carlos Marighela

A collection of writings by the man who, more than any other, shifted guerilla opposition to Brazil's fascist regime into the towns.

Guatemala - Another Vietnam?*

Thomas and Marjorie Melville

In this book two missionaries, whose ministry was terminated when they backed the cause if the landless Indian peasantry in Guatemala, describe the way in which the U.S. government engineered the now notorious coup which brought an oppressive right-wing junta to power in place of the liberal government of President Arbenz.

*Not for sale in the U.S.A.